T0360838

Metropolitan Governance in Latin America

This book represents a powerful analysis of the challenges of metropolitan governance in all its messiness and complexity. It examines Latin American metropolitan governance by focusing on the issue of public service provision and comparatively examining five of the largest and most complex urban agglomerations in the region: Buenos Aires, Bogota, Lima, Mexico City and Santiago.

The volume identifies and discusses the most pressing challenges associated with metropolitan coordination and the coverage, quality and financial sustainability of service delivery. It also reveals a number of spatial inequalities associated with inadequate provision, which may perpetuate poverty and other inequalities.

Metropolitan Governance in Latin America will be valuable reading for advanced students, researchers and policymakers tackling themes of urban planning, spatial inequality, public service provision and Latin American urban development.

Alejandra Trejo Nieto is a Professor at El Colegio de Mexico's Centre for Demographic, Urban and Environmental Studies.

Jose L. Niño Amézquita is a member of the Humanities and Social Sciences Faculty at EAN University, Colombia.

Regions and Cities
Series Editor in Chief
Joan Fitzgerald, *Northeastern University, USA*

Editors
Roberta Capello, *Politecnico di Milano, Italy*
Rob Kitchin, *Maynooth University, Ireland*
Jörg Knieling, *HafenCity University Hamburg, Germany*
Nichola Lowe, *University of North Carolina at Chapel Hill, USA*

In today's globalised, knowledge-driven and networked world, regions and cities have assumed heightened significance as the interconnected nodes of economic, social and cultural production, and as sites of new modes of economic and territorial governance and policy experimentation. This book series brings together incisive and critically engaged international and interdisciplinary research on this resurgence of regions and cities, and should be of interest to geographers, economists, sociologists, political scientists and cultural scholars, as well as to policy-makers involved in regional and urban development.

About the Regional Studies Association (RSA)

The Regions and Cities Book Series is a series of the Regional Studies Association (RSA). The RSA is a global and interdisciplinary network for regional and urban research, policy and development. The RSA is a registered not-for-profit organisation, a learned society and membership body that aims to advance regional studies and science. The RSA's publishing portfolio includes five academic journals, two book series, a Blog and an online magazine. For more information on the Regional Studies Association, visit www.regionalstudies.org.

There is a **30% discount** available to RSA members on books in the *Regions and Cities* series, and other subject-related Taylor and Francis books and e-books including Routledge titles. To order, simply email Luke McNicholas (Luke.McNicholas@tandf.co.uk), or phone on +44 (0)20 701 77545 and declare your RSA membership. You can also visit the series page at www.routledge.com/Regions-and-Cities/book-series/RSA and use the discount code: **RSA225**.

For more information about this series, please visit: www.routledge.com/Regions-and-Cities/book-series/RSA.

Metropolitan Governance in Latin America

Edited by Alejandra Trejo Nieto
and Jose L. Niño Amézquita

Routledge
Taylor & Francis Group

LONDON AND NEW YORK

First published 2022
by Routledge
2 Park Square, Milton Park, Abingdon, Oxon OX14 4RN

and by Routledge
605 Third Avenue, New York, NY 10158

Routledge is an imprint of the Taylor & Francis Group, an informa business

© 2022 selection and editorial matter, Alejandra Trejo Nieto and Jose L.
Niño Amézquita; individual chapters, the contributors

British Library Cataloguing-in-Publication Data
A catalogue record for this book is available from the British Library

Library of Congress Cataloging-in-Publication Data
Names: Trejo Nieto, Alejandra, editor. | Niño Amézquita, Jose L., editor.
Title: Metropolitan governance in Latin America / edited by Alejandra
    Trejo Nieto and Jose L. Niño Amézquita.
Description: Abingdon, Oxon; New York, NY: Routledge, 2022. | Series:
    Regions and cities | Includes bibliographical references and index. |
    Contents: Introduction / Alejandra Trejo Nieto and Jose L.
    Niño Amézquita—A framework for contextualising metropolitan
    governance in Latin America / Alejandra Trejo Nieto—Bogotá:
    metropolitan centralism, governance and service delivery / Jose L.
    Niño Amézquita—Governance stuctures and the unequal provision of
    services in metropolitan Lima / Matteo Stiglich-Labarthe and María
    Vásquez—Fragmented governance, service provision and inequality in
    Mexico City metropolitan area / Alejandra Trejo Nieto—The challenging
    evolution of integrated governance in metropolitan Buenos Aires /
    Gabriel Lanfranchi—Metropolitan Santiago: from dispersion and
    inequality to the challenge of effective intergovernmental governance /
    Esteban Valenzuela VT, Claudia Toledo A. and Osvaldo Henríquez O.—An
    assessment of metropolitan governance and service provision in Latin
    America / Alejandra Trejo Nieto.
Identifiers: LCCN 2021030997 (print) | LCCN 2021030998 (ebook) | SBN
    9780367615673 (hardback) | ISBN 9780367615697 (paperback) | ISBN
    9781003105541 (ebook)
Subjects: LCSH: Metropolitan government—Latin America. | Metropolitan
    government—Latin America—Case studies. | Municipal services—Latin
    America. | Municipal services—Latin America—Case studies.
Classification: LCC JS2061 .M47 2022 (print) | LCC JS2061 (ebook) | DDC
    320.8/5098—dcundefined
LC record available at https://lccn.loc.gov/2021030997
LC ebook record available at https://lccn.loc.gov/2021030998

ISBN: 978-0-367-61567-3 (hbk)
ISBN: 978-0-367-61569-7 (pbk)
ISBN: 978-1-003-10554-1 (ebk)

DOI: 10.4324/9781003105541

Typeset in Bembo
by KnowledgeWorks Global Ltd.

Contents

List of figures

List of tables

Foreword

I met Alejandra Trejo Nieto and Jose L. Niño Amézquita at Brown University at research workshops in 2012 and 2015, respectively. I still vividly remember comparing notes on the complexities of urban governance in India and Latin America, marvelling at the similarities of the challenges and bemoaning the lack of good, comparative work. Going back to the classics (Weber and Marx), social scientists have always celebrated the importance of having comparative frames, but the fact remains that comparative work is really hard. It is hard because at heart we are all parochialists, instinctively drawn to generalise from the cases we know best and have invested so much time and effort in learning about. It is hard because to take up new cases is a huge investment of time and resources. It is hard because comparing complex questions such as urban governance across such varied contexts is inherently challenging. And it is hard because it takes longer, and because the best comparative work begins through collaborations. So the invitation to write a foreword to this book is as much a celebration of an amazing collaborative achievement with in-depth studies of five Latin American megacities as it is an opportunity to comment on this remarkable book.

Can there be any doubt that the greatest governance challenge of the twenty-first century is the challenge of governing the world's great metropolitan areas? As this book makes clear, there are really three massive challenges at hand. The first is institutional. How does one govern a rapidly growing city-region? As the authors say 'urbanisation now is more intense, accelerated, and turbulent than ever before' a point underscored by recent urban protests in Latin America that have rocked even its most prosperous cities. Urbanisation in Latin America, and indeed throughout the Global South, has simply outpaced the capacity of public institutions to actually govern new urban conglomerations and in particular the peripheries of these sprawling megacities. The problem is not, as Trejo Nieto and Niño Amézquita point out one of traditional, territorially defined government, but rather one of governance, that is having to coordinate across multiple jurisdictions and to do so by involving a range of private sector and civil society actors. The massive challenges of managing competing interests, reconciling contradictory sectoral pulls (growth, equity and sustainability) and realigning functional needs with actual administrative capacity, requires a whole new way of governing, one that requires both integration (coordination across governmental layers and entities) and embeddedness (coordination between state and society).

The second challenge is the almost inexorable way that cities are contributing to increasing inequality and precarity. Cities are force multipliers. They attract resources and people because they amplify the returns to the division of labour, accelerate innovation and nourish associational and cultural life. But by the same token, cities are rationed. Dominant groups have a stake in limiting or at least in differentiating access to the city. This is why patterns of urban spatial inequality and segregation are becoming more pronounced than ever. Accessing the city today for those who do not have significant resources basically means having to accept substandard (and often subhuman) conditions of belonging, or what we have more politely come to simply call informality.

The new problems of governance and growing inequality vector neatly and very concretely into the third challenge, which is providing basic services. The potential of cities as force multipliers depends on the provision of basic public services. Dense and highly interdependent populations need good transport and access to water and sanitation just to provide baseline functionality. But these services are also critical to enhancing basic capabilities. The quality and inclusivity of all these services are vital to giving the urban poor a chance at decent work and decent lives. Yet as the institutional challenges of governance increase and the logic of spatial inequality accelerates, providing these services has become more challenging than ever.

Metropolitan Governance in Latin America is timely, innovative and essential. In recent years, urban scholars have started to focus on the specific challenges of metropolitan governance, recognising in particular that our conventional government-focused lenses of analysis were inadequate. But as is all too often the case, this initial burst of interest has produced more theories and models than actual empirical analysis. And conspicuously missing has been a careful, systematic effort at cross-national analysis of megacities. Working with a carefully and painstakingly developed frame of analysis that looks specifically at the links between urban services, metropolitan governance and increasing inequality, Trejo Nieto and Niño Amézquita and their collaborators – Esteban Valenzuela Van Treek, Claudia Toledo A., Osvaldo Henríquez O., Gabriel Lanfranchi, Matteo Stiglich-Labarthe and María Vásquez – provide comprehensive and granular case studies of Mexico City, Buenos Aires, Santiago, Bogota and Lima. As the authors show, each city is embedded in a unique political and institutional system, all of which have produced varied efforts to develop new metropolitan-level responses to the challenges of governance. Each study could stand on its own, but the cross-city framing brings to light exactly how governance, spatialised inequality and patterns of service provisioning are dynamically and mutually intertwined. What emerges is a powerful analysis of the challenges of metropolitan governance in all its messiness and complexity but also a clear-eyed sense of what is to be done.

Patrick Heller
Professor of Sociology and International Affairs, Brown University
Providence, April 20, 2021

Acknowledgements

We start by thanking our families for their love and support. We are also grateful to the contributors to this volume, Esteban Valenzuela, Claudia Toledo A., Osvaldo Henríquez O., Matteo Stiglich-Labarthe, María Vásquez and Gabriel Lanfranchi, for their commitment and dedication to this project. Also thanks to Natalie Tomlinson and Kristina Abbotts, our editors at Routledge, and Christiana Mandizha, the editorial assistant, for their guidance; you are brilliant.

This book grew out of the 2016 research project titled "Intra-Metropolitan Dynamics in Latin America: Challenges and Problems of Cooperation and Coordination between Existing Administrative Territorial Units" sponsored by Brown International Advanced Research Institutes (BIARI) as part of its annual grants. We thank BIARI for funding that project in which the cases of Bogota, Lima and Mexico City were analysed. Special gratitude to Professor Patrick Heller, at Brown University, for writing a kind foreword for this volume, commenting our research and participating in a seminar that took place in Mexico City in 2016. His views and critics were invaluable.

Most of the writing and editing process of this book took place in the middle of a global pandemic. COVID-19 faced us with difficult and stressful circumstances in our academic work and daily life. At times, our spirits and health were affected in different ways. Thanks to all those, including loved ones, friends, medical doctors, counsellors, research assistants and proof readers, who were encouraging, friendly and kind during the lockdown. Thanks to all of you.

Alejandra Trejo Nieto, Mexico City
Jose Luis Niño Amézquita, Bogotá
May 16, 2021

About the editors

Alejandra Trejo Nieto is an Economist with a master's degree in Regional Economics and a Ph.D. in Development Studies from the University of East Anglia in the United Kingdom. She is currently a professor at El Colegio de Mexico's Centre for Demographic, Urban and Environmental Studies, where she was academic coordinator of the master's program in Urban Studies in 2013–2015. She was awarded the Mexico Studies Chair with a Fulbright-Garcia Robles Grant at the University of California in San Diego (January–May 2018). She has been a visiting research fellow at the Brussels Centre for Urban Studies, Vrije Universiteit (January–April 2019) and a visiting researcher at CREPIB in Colombia (October–December 2018). She is a Level II member of the National Researchers System in Mexico, the Regional Studies Association's Latin American division chair and an ambassador to Mexico, and a United Kingdom Research and Innovation International Development peer-review college member. Her areas of expertise include urbanisation and metropolitan areas; industrialisation; urban markets; and urban and regional economic development. Her research agenda reflects significant interdisciplinary concerns about urbanisation, urban and regional economic development, governance and policy.

Jose L. Niño Amézquita holds a bachelor's degree in Economics, a Ph.D. in Regional Studies and a postdoctoral fellowship in Geography. He works as a member of the Humanities and Social Sciences Faculty at EAN University in Colombia. Professor Niño Amézquita leads the Politics and Sustainability Research Group and is the editor of the journal *Comunicación, Cultura y Política*. He has over ten years of professional, academic and consultative experience in the public sector, in academia, and in the non-governmental sector. His research focuses on the economic and political role of sub-national territories and their functions. He also analyses the functional and administrative integration of continuous and non-continuous territories, territorial internationalisation and the territorialisation of national public policy. He has been a visiting scholar in ILAS at Columbia University and a guest researcher at Humboldt University.

List of contributors

Osvaldo Henríquez O. is a Professor at the University of Talca, Chile

Gabriel Lanfranchi is a Professor of Urban Planning at the University of Buenos Aires, Argentina

Jose L. Niño Amézquita is a member of the Humanities and Social Sciences Faculty at the EAN University, Colombia

Matteo Stiglich-Labarthe is a Professor of Urbanism at the Pontifical Catholic University of Peru, Peru

Claudia Toledo A. is a Research Associate at CREASUR, University of Concepción, Chile

Alejandra Trejo Nieto is a Professor of Urban and Regional Economics at the Centre for Demographic, Urban and Environmental Studies, El Colegio de Mexico, Mexico

Esteban Valenzuela Van Treek is the Director of CREASUR, University of Concepción, Chile

María Vásquez is a Private Consultant in Lima, Peru

Part I

Introduction

Alejandra Trejo Nieto and Jose L. Niño Amézquita

Metropolitan governance in Latin America: Unravelling the links with service provision and inequality

Latin America is the most urbanised region in the developing world, with 80 per cent of its population living in cities. Three of its megacities, Buenos Aires, Mexico and Sao Paulo, are among the world's largest, while other sprawling metropolises including Bogotá, Lima, Santiago and Rio de Janeiro are not far behind. Several of these and other large cities in the region are struggling to keep pace with the social demands accompanying their expansion into neighbouring areas outside their jurisdiction. In most cases, metropolitan areas that have grown beyond their parent city's political-administrative boundaries are not politically, legally or fiscally recognised. The resulting fragmented political structure of metropolitan areas spreads the responsibility for urban management across the authorities of multiple jurisdictions and at different government levels (Wilson, 2012). As a result, urban agglomerations have outgrown the capacity of their governments to deliver adequate public policies (Trejo Nieto, Niño Amézquita & Vasquez, 2018). Although metropolitan-wide administrative, political and fiscal arrangements are key to addressing the growing challenges that accompany urban expansion, these have been frequently held back by decentralisation, intergovernmental relations and political factors (Rodriguez-Acosta & Rosenbaum, 2005; Wilson, 2012).

Since the 1980s, the region began its journey towards political, administrative and fiscal decentralisation, and the possibility of privatisation of public service delivery and infrastructure development. However, the effectiveness and sustainability of these trends are disputed. It is broadly recognised that the metropolitan condition of many large Latin American cities has made urban governance and the provision of public goods and services an extraordinarily challenging undertaking. In point of fact, poor metropolitan management has been blamed for recent social unrest in Latin American cities.

In 2019, there were massive protests in cities in Chile, Colombia and Ecuador and other Latin American countries due to general discontent in the population as manifestations of inequality such as segregation and slow social mobility and the lack of voice in politics became more evident

DOI: 10.4324/9781003105541-2

(Sachs, 2019). Santiago de Chile was one of the cities that experienced the most violent protests and unrest in 2019. Despite living in a country regarded as a paragon of economic success, Chileans expressed their dissatisfaction about key aspects of their lives. Reports highlighted how a rise in underground fares ignited the protest, unveiling one of the city's most intrinsic failures: its spatial segregation and fragmentation. Many living in the central city, especially young people already struggling to find work and affordable housing, were pushed out of the centre by the high cost of housing. As a result they needed private or public transport to get to work, and a relatively small addition to the underground fare implied a substantive increase for low-income families commuting from urban districts far from employment centres (Carey, 2019; Garnham, 2019; Morales, 2019; Moyano, 2019; Sachs, 2019; Sehnbruch, 2019).

La Paz, in Bolivia, also brought demonstrations against inequality and criticism of the municipalities' dysfunctional provision of sanitation services, clean drinking water, electricity, healthcare and education (Carey, 2019). Poor quality and coverage of services and the growing feeling of exclusion from wellbeing led to protests in the streets of cities in Ecuador and Argentina (Morales, 2019), and in Colombia the population also protested against inequality and segregation (Peñaranda & Gómez-Delgado, 2019).

In 2020, in the midst of the COVID pandemic crisis it became even more apparent that maintaining infrastructure and providing public services such as waste management, public transport, access to housing, water and sanitation are of the utmost importance both to citizens' wellbeing and to underpin health policies in Latin American countries that had been badly hit.

Metropolitan governance arrangements and policies – or their absence – can explain an important part of such city dynamics and failures in the region. Metropolises are characterised by manifold spatial and functional connections and interdependencies that are often not reflected in the way they are governed. Quality of life and economic outcomes can be profoundly affected if their management fails to acknowledge these links. Inequalities tend to be more visible than in smaller cities, and rapid and unplanned urbanisation can lead to violence and social unrest. The combination of inequality, competition for scarce resources such as land, lack of infrastructure, inadequate urban services and weak city governance increases the risk of violence and law and order breakdown, as has been seen in Latin American cities in recent years.

Given that urban main concerns in metropolitan contexts are linked to both, a classic urban agenda that addresses housing, mobility, the urban labour market, the delivery of infrastructure and services, informality and inequality, and to an agenda arising in the new context of urban expansion to tackle governance, coordination, citizenship, participation, transparency and funding, we observe that one of the fundamental questions still facing metropolitan areas in Latin America and bringing the old and the new agendas together is the design and management of the provision of the most basic urban services (Slack, 2007). But systematic evidence and research are still scarce.

There are relatively few analyses of metropolitan areas in Latin America that identify and explain the realities and challenges imposed by prevailing metropolitan structures (see for instance Paiva, 2003; Rodriguez-Acosta & Rosenbaum, 2005; Rojas, 2005; Frey, 2012; Wilson, 2012; Lanfranchi & Bidart, 2016; Grin et al., 2017; Fuentes & Durán, 2018; Trejo Nieto, Niño Amézquita & Vasquez, 2018). This book presents a number of studies on metropolitan governance in the region. Using a cross-metropolitan approach it examines the governance structures operating in the largest metropolises of Argentina, Colombia, Chile, Mexico and Peru. We discuss various aspects of the existing institutional structures, political systems and local practice, and explore how these shape outcomes in the delivery of strategic public services.

The book grew out of the 2016 project titled Intra-Metropolitan Dynamics in Latin America: Challenges and Problems of Cooperation and Coordination between Existing Administrative Territorial Units, sponsored by Brown International Advanced Research Institutes (BIARI) as part of its grant competition. The project addressed the relationship between institutional fragmentation and unequal urban service provision in metropolitan regions. It was based on the premise that such metropolitan fragmentation can produce, via different channels, significant spatial disparities in the provision of and access to public services, perpetuating inequality, and advocated discussion and analysis of the role of metropolitan governance in tackling territorial inequalities and improving urban efficiency. It analysed how the governance structures of three metropolitan areas, Mexico City, Bogotá and Lima, affect the provision of public services, and particularly the ability of regional/local governments to expand their public service coverage as the cities grow and gradually incorporate new areas and peripheries. The three participants in this project have also contributed chapters to this book. The above three case studies provided the initial material for an exploration, but more cases were needed to deepen the analysis.

This volume contributes to developing the debate on metropolitan governance with its analysis of relevant case studies in the Latin American region and evaluation of the extent to which the governance setup in metropolitan areas fosters the inclusive and sustainable provision of public services. We also include Santiago and Buenos Aires, other two capital cities with the largest populations in Spanish-speaking Latin America. We evaluate the different realities and practices of metropolitan governance and apply a comprehensive assessment. The focus is on identifying the most pressing governance challenges associated with metropolitan coordination, sustainability, and coverage of urban service delivery. Importantly, because the region suffers from multiple socioeconomic inequalities that have been blamed for increasing social unrest in several Latin American countries we identify a number of spatial inequalities associated with service provision. This examination contributes to understanding the problems and prospects of rapidly urbanising countries across the Global South where not only urbanisation but also governance pose enormous challenges to service provision and equity. Thus we lay the foundation for further analysis with the aim of providing significant insights and guidance for metropolitan service delivery.

The importance of metropolitan governance in the Global South

In *The City in History* (1961) Lewis Mumford outlines a fascinating interpretation of the origin, nature and evolution of cities. Rather than seeing the destiny of urban centres as large metropolitan concentrations derived from the uncontrolled expansion of peripheries in which inequality and economic and social backwardness prevail, Mumford envisions an urban order that integrates technical development with all of humanity's biological, social and intellectual needs. But these first decades of the twenty-first century have shown a variety of trends and patterns of urban development that are significantly different from the most orderly past urbanisation. Urbanisation now is more intense, accelerated and turbulent than ever before, signalling the need for new and evolving urban management arrangements.

In 2020 global urbanisation reached 56.2 per cent, and it is estimated that by 2050 more than 68 per cent of the world's population will live in cities (UN, 2020). This high and increasing rate of urbanisation is not without consequences. While the many social and economic benefits of urban life in organised and efficient cities are recognised, intense and unplanned urbanisation brings challenges and dangers. How effectively urban problems and opportunities can be addressed will increasingly be determined by how well urban agglomerations are governed and planned; however, the speed at which urbanisation is happening challenges the governments' capacity for managing cities (Klüber & Heinelt, 2005).

If urbanisation is to provide inclusive and sustainable development it must be accompanied by carefully considered urban planning and effective regulatory frameworks. The inability of governments and authorities at all levels to provide appropriate infrastructure and public services is at the core of many current urban challenges. This is particularly true in economies in the Global South where urbanisation has at different times and to varying degrees led to increasing urban poverty and inequality, deterioration of the quality of the urban environment, and deficiencies in access to basic urban services including water supply and sanitation, housing, waste management, energy, transport and health. In the face of other risk factors accompanying urban development such as diseases and epidemics, the increased concentration of population, infrastructure and economic activities mean that the risks materialising in the cities have far greater potential to disrupt society than ever before (WEF, 2015). Latin America's urban agglomerations, for instance, face considerable challenges to reduce the difference between socioeconomic classes, improve the living conditions of their most vulnerable communities and improve their institutions so that they can be more effective and active in development (Loibl et al., 2018).

Metropolitan areas have increasingly become the key sites for wealth generation and they concentrate most population in many countries of the world (Florida, Mellander & Gulden, 2009; Wilson, 2012; Bouchet, Lius & Parilla, 2018; OECD, 2018; WEF, 2018). Therefore the metropolitan scale is often identified as the operative scale for many city government measures such as formulating master plans, planning infrastructure and providing services (Harrison & Hoyler, 2014). This responds to the functional dynamics of the city that extends beyond its administrative boundaries. For many city functions it can be more advantageous if urban policies and strategic planning for housing, public transport, water provision, sewerage and environmental control are organised by an integrated authority that match better with the spatial dynamic of the metropolis. Effective management, political interests, efficiency and social wellbeing are valid arguments for advocating metropolitan scale institutions. The role of governance is important for the urban economy because service provision and strategies for urban development affect firms and households' location decisions (Paiva, 2003). Metropolitan-wide planning efforts can also ameliorate many inequalities (Wilson, 2012).

Metropolitan areas and urban functions involve jurisdiction boundaries, administrative and political responsibility for services and infrastructure, resource bases and mobilisation, performance in service delivery and access to services, political representation, accountability and citizen participation (Devas, 2005). Experience has shown that the proper metropolitan model or the best institutional architecture that can offer policy development and implementation across an urban functional unity often administratively divided are highly complex issues (Wilson, 2012; Harrison & Hoyler, 2014). The general understanding has been that metropolitan-wide government is desirable; however, the formation of integrated metropolitan governments has long faced political, legal and administrative barriers that are difficult to overcome. Despite the de facto existence of metropolitan areas, they commonly lack a legal foundation and so are seldom recognised as formal political entities that could be the recipients of decentralised resources (Slack, 2007). This largely explains why the formation of metropolitan institutions has been omitted from both the theory and the practice of decentralisation. Generally decentralisation policies target formal units of government that have taxing and spending powers and some degree of political autonomy. Policymakers design decentralisation policies for states and municipalities, altogether ignoring the existence of metropolitan or any other kind of intermediate formation. This has had important consequences for areas such as planning and the provision of services, because jurisdictions have differing capacities for dealing with decentralised functions and responsibilities and consequently their service provision is often uncoordinated (Raich, 2006).

Metropolitan governance is a conceptual category that encompasses public and private action for metropolitan management and planning (Paiva, 2003; Feiock, 2004; Oakerson, 2004). While some authors refer more generally to 'metropolitan management' (Andersson, 2012), 'governance' defines the participation of interest groups and different sectors of civil and political society in the decision-making process and in verifying the performance and assessment of urban action (Paiva, 2003; Wilson, 2012). It has become a meaningful tool for tackling the increasing need for metropolitan-scale coordination, joint decision-making and integrated planning of urban functions and services (Andersson, 2012; Da Cruz, Rode & McQuarrie, 2019).

Harrison and Hoyler (2014) underscore how empirical and conceptual literature on metropolitan governance gravitates towards a number of large cities in Europe and North America, many of which are considered global cities, while city-regionalism in non-global cities and those in developing countries is often overlooked. But metropolitan expansion is more significant in many cities in the less-developed world, where metropolitan areas are a main characteristic. Essentially, the urban population of the world is increasingly concentrating and growing in metropolitan areas in the Global South, with the demographic and economic weight of metropolitan agglomerations now recognised as a fundamental feature of contemporary Latin American and Asian societies (Cohen, 2006; Jones, Clench & Harris, 2014; UN, 2019).

Governance should be a central concern for metropolitan areas in the Global South, which are daily confronted with the urgent need to rethink and redesign the management of their basic urban functions. In Latin America the huge and concentrated populations already living in metropolitan areas both intensify the need for and complicate the supply of services and infrastructure (Trejo Nieto, Niño Amézquita & Vasquez, 2018). Inadequate governance structures can produce significant spatial disparities in the provision of and access to public services, perpetuating other inequalities and poverty (Devas, 2005; Wilson, 2012). The role of metropolitan governance in tackling service provision and territorial inequalities in the Global South has not yet been systematically and exhaustively studied. This book advances in that direction by exploring these questions in relation to a number of Latin America's metropolises, examining how their spatial inequalities are related to disparities in urban service supply and access. Analysing how the governance setups of large urban centres impede or facilitate the provision of inclusive public services is necessary to understanding some of the contradictions in the development of the region's large metropolitan areas. This perspective is also relevant to the growing urban agglomerations in other countries in the Global South and to metropolitan areas with complex territorial, political and legal compositions.

Overview of the changing debates and approaches to metropolitan governance

'Governance' has been used as an umbrella concept that covers multifaceted processes pursuing social goals in specific areas of development through the promotion of dialogue in decision-making and the participation of multiple actors. Oakerson (2004) defines governance as the process by which human beings regulate their interdependencies in the context of shared environments. It is not a synonym for government, as it describes a more complex multilevel participation process beyond the state which includes not only public institutions but also the private sector, non-governmental organisations and civil society. Governance involves ethical principles such as transparency, accountability, responsibility, equity and justice, and is not simply the execution of public policies (Tortajada, 2006). Behind the concept of governance is the powerful idea of the action and interaction of different social groups (civil society, the state and the private sector) as resources to overcome governmental limitations. Allusion to governance refers mainly to the method, the practice and the means for achieving better cooperation between the actors on the urban scene to achieve satisfactory outcomes (Jouve & Lefèvre, 2004).

Metropolitan areas are shaping the contemporary urban governance debate as a prominent locus through which societies should address various socio-economic, spatial and political issues (Harrison & Hoyler, 2014; Zimmermann, Galland & John, 2020). Metropolitan governance has been defined as the process by which a set of governmental and non-governmental actors interact on the formulation of policies and the provision of collective goods on a metropolitan scale. It is a complicated process because it involves not only different levels of government and actors that do not belong to the public sphere but also several local governments in the same urban area. This means that adjoining municipalities provide services that often generate externalities, necessitating intergovernmental coordination (Slack, 2007).

With the ongoing growth of urban agglomerations, metropolitan governance becomes more complex. Large cities have to coordinate their activities through local units to meet the interests of their inhabitants. They need to attenuate conflicts between the core city and its suburbs and between districts with different sizes, levels of income and economic functions. Governance is an appealing concept as within it local authorities must negotiate their way through the policy process, are subject to the influences of other levels of government, need to coordinate with other local governments, and are prone to lobbying pressures. It emphasises the relationships and interactions between actors as well as the conditions and rules that frame those relationships and interactions (Da Cruz, Rode & McQuarrie, 2019).

Even if they occupy a space of major relevance in the metropolitan area to address economic and social problems, local governments become just one part of a broader multilevel and multi-actor governance process. Metropolitan governance depends on the type of government or institutional and political framework, the way in which coordination is handled, the funding bodies, and the form of private-sector and civil-society participation (Feiock, 2004). It can contribute to solving difficulties arising from the lack of unified government in a metropolis and strengthen the structures of an existing metropolitan government, and plays a critical role in how well metropolitan areas function. Governance can regulate how services are delivered and coordinated across local government boundaries, where and how decisions are made, and how costs are shared throughout the metropolitan area (Slack, 2007). It also produces certain patterns of accountability, citizen participation, representation and community differentiation (Lewis, 2004; Oakerson, 2004). Consequently, the analysis of institutions, as structures and contexts of agency, should be the basis for all governance examinations as they determine the characteristics and administration models to which different cities ascribe. But the study of metropolitan governance allows for a multiplicity of perspectives for discussion, ranging from the financial sphere and management instruments to the incidence of community actors' participation in decision processes, among others (Fuentes & Durán, 2018).

The issue of metropolitan governance has been redefined over the years and practice offers a rich collection of experiences and a variety of institutional forms, planning practices and episodes around the world. In the past the emphasis of most analyses of metropolitan management has been on the general problem of political–territorial fragmentation and overlapping jurisdictions (Klüber & Heinelt, 2005). More recent studies have examined emerging and more consolidated patterns of metropolitan organisation, along with its institutional frameworks, modes of governance, policy instruments and spatial strategies, all aiming to increase productivity, efficiency, sustainability and democracy (Feiock, 2004; Heinelt & Kübler, 2005; De Vries, Reddy & Haque, 2008; Spink, Ward & Wilson, 2012; Harrison & Hoyler, 2014; Zimmermann, Galland & John, 2020).

The first wave of metropolitan analysis in the 1960s focused on metropolitan realities in Europe and the US, debating whether metropolitan areas should be governed by separate or consolidated authorities (Feiock, 2004). Accordingly, the long-running debate on metropolitan models confronted two different intellectual traditions: the metropolitan reform tradition and the public choice approach. Reformers advocated governmental consolidation, with the administrative boundaries of the city matching those of the whole urban area. Consolidation would be achieved through the annexation of local jurisdictions or by creating a single government. In contrast, the public choice school argued that institutional fragmentation into autonomous local jurisdictions was more beneficial for efficient metropolitan service delivery. Drawing on Tiebout's hypothesis, public choice scholars claimed that competition between local governments to attract new residents by providing better services led to the efficient allocation of public resources and better matching of urban services to demand (Klüber & Heinelt, 2005).

This long-standing debate on whether metropolitan areas are best governed and managed via decentralised or consolidated structures was framed mostly in the theoretical discussion around government decentralisation and its consequences for economic efficiency and equity (Bird & Slack, 2007). On the one hand, decentralisation favours accountability and triggers a better supply of public goods by means of local competition (Tiebout, 1956); on the other, consolidation facilitates the exploitation of economies of scale, the management of externalities and equity (Treisman, 2000). According to the empirical evidence, each of these extreme approaches lacked empirical underpinning, and such excessive dichotomising provided limited guidance for contemporary issues of metropolitan governance (Lewis, 2004).

New regionalists in the 1990s argued that effective metropolitan governance does not necessarily require institutional consolidation and can be achieved through cooperative arrangements between policy-relevant actors involved in the delivery of urban services. Institutional structures are important for the achievement of area-wide governance, but so are relations between actors at different territorial levels (Feiock, 2004; Oakerson, 2004; Klüber & Heinelt, 2005). This decentralised approach to governance based on cooperation emphasises the presence of horizontally and vertically linked actors and institutions, overcoming the assumption that competition makes cooperation close to impossible. In practice this means that metropolitan problems can be addressed through a variety of schemes that often involve networks of coordination and collaboration between local governments, agencies and non-public actors at various levels (Feiock, 2004).

Thus, beyond the traditional focus on ideal metropolitan government models, more recent discussions have dealt with the identification of concrete governance practices for addressing the challenges facing contemporary metropolises. Effective metropolitan governance – intervention in and management of the urban territory efficiently and fairly to reverse urban disorder and produce consistent sustainable development – rather than an ideal model to govern urban regions, is the core of the renewed deliberations (Harrison & Hoyler, 2014).

Storper (2014) argues that fragmentation is an inevitable condition of metropolitan areas, and regulation of all urban interdependent relations in the absence of an overarching political authority is highly problematic. The enduring gap between functional and administrative boundaries mean that there will always be governance problems, and neither complete consolidation nor complete fragmentation are likely to resolve these fundamental metropolitan issues. According to Storper (ibid) there is no optimal metropolitan solution whether from the standpoint of efficiency, satisfaction or justice. Similarly, others have argued that there are no general linear processes in metropolitan governance, which is always incomplete and prone to discontinuities (Le Galès & Vitale, 2013). Efficient scales and preferences for providing public services, which are diverse in the size of their effects, production functions, and financial and cost structures, are multiple, heterogeneous and evolve over time (Parks & Oakerson, 1989; Slack, 2007). There is no single right way to organise metropolitan areas, no single geography or organisation of governance, and solutions to service provision can be place- and time-specific (Parks & Oakerson, 1989, 1993; Slack, 2007; Bahl, 2013).

Parks and Oakerson (1989, 1993) say that the metropolitan areas that are more fragmented and cover multiple jurisdictions tend to be complexly organised. However, organisational diversity and complexity do not necessarily imply institutional failure and in fact can lead to greater efficiency, and therefore jurisdictional fragmentation alone does not account for organisational complexity. A distinction between the production and the provision of public services makes the case for organisational metropolitan structures that allow for a more complete depiction of governance. Governments are provision units that can use a variety of alternative production arrangements: direct production, private concessions, coordinated or joint production and franchising. Metropolitan areas are usually complicatedly organised as multiple provision units (i.e. governments) linked in numerous ways to a variety of production units. Different production arrangements can be rational accommodations to diversity so that the choice of governance arrangements depends on variable environmental factors including the capacity to elaborate, change and enforce the rules within which provision and production take place (Parks & Oakerson, 1989). From this perspective levels of governance rather than types of government structure are the relevant focus.

Shared governance structures can transcend municipal boundaries and permit problem-solving and rule-making on a metropolitan basis, allowing greater efficiency. When voluntary cooperation and overlying governmental bodies are not achieved, metropolitan governance is weak (Parks & Oakerson, 1993).

Thus, studies are increasingly using analytical frameworks such as collective action approaches, which provide guidance through a variety of empirical possibilities (Feiock, 2004; Klüber & Heinelt, 2005) because a metropolitan area is an environment characterised by variable conditions and requires structures of governance that are sufficiently open to allow for diverse solutions (Parks & Oakerson, 1989; Storper, 2014). Approaches should allow for contextual conditions such as nationally specific government traditions and state-society relations, as well as a set of environmental factors whose combination and interactions are locally specific (Feiock, 2004).

The institutional collective action framework provides a way of understanding a system of metropolitan governance in the absence of a single overarching metropolitan government. Vertical and horizontal coordination in fragmented city-regions or metropolitan areas can be achieved by local governments acting collectively to integrate the area via a web of voluntary agreements or associations. Cooperation can also be attained between levels of government and between local governments and other actors in the city and may involve both formal and informal collective action. Neither coordination nor cooperation are always voluntary, and they often reflect strategic interactions among actors, when incentive structures, political leadership, common goals and strategies are needed to open up the path to governance. Even the existence of common goals and interests may be insufficient to motivate collective action for integrated metropolitan governance because contextual factors such as economic conditions, local political culture and state-level rules shape the institutional outcome. Cooperative action and institutions arise when the potential benefits outweigh the transaction costs of forming new institutions and structures. Transaction costs are minimised in small groups, whereas in big groups collective action requires a third party (an upper-level government or other actor) to absorb the costs and apply coercion or provide incentives. Collective action is also possible where internal mechanisms induce cooperation and overcome social dilemmas; i.e., trust, cooperative norms, exchange of commitments, collective identity and so on (Feiock, 2004).

Political power all over the world has increasingly been transferred from central to local governments due to decentralisation and neoliberal thinking, in many cases moving previously centralised service provision to subnational authorities (Gilbert, 2006; Wilson, 2012). However, complex layers of administration and high poverty levels in metropolitan areas have prevented their adequate management. Moreover, as demand for more appropriate, flexible, networked and smart forms of planning and governance increases, new expressions of territorial cooperation and conflict are emerging (Harrison & Hoyler, 2014).

Government structures and political-administrative power still imply an imbricated context, but approaches to metropolitan management and planning that rely on alternative formal or informal arrangements through which effective governance can be achieved have been identified worldwide. Such arrangements and practices are gradually equipping metropolitan areas with political, functional and operational legitimacy, even though they are not legally recognised in national constitutions or are not included as a formal tier of government (Feiock, 2004; Heinelt & Kübler, 2005). Emergent urban politics and development frameworks are presenting these possibilities for achieving metropolitan order, although they are intermingled with old and rigid structures that must be overcome. Varied institutional organisations and political administrations may lead to a rich mixture of experiences across the globe, but the key elements of effective governance should be pinpointed and systematised in an orderly way, because many metropolitan areas still lack effective coordinating agencies (Zimmermann, Galland & John, 2020). Latin America, for example, has many megacities, but their metropolitan governance frameworks – with exceptions such as the Metropolitan District of Quito in Ecuador – are lacking or weak (Andersson, 2012).

Empirical strategy for analysing metropolitan governance and the delivery of urban services

Some researchers, including Spink, Ward and Wilson (2012), have highlighted that despite rapid metropolisation and widespread interest in megacities, few studies have examined their governance and the challenging question of public service provision. Jones, Clench and Harris (2014) point out that governance analysis is important for determining the effective delivery of public services in urban areas. In an increasingly urbanised world public services to the wider population must be assured, and it is well known that governance factors play an important part in constraining or enabling effective service delivery. However, the body of knowledge about the key governance challenges specific to urban environments remains weak, and empirical and comparative studies in this area are needed to identify, understand and address the pressing challenges associated with the delivery of urban services in the developing world, with specific attention to the urban services most critical to broader development goals, and those whose provision is uniquely challenging in urban environments.

The main objective of this book is to examine the realities and practices of metropolitan governance and how the governance setting shapes the process and outcomes of public service provision in a number of case studies in Latin America. The way of approaching these issues has been to look at the general characteristics of metropolitan governance and the extent of its legitimacy; then, to assess the deficits in local government capacity to provide and finance specific public services, and in metropolitan coordination. The focus is on pinpointing the most pressing challenges to the metropolitan coordination of strategic urban service provision. Importantly, because the increasing social unrest in various cities in the region has been attributed to widespread socioeconomic inequality, we identify spatial inequalities associated with inadequate service provision.

In the BIARI project we used a '3×3×3' framework to address metropolitan problems and challenges. The first three referred to the number of metropolises selected for analysis (Bogotá, Mexico City and Lima); the second indicated the number of services or sectors analysed (water, transport, and waste collection), and the third represented the aspects of governance on which we focused.

In this book, we examine the cases of Buenos Aires, Bogotá, Lima, Mexico City and Santiago, five of the largest and most complex urban agglomerations in the region. These urban areas have experienced rapid urban growth, which in turn has engendered significant challenges in the provision of public services and infrastructure. Even though their respective countries operate under different political systems, with unitary governments in Colombia, Chile and Peru and federal governments in Mexico and Argentina, they have all carried out important decentralisation processes and stimulated private investment in public services. These metropolises belong to Spanish-speaking Latin America and have some cultural background and roots in common; they are capital cities with special political-administrative status, and they all have a fragmented metropolitan government structures. At the same time, the five cities show different historical forms of metropolitan expansion and are of various sizes and varying complexity. These cases exhibit different forms of territorial and administrative organisation, making it possible to obtain research results with some degree of contrast. Our analyses deal with entire metropolitan areas that usually bear the name of their core city.

The literature on urban service delivery tends to focus on a subset of government services with particular attention to housing, water and sanitation, solid waste management and transport management. Although the list of services to be provided on the metropolitan scale can be extensive, we focus on these three archetypal urban sectors: public transport, solid waste collection and water supply, strategic services that affect the daily life of urban populations. They denote the kinds of service that present unique technical, political and financial challenges in metropolitan and urban environments. Transportation, for instance, is a sector with clear metropolitan relevance because it connects people to different parts of the metropolitan area, and coordination of accessible transportation across municipal boundaries is necessary to ensure access to employment and services. Metropolitan areas also need to define where water provision facilities and garbage disposal sites are to be located, and how these services will be provided (Jones, Clench & Harris, 2014). To some extent, attention is given in some chapters to environmental and housing-related issues. Each service raises its own political and governance challenges according to the distinctive nature of the good being delivered (Batley & Mcloughlin, 2015).

Metropolitan areas contain a constellation of private, political-interest-group, government and civil-society actors and involve societal challenges that are often incompatible with a fragmentary approach. They require coordinated and collaborative solutions and their governance plays an important role in the effective delivery of services (Jones, Clench & Harris, 2014). Metropolitan governance involves various and complex facets of the delivery of strategic services: service quantity and quality, inclusive access, technical efficiency, costs and financial management, government accountability, and inclusive decision-making (Slack, 2007). Wilson (2012) suggests that governance for the delivery of public services is important for three reasons: concern about the ability of government to efficiently provide better-than-adequate public services in highly complex settings; concern about the institutional dynamics of planning the provision of services in areas where multiple governments often require interjurisdictional coordination mechanisms; and concern about the capacity of existing political systems to effectively incorporate citizens' preferences and participation in metropolitan-wide affairs. We mostly deal with Wilson's (ibid) first two concerns, concentrating on factors that reveal fundamental issues in the functioning of governance: coverage and quality; sustainability (reflecting adequate and efficient provision), and coordination (institutional, vertical and horizontal). In doing so, we follow Boex, Lane and Yao (2013) in that we focus on specifically defined governance factors. The practical answers to these concerns about how adequately and efficiently services are provided and coordinated are based on some of the recent analytical developments in metropolitan governance.

Using this methodology the book seeks to answer the following questions: What governance structures exist in Latin American metropolises? How do they work? Who/what is involved? How do public and private, formal and informal entities participate? How and to what extent metropolitan governance structures promote cooperation and coordination? And how do multi-jurisdictional dynamics interact with service provision outcomes? From this analysis a collective understanding of the relationship between metropolitan governance structures and the delivery of public services can be introduced.

Furthermore inequality in service provision is discussed in various ways in the case studies. The institutional structure that provides urban services produces different forms of inequality within metropolitan areas and has a spatial impact, with areas where services are poor or inadequate coinciding with low-income locations. This reinforces patterns of segregation and the spatial manifestation of socioeconomic disparities (Wilson, 2012), very much in line with the idea that complex institutional arrangements and fragmentation tend to produce gross inequities in the delivery of urban services and perpetuate inequalities among the residents of metropolitan areas (Ostrom, 1983).

A diversity of governance structures can emerge from the many forms of organisation for the provision of services, and we need an insightful parameter with which to classify governance. Metropolitan governance for service provision is then classified into three categories: (1) fragmented, where the organisation of provision and production preserves the metropolitan area's administrative structure, there are no coordination arrangements or other formal or informal efforts to deliver metropolitan wide services; (2) consolidated, where a service is provided and produced completely or mainly by a single entity, even if this is not a local government or public metropolitan agency; and (3) in consolidation, where different public or private, formal or informal schemes are being developed to build a metropolitan service supply approach and gradually incorporating metropolitan areas into the service supply coverage.

Pierre (2005) claims that comparative urban governance has tremendous potential, not only for uncovering causal mechanisms but also for exploring the drivers of urban political, economic and social change. However, comparative research necessarily entails some degree of reductionism and requires robust definition of the variables that excludes as much contextual noise as possible, and is therefore more parsimonious than in-depth. The analytical categories that we predominantly employ to look at the efficiency criteria (coverage/quality and financial sustainability) and coordination form the basis of a collective language across chapters for comparative assessment, although each empirical chapter focuses on specific issues of its interest.

As part of the BIARI project we collected data on Mexico City, Bogotá and Lima. This data collection was carried out between 2016 and 2017 and consisted of two types of information: databases, statistics, reports and documents containing indicators of access, coverage and other aspects of the provision of services, including information from national and local statistics offices and reports by international or local organisations, non-governmental organisations and think tanks; and primary data gathered during field research in Bogotá, Lima and Mexico City that included workshops, interviews and technical visits to a few municipalities in their peripheries. A workshop on each sector – transportation, water and waste collection – was organized in the three cities. Four sectors of society participated in each workshop: academia, civil society, government and private companies. The workshops were spaces for reporting and discussing the situation, the problems and the challenges of each specific public service, as perceived by different actors. We had prepared a number of guiding questions, but we allowed different issues to emerge. Varying numbers of semi-structured interviews were carried out in each city depending on access to informants (local authorities such as municipal mayors, community leaders in peripheral neighbourhoods, government or sector-specific managers, etc.). At least one technical visit to a municipality or neighbourhood in the periphery was included in each city. Information from statistics, reports and relevant indicators has been updated for this book. For Santiago and Buenos Aires extensive literature reviews, data collection from different sources and field research were used to analyse and collect relevant information.

Contents and structure

Metropolitan governance has a critical influence on urban inhabitants' quality of life and development outcomes. In a highly urbanised developing region such as Latin America, improving the quality and coverage of public services should be a priority when designing urban policies that promote overcoming poverty, improving the quality of life and economic and social development.

This book is timely and significant because the evolving patterns of urbanisation and the restructuring of national states have shaped the context for policymaking, management and collective action in Latin American cities and metropolises. Such book is an essential reading for anyone seeking to increase their knowledge of the spatial, administrative and social organisation of large metropolitan areas in Latin America, as well as for those interested in comprehensive discussion and empirical work on metropolitan governance and the delivery of urban services. Answers to the question of how public service provision is linked to spatial inequalities in large and fragmented urban agglomerations of the developing world are investigated. These issues are of the utmost interest to many researchers and policymakers. The extensive significance of metropolitan governance and urban policy and the book's empirical perspective give it both regional and international appeal.

This introductory chapter has expounded the relevance of developing a book on the governance of metropolises in the Global South and the salient issues of urbanisation, governance and inequality that emerge from the examination of five Latin American case studies. The next seven chapters, five of which focus on the case studies, discuss experiences of decentralisation, metropolitan governance and the provision of urban services in Latin America.

In Chapter 1, Alejandra Trejo Nieto introduces urbanisation, decentralisation and metropolisation in Latin America and explores the conditions underlying the provision of urban services during two different stages: (1) central-state-driven provision and (2) decentralised provision linked to a new political dynamic in which subnational governments are responsible for providing a variety of public services. Scrutinising the distinctiveness and flaws of urbanisation and decentralisation in this region, the chapter includes a discussion on potential links between governance in the provision of services and metropolitan spatial inequalities.

The five empirical chapters in the book examine metropolitan governance of public service delivery in Latin America. In Chapter 2, Jose L. Niño Amézquita discusses the challenge of providing efficient public services to the rapidly growing population of Bogotá and the surrounding metropolitan area. Colombia's capital city's evolving urban expansion has jeopardized the capacity to internalise urban effects in the Capital District of Bogotá. Integrating metropolitan governance into the public provision of services by the Capital District's public companies is reconsidered as a solution to improving the quality and equity of public service delivery.

In Chapter 3, Matteo Stiglich-Labarthe and María Vásquez examine the governance of service provision in the metropolitan area of Lima and provide insights into how governance contributes to the reproduction of unequal access to good-quality public services. Although the governance structures for water, transport and waste management are heterogeneous, the authors argue that the lack of metropolitan planning and the local political economy dynamics with private companies are recurring issues across these sectors.

In Chapter 4, Alejandra Trejo Nieto focuses on assessing the extent to which Mexico City Metropolitan Area has been able to provide adequate public transport, water, and waste collection services. The chapter highlights the link between governance and urban inequalities through the lens of public service delivery. This case study provides insights into the problematic governance of large and highly fragmented metropolitan areas in emerging economies. Several coordination failures, rigid intergovernmental relations, political struggles and entrenched power overlaps have led to deficient outcomes in metropolitan service delivery and to growing inequalities.

Gabriel Lanfranchi analyses metropolitan governance in the capital city of Argentina in Chapter 5. He explains how the Metropolitan Region of Buenos Aires has been unable to fully develop a structure or organisation for integrated metropolitan governance. The chapter assesses Buenos Aires' advances in metropolitan management and service provision, and offers a series of recommendations for the governance of sustainable and inclusive metropolitan development.

In Chapter 6, Esteban Valenzuela Van Treek, Claudia Toledo A. and Osvaldo Henríquez O. review the long-standing challenges facing coordinated governance of the Santiago Metropolitan Area and their implications for social equity and sustainability both of which threaten both the citizens' quality of life and urban competitiveness. Based on this analysis they explain a roadmap that has been already designed to build the institutional spaces and strategies in which multilevel governance and local coordination can advance a shared long-term vision of more inclusive and sustainable metropolitan development and service provision.

In the concluding chapter, Alejandra Trejo Nieto summarises the most meaningful findings and offers an assessment of the variegated forms of metropolitan governance across the case studies, based on a number of common analytical categories. The five metropolitan areas in Latin America examined in the book are evaluated in the light of the collective concern about the relationship between governance, service delivery and metropolitan inequalities. The governance of service provision is place- and sector-specific and depends heavily on the evolution of metropolitan territories' legal status, political culture, legal framework and national urban policies. However, metropolitan realities are facing common challenges such as political struggles, ambiguous governmental structures, financial restrictions, inequality and spatial segmentation.

Lessons learnt from the largest metropolises in Latin America about how the provision of urban services in expanding territories has been managed can inform other metropolises in the Global South, making it possible to develop new models of comparative empirical analysis.

References

Andersson, M. (2012). *Metropolitan Management: Approaches and implications*. Sixth Urban Research and Knowledge Symposium, Washington, DC.

Bahl, R. (2013). 'The Decentralization of Governance in Metropolitan Areas'. In Bahl, R., Linn, J., Wetzel, D., (eds.) *Financing Metropolitan Governments in Developing Countries*. Cambridge: Lincoln Institute of Land Policy, pp. 85–106.

Batley, R. & Mcloughlin, C. (2015). 'The Politics of Public Services: A Service Characteristics Approach'. *World Development*, 74, 275–285.

Bird, R. & Slack, E. (2007). 'An Approach to Metropolitan Governance and Finance'. *Environment and Planning C: Government and Policy*, 25(5), 729–755.

Boex, J., Lane, B., & Yao, G. (2013). 'An Assessment of Urban Public Service Delivery in South Asia: An Analysis of Institutional and Fiscal Constraints'. *Urban Institute Center on International Development and Governance Research Report*. Washington DC: The Urban Institute.

Bouchet, M., Lius, S. & Parilla, J. (2018). '*Global Metro Monitor 2018*'. Washington, DC: Brookings. At: www.brookings.edu/wp-content/uploads/2018/06/Brookings-Metro_Global-Metro-Monitor-2018.pdf

Carey, F. H. (2019). Urban Unrest Propels Global Wave of Protests. *The Conversation*, November 12 2019. At: https://theconversation.com/urban-unrest-propels-global-wave-of-protests-126306

Cohen, B. (2006). 'Urbanization in Developing Countries: Current Trends, Future Projections, and Key Challenges for Sustainability'. *Technology in Society*, 28(1), 63–80. At: https://www.sciencedirect.com/science/article/pii/S0160791X05000588#!

Da Cruz, N. F., Rode, P. & McQuarrie, M. (2019). 'New Urban Governance: A Review of Current Themes and Future Priorities'. *Journal of Urban Affairs*, 41(1), 1–19. DOI: 10.1080/07352166.2018.1499416

De Vries, M., Reddy, P. & Haque, S. (eds.) (2008). *Improving Local Government: Outcomes of Comparative Research*. New York: Palgrave Macmillan.

Devas, N. (2005). 'Metropolitan Governance and Urban Poverty'. *Public Administration and Development*, 25(4), 351–361. At: https://doi.org/10.1002/pad.388

Feiock, R. (2004). *Metropolitan Governance: Conflict, Competition, and Cooperation*. Washington, DC: Georgetown University Press.

Florida, R., Mellander, C. & Gulden, T. (2009). 'The role of cities and metropolitan areas in the global economy'. Working Paper Series: Martin Prosperity Research MPIWP-002. Martin Prosperity Institute. At: www.creativeclass.com/rfcgdb/articles/Global%20metropolis.pdf

Frey, K. (2012). 'Abordagens de governança em áreas metropolitanas da América Latina: Avanços e entraves'. *Urbe, Revista Brasileira de Gestão Urbana*, 4(1), 87–102.

Fuentes, L. & Durán, G. (2018). *La institucionalidad metropolitana frente al desafío del desarrollo en Latinoamérica: Los modelos de gestión urbana de Bogotá, Lima, Quito y Santiago en cuestión*. IX Congreso Internacional en Gobierno, Administración y Políticas Públicas GIGAPP, Madrid, España.

Garnham, J. P. (2019). 'Why Chile's Massive Protests Started with a Subway Fare Hike'. *City Lab*, October 16 2019. At: https://www.bloomberg.com/news/articles/2019-10-26/why-chile-s-protests-started-with-the-metro

Gilbert, A. (2006). 'Good Urban Governance: Evidence from a Model City?' *Bulletin of Latin American Research*, 25(3), 392–419. At: https://doi.org/10.1111/j.0261-3050.2006.00204.x

Grin, E. J., Hernández Bonivento, J. & Abrucio, F. (eds.) (2017). *El Gobierno de las grandes ciudades: Gobernanza y Descentralización en las Metrópolis de América Latina*. CLAD Centro Latinoamericano de Administración para el Desarrollo and Universidad Autónoma de Chile, Santiago.

Harrison, J. & Hoyler, M. (2014). 'Governing the New Metropolis'. *Urban Studies*, 51(11), 2249–2266. DOI:10.1177/0042098013500699

Heinelt, H. & Kübler, D. (eds.) (2005). *Metropolitan Governance in the 21st Century. Capacity, Democracy and the Dynamics of Place*. London: Routledge. At: https://www.routledge.com/Metropolitan-Governance-in-the-21st-Century-Capacity-Democracy-and-the/Heinelt-Kubler/p/book/9780415498951

Jones, H., Clench, B. & Harris, D. (2014). 'The governance of urban service delivery in developing countries'. Overseas Development Institute Report. [Online] At: https://www.odi.org/publications/8329-urban-services-poverty

Jouve, B. & Lefèvre, C. (eds.) (2004). *Horizons Metropolitains*. Lausanne: Editions Presses Polytechniques et Universitaires romandes.

Klüber, D. & Heinelt, H. (2005). Introduction. In Heinelt, H. and Kübler, D. (eds.) *Metropolitan Governance in the 21st Century. Capacity, Democracy and the Dynamics of Place*. London: Routledge, pp. 1–7.

Lanfranchi, G. & Bidart, M. (2016). *Gobernanza metropolitana en América Latina y el Caribe*. Documento de Trabajo No. 151. CIPPEC.

Le Galès, P. & Vitale, T. (2013). 'Governing the large metropolis: A research agenda'. Working paper of Cities are Back in Town Programme No. 2013-8. [Online] At: https://hal-sciencespo.archives-ouvertes.fr/hal-01070523

Lewis, P. G. (2004). 'An Old Debate Confronts New Realities: Large Suburbs and Economic Development in the Metropolis'. In Feiock, R. C. (ed.). *Metropolitan Governance in the 21st Century. Capacity, Democracy and the Dynamics of Place*. Washington D.C.: Georgetown University Press, pp. 95–123.

Loibl, W. et al. (2018). 'Characteristics of Urban Agglomerations in Different Continents: History, Patterns, Dynamics, Drivers and Trends'. In Ergen, M. (ed.) *Urban Agglomeration*. [Online] At: https://www.intechopen.com/books/urban-agglomeration/characteristics-of-urban-agglomerations-in-different-continents-history-patterns-dynamics-drivers-an

Morales, L. (2019). La desigualdad que vivimos es insostenible. *El Espectador*, November 6 2019. At: https://www.elespectador.com/noticias/educacion/la-desigualdad-que-vivimos-es-insostenible-profesor-u-catolica-de-chile/

Moyano, R. (2019). Testigos de la historia de Chile. *El País*, October 18 2019. At: https://elpais.com/elpais/2019/12/03/3500_millones/1575362083_494071.html

Mumford, L. (1961). *The City in History: Its Origins, its Transformations, and its Prospects*. New York: Harcourt, Brace and World.

Oakerson, R. J. (2004). 'The Study of Metropolitan Governance'. In Feiock, R. C. (ed.) *Metropolitan Governance in the 21st Century. Capacity, Democracy and the Dynamics of Place*. Washington, DC: Georgetown University Press, pp. 17–45.

OECD. (2018). *OECD Regions and Cities at a Glance 2018*. Paris: OECD Publishing. At: https://doi.org/10.1787/reg_cit_glance-2018-en

Ostrom, E. (1983). 'The Social Stratification-Government Inequality Thesis Explored'. *Urban Affairs Quarterly*, 19(1), 91–112. At: https://doi.org/10.1177/004208168301900107

Paiva, A. (2003). *Relevance of Metropolitan Government in Latin American Cities: Interinstitutional Coordination in Caracas, Venezuela and Monterrey, Mexico*. Utrecht: Eburon.

Parks, R. & Oakerson, R. (1989). 'Metropolitan Organization and Governance: A Local Public Economy Approach'. *Urban Affairs Quarterly*, 25(1), 18–29.

Parks, R. B. & Oakerson, R. J. (1993). 'Comparative Metropolitan Organization: Service Production and Governance Structures in St. Louis (MO) and Allegheny County (PA)'. *Publius: The Journal of Federalism*, 23(1), 19–40.

Peñaranda, I. & Gómez-Delgado, J. (2019). 'Colombia's New Awakening'. *Jacobin*, August 12 2019. At: https://www.jacobinmag.com/2019/12/colombia-protests-paro-nacional-ivan-duque-farc

Pierre, J. (2005). 'Comparative Urban Governance: Uncovering Complex Causalities'. *Urban Affairs Review*, 40(4), 446–462. At: https://doi.org/10.1177/1078087404273442

Raich, U. (2006). 'Unequal development: Decentralization and Fiscal Disparities in the Metropolitan Zone of the Valley of Mexico'. PhD Thesis, Department of Urban Studies and Planning, Massachusetts Institute of Technology.

Rodriguez-Acosta, C. A. & Rosenbaum, A. (2005). 'Local Government and the Governance of Metropolitan Areas in Latin America'. *Public Administration and Development*, 25(4), 295–306. At: https://doi.org/10.1002/pad.387

Rojas, E. (2005). 'Las regiones metropolitanas de América Latina. Problemas de gobierno y desarrollo'. In Rojas, E., Cuadrado-Roura, J. R. and Fernández Güell, J. M. (eds.) *Gobernar las metropolis*. Washington, DC: Inter-American Development Bank. At: http://site.ebrary.com/id/10201140

Sachs, J. (2019). 'Why Rich Cities Rebel'. Project Syndicate, October 22, 2019. At: https://www.project-syndicate.org/commentary/explaining-social-protest-in-paris-hong-kong-santiago-by-jeffrey-d-sachs-2019-10?barrier=accesspaylog

Sehnbruch, K. (2019). 'How Pinochet's economic model led to the current crisis engulfing Chile'. *The Guardian*, October 30 2019. At: https://www.theguardian.com/world/2019/oct/30/pinochet-economic-model-current-crisis-chile

Slack, E. (2007). 'Managing the Coordination of Service Delivery in Metropolitan Cities: The Role of Metropolitan Governance'. Policy Research Working Paper, No. 4317. Washington, DC: World Bank. At: https://openknowledge.worldbank.org/handle/10986/7264

Spink, P. K., Ward, P. & Wilson, R. (2012). *Metropolitan Governance in the Federalist Americas: Strategies for Equitable and Integrated Development*. Notre Dame, IN: University of Notre Dame Press.

Storper, M. (2014). 'Governing the Large Metropolis'. *Territory, Politics and Governance*, 2(2), 115–134. DOI: 10.1080/21622671.2014.919874

Tortajada, C. (2006). *Water Governance with Equity: Is Decentralisation the Answer? Decentralisation of the Water Sector in Mexico and Intercomparison with Practices from Turkey and Brazil*. Nueva York: United Nations Development Programme (UNDP), Human Development Reports (Ocassional Paper). At: http://hdr.undp.org/sites/default/files/tortajada_b.pdf

Tiebout, C. (1956). 'A Pure Theory of Local Expenditures'. *Journal of Political Economy*, 64(5), 416–424.

Treisman, D. (2000). 'Decentralization and the quality of government'. Unpublished paper, University of California, Los Angeles. [Online] At: https://www.imf.org/external/pubs/ft/seminar/2000/fiscal/treisman.pdf

Trejo Nieto, A., Niño Amézquita, J. L. & Vasquez, M. L. (2018). 'Governance of Metropolitan Areas for Delivery of Public Services: The Cases of Bogotá, Lima and Mexico City'. *Region*, 5(3), 49–73. At: https://openjournals.wu.ac.at/region/paper_224/224.html

UN. (2019). *World Urbanization Prospects: The 2018 Revision*. United Nations Department of Economic and Social Affairs, Population Division. New York: UN. At: https://population.un.org/wup/Publications/Files/WUP2018-Report.pdf

UN. (2020). *World Urbanization Prospects: The 2019 Revision*. United Nations Department of Economic and Social Affairs, Population Division. New York: UN. At: https://population.un.org/wpp/DataQuery/

WEF. (2018). 'Cities and urbanisation: Urban economies'. World Economic Forum. [Online] At: https://toplink.weforum.org/knowledge/insight/a1Gb0000000LiPhEAK/explore/dimension/a1G0X000004Pz5WUAS/summary

WEF. (2015). 'Global Risks 2015'. Geneva: World Economic Forum. At: http://www3.weforum.org/docs/WEF_Global_Risks_2015_Report15.pdf

Wilson, R. H. (2012). 'Metropolitan governance systems in the Global South: forms and effectiveness'. Paper presented at the 2012 Regional Studies Association Global Conference in Beijing, China, 24–26 June.

Zimmermann, K., Galland, D. & John, H. (eds.) (2020). *Metropolitan Regions, Planning and Governance*. Berlin: Springer.

1 A framework for contextualising metropolitan governance in Latin America

Alejandra Trejo Nieto

Introduction

Over the course of a half a century, rapid urban growth, socio-political upheavals and economic, political and democratic transitions, including decentralisation, have dramatically reshaped the landscape of Latin America's societies. With 80 per cent of its population living in urban areas, Latin America is the most urbanised region in the Global South in comparison to other regions such as Asia and Africa. But while its urban transition is almost complete, acceptable levels of development have not been reached. Urbanisation has historically been seen as an opportunity for development, and abundant evidence has been found in support of the positive impacts of cities; however, accelerated and concentrated urbanisation generate multiple challenges among which urban poverty, informality, precarious housing, irregular settlements, insufficient infrastructure and public spaces and inadequate basic services particularly stand out. From the point of view of public policy, a key implication of the advance of urbanisation is that social demands and requirements increase and diversify. Two challenges emerge at this level. One is the absence of politically legitimate, financially solvent and technically and administratively well-endowed urban governments; the other is insufficient experience, weak political will and a lack of instruments with which to act on pressing economic, social, environmental, cultural and political issues.

In the last three decades, the dynamics of urban development in the region have taken on new and complex spatial forms. While the extensive and intensive expansion of cities during most of the twentieth century has resulted in the geographical spread of cities and formation of metropolitan areas, mainly via sprawl, countries in the region have made little progress towards effective metropolitan planning and governance. The kind of decentralisation that has been taking place since the 1980s has led to cities that lack government institutions on the appropriate metropolitan scale. Only some countries have witnessed the emergence of efforts towards a properly run metropolitan city with a metropolitan scale of institutions.

Scrutinising the distinctiveness and flaws of urbanisation in Latin America, this chapter describes the current state of urban trends in the region and

DOI: 10.4324/9781003105541-3

discusses the complexities underlying the provision of urban services in the context of decentralisation and metropolisation. Metropolitan governance is the fundamental analytical device from which to investigate the problems and challenges in the delivery of services in the extended and complex urban environments that have arisen in several Latin American societies.

Contemporary patterns of metropolitan urbanisation, urban failure and unequal cities

Metropolitan areas have rapidly and incrementally become an established phenomenon in Latin America (Rojas, 2005; Lanfranchi & Bidart, 2016; Mashini, 2020; Trejo Nieto, 2020). Plenty of publications describe and explain the magnitude and distinctive urbanisation patterns and trends in Latin America, and how it evolved so rapidly and dramatically during the twentieth century (e.g. Lattes, 1995, 2000; Pinto da Cunha, 2002; Cerrutti & Bertoncello, 2003; UN-Habitat, 2012; Trejo Nieto, 2020).

Cities in Mesoamerica and South America have been important for more than 1,500 years; the main pre-Columbian cultures developed inner urban systems with cities as the focal point of social interaction and as administrative, religious and commercial centres (Hardoy, 1982; Zarate Martín, 1989). During colonial times, the Spanish Crown developed cities and urban systems based on European standards of urban planning and design. While these factors contributed to contemporary urbanisation in Latin America and the Caribbean (Rodgers, Beall & Kanbur, 2011), the current urbanisation is the result of the urban explosion after the Second World War caused by industrialisation strategies based on import substitution, by natural population growth and by massive rural migration to cities (Zarate Martín, 1989; Trejo Nieto, 2020). In many countries, central government employed macroeconomic policies as channels directing resources and investment towards cities and the manufacturing sector, feeding a massive rural-urban movement (Trejo Nieto, 2017).

The first thing that stands out in the urban evolution of Latin America is the current high rates of urbanisation (Lattes, 1995). Today around 81 per cent of Latin America's population lives in cities in comparison to 51 per cent in Asia and 44 per cent in Africa, and this is predicted to rise to 88 per cent by 2050. Despite being a developing region, its overall rate of urbanisation is second only to that of North America and similar to that of Europe (Figure 1.1).

Urbanisation varies across the countries, but the regional trends are largely determined by the largest countries: Brazil, Mexico, Colombia, Argentina, Venezuela and Chile (Figure 1.2). In most of Latin American countries more than 50 per cent of the total population is urban, although in some it exceeds 90 per cent (Argentina and Uruguay), and in others in the Caribbean such as Barbados and Trinidad it is under 33 per cent (UN, 2016). This heterogeneity may be accounted for by variations in the implementation of economic models and demographic transitions (Trejo Nieto, 2020).

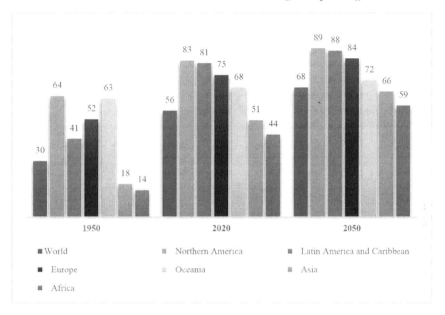

Figure 1.1 Urbanisation by region (per cent)
Source: UN (2020).

The second distinctive characteristic of Latin America is its explosive urbanisation in the second half of the twentieth century. The speed of urbanisation has been remarkable: the region was urbanised in less than two generations due to its rapid (4–5 per cent) rate of urban growth in the 1950s and '60s. No other region in the world has become urbanised so quickly (Zarate Martín, 1989; Lattes, 2000; Trejo Nieto, 2020). In 1950, there were only 66 cities with more than 100,000 inhabitants, and only 1 with more than 5 million; in 1980, this had risen to 245 and 5 cities, respectively (Zarate Martín, 1989). Today, there are 6 megacities with more than 10 million inhabitants, 3 cities have 5–10 million, and 65 have more than 1 million, between them totalling 248 million people. The largest agglomerations are Mexico City (21 million), Sao Paulo (19 million), Rio de Janeiro (11 million) and Buenos Aires (12 million) (Trejo Nieto, 2020). Compared to other regions of the world, the distribution of these urban populations is marked by the outstanding importance of megacities, which contain around 15 per cent of Latin America's entire urban population (UN-Habitat, 2012; Lanfranchi & Bidart, 2016).

Latin America's megacities are associated with excessive primacy, another characteristic of its urbanisation, which creates major imbalances in city systems. Latin America's macrocephalic and bicephalic urban systems are the result of inherited models of centralisation and concentration in one or a small number of cities, and the state's tendency to concentrate investment and resources in consolidated urban agglomerations, usually the capital city

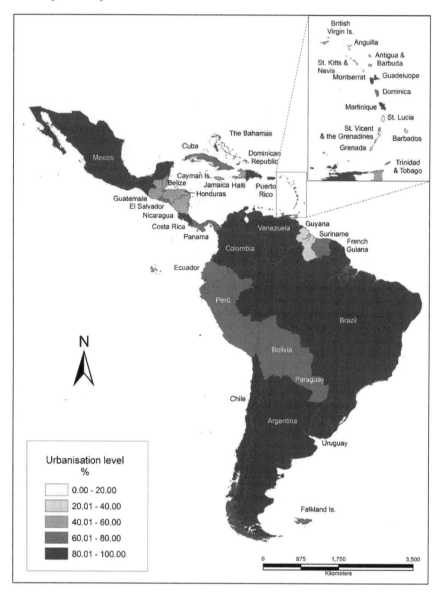

Figure 1.2 Urbanisation in Latin American countries (per cent)

Source: UN (2020).

(Zarate Martín, 1989; Angotti, 1996). Argentina is a typical macrocephalic urban system, whereas Brazil has consolidated into a bicephalic structure which is led by Sao Paulo and Rio de Janeiro (Trejo Nieto, 2020).

Urbanisation in the 1980s started to appear with the significant transformation of cities' form and size: (1) the expansion of urban centres with a tendency to intensive use of land in the peripheries; (2) the deterioration and abandonment of historic centres (e.g. in Havana, Montevideo, Panama and Cartagena) accompanied by gentrification and (3) the proliferation of illegal and marginal settlements in the peripheries (Zarate Martín, 1989). Phenomena such as the growth of lower-class peripheral settlements were observed in the 1950s and '60s (Portes, 1971) and later became the distinctive expression of Latin America's urban pathway. Over time the urban challenge evolved as new city forms emerged. Expansion, peri-urbanisation and conurbation blurred the urban-rural divide and imposed a new character on traditional urban problems. These changes are largely associated with metropolisation: the physical expansion of cities beyond their administrative boundaries. With the construction of new residential complexes, shopping centres, industrial zones and irregular settlements, cities are physically expanding at high speed and the urban footprint is growing up to twice or three times as fast as the population (Trejo Nieto, 2020). Low-density and frequently discontinuous peripheral growth extends over a vast urban space beyond the municipal limits, requiring the expansion of infrastructure networks and increasing the cost of travel and public service provision (Rojas, 2005).

In 2010, there were 320 metropolitan areas in Latin America, 113 more than in 2000. The most extensive were Sao Paulo (4,360 km^2), Buenos Aires (3,300 km^2) and Mexico City (3,180 km^2) (Vargas et al., 2017). Approximately 22 of the 300 world's biggest metropolitan economies are in Latin America and account for 30 per cent of its population and 40 per cent of its economic output (Parilla, Leal & Berube, 2015). In countries like Argentina, the three most important metropolitan areas generate 75 per cent of total GDP (Lanfranchi & Bidart, 2016).

Rapid urbanisation and urban expansion in most Latin American countries have created a large number of problems, such cities often being regarded as the most dangerous and unequal in the world, with social, economic and spatial divisions deeply rooted in their society (Trejo Nieto, 2020). Angotti (1995) describes urban life in Latin America as flawed by poverty, inequality and lack of basic services. They face significant socio-environmental challenges including disorderly growth, segregation, poverty, environmental deterioration, violence and citizen insecurity, institutional and planning struggles and great deficits of social participation (Antúnez & Galilea, 2003). In general, precarious urbanisation, high levels of inequality and highly differentiated access to opportunities and urban services are the norm. Informal neighbourhoods, most lacking basic urban services, proliferate, their housing inadequate and overcrowded. Urbanisation has been accompanied by the impoverishment of social groups and considerable segments of the urban population are excluded from the formal labour market or earn an extremely low income. The dichotomy between the formal and informal economy and productive and unproductive activities is a predominant characteristic of urban economies in the region (Pírez, 2000; Trejo Nieto, 2020). Low tax collection and insufficient investment in infrastructure further challenge the region's cities (UN, 2016).

Unlike in developed countries, industry has not driven urbanisation; in many cases, it came later and is often incomplete. Instead of a direct relationship between industrial employment and urbanisation, the association between urban production and urban growth through the informal sector of the economy shows an extraordinary capacity to generate nonproductive jobs, substituting increased productivity with the employment of cheap and abundant labour (Zarate Martín, 1989). Urbanisation in Latin America has not reinforced economic growth and industrial development. This weaker correspondence between urbanisation and economic performance, compared to developed countries, denotes the failure of urban transitions in the region (Trejo Nieto, 2020). Since the 1970s, authors such as Firebaugh (1979) have discussed how economic development alone is an inadequate explanation of Latin America's urbanisation. Portes (1971) argues that in contrast to the experience of most developed societies, urbanisation in Latin America is less an indicator of economic and social advancement than a sign of the accelerating contradictions generated by underdeveloped economies.

As mentioned, Latin America is recognised as the world's most unequal region. Social and economic inequalities, largely resulting from extremely unequal income distribution, are major challenges currently facing the region, all of whose countries and major cities have high economic inequality with an average Gini coefficient of approximately 0.40. Inequality is also evident in the access to urban services. Large parts of the urban population live without access to good quality and sufficient public services. The spatial expression of these inequalities illustrates the socio-spatial exclusion and territorial segregation that strongly characterise the region (UN, 2016).

A few cities are exceptional in that they have overcome some of these common features via persistent comprehensive policies. Curitiba in Brazil and Medellín in Colombia have applied thought-provoking urban policies. However, as a rule the problems and structural deficiencies are persistent and worsening, particularly in public services (Antúnez & Galilea, 2003).

Many of the flaws in Latin America's urbanisation have been attributed to the lack of adequate institutional and planning frameworks. The region has lacked adequate urban planning that can deliver economic growth and a good quality of life to its populations (Trejo Nieto, 2020). Other interpretations suggest that despite the widespread perception that cities are unplanned and unmanageable, both government agencies and the private sector have historically engaged in considerable planning; this, however, has mostly benefited the wealthy and the powerful (Angotti, 1995).

Decentralisation and pressing issues for local governments

Decentralisation has been the centre stage in a large number of developing nations' policy reform for some decades. It has structured intergovernmental relations, subnational functions and local government financing in several countries. After experiencing a historical tradition of strong centralisation and authoritarianism, from the 1980s calls for increased government efficiency drove a Latin American region-wide transfer of power and resources to subnational rather than national policymakers, for instance in Chile and Mexico. Although only Argentina, Mexico, Brazil and Venezuela have federal governments and a greater proportion of Latin American countries are under unitary governments, decentralisation took place in most national states in the region (Mascareño, Balbi & Cunill, 1995). Stimulated by high levels of dissatisfaction with democracy, bureaucracy and clientelism and a high concentration of political power and discretion, the responsiveness of policymakers closer to citizens started to be included in a new wave of political and administrative transformation (Simon & Sweigart, 2020). Thus during the 1980s and '90s, Latin America saw great institutional changes that transformed the dynamics of power in the region. With the fall of military governments and the emergence of a democratic wave, countries carried out reforms that included a so-called Silent Revolution: the decentralisation of the state (Grin, Hernández Bonivento & Abrucio, 2017).

Decentralisation, broadly defined as the transfer of responsibility for planning, management and the raising and allocation of resources from central government to (a) field units of central government ministries or agencies; (b) subordinate units or levels of government; (c) semi-autonomous public authorities and corporations; (d) area-wide regional and functional authorities or (e) Non-Governmental Organisation (Rondinelli, 1981), was widely alleged to create a range of social welfare and efficiency benefits by means of incremental institutional capacity-building. Proponents advocated the decentralisation of political authority and public resources to subnational governments through the reduction of central government, making them responsive and accountable (Rondinelli, Nellis & Shabbir Cheema, 1983). Decentralisation would also help to deepen and consolidate democracy by devolving power to local government. Moreover, economists argued that decentralisation would help to improve resource allocation and service provision through better knowledge of local preferences and competition among local governments (Falleti, 2005).

In the case of Latin America, common political, economic and administrative reasons explain the wave of decentralisation. The economic reasons for decentralisation stemmed from the economic crisis in the 1980s, which directly affected the region's centralised development models. The political reasons were related to the increasing demands for democratisation: Latin America was a region plagued by authoritarian military governments in the 1970s. Political decentralisation included the election of local authorities by popular vote, deepening democracy and the legitimacy of governmental action. The administrative reasons for decentralisation came from the need to adapt to the complexity of modern societies and greater concern for citizens' needs (Grin, Hernández Bonivento & Abrucio, 2017).

Across the region, decentralisation has been both quantitatively and qualitatively unequal. The magnitude of change in the fiscal, administrative and political areas of decentralisation has ranged from insignificant to substantial, leading to differing intergovernmental balances of power across countries, a mixed transfer of functions and taxing powers, and varying levels of accountability to their constituencies on the part of governors and mayors (ibid). As a consequence of this heterogeneity, the main features of local governments are their uneven resources, state capacity, democratisation and relative strength and autonomy in relation to their central government (Moscovich, 2015).

The Peruvian state, for instance, embarked on a decentralisation strongly based on the transfer of tax revenue and several regulatory attributions from Lima to local governments (Simon & Sweigart, 2020). Even though the movement towards decentralisation in Peru was initiated from below with a sequence of political, administrative and fiscal decentralisation moves, the intergovernmental balance of power saw little change.

Decentralisation in Colombia followed a sequence of reforms: political autonomy was devolved first, followed by fiscal decentralisation. Administrative decentralisation was the last reform, with subnational actors obtaining the guaranteed fiscal resources necessary to afford the costs of the transferred services. In contrast, Argentina's sequence of administrative, fiscal and political reforms produced only a small change in the intergovernmental balance of power: while local expenditure increased, it did so by less than the changes in local spending in Colombia, Mexico or Brazil, and the subnational share of revenue decreased (Falleti, 2005). In Chile, early deconcentration under the authoritarian regime preceded an incremental top-down decentralisation that mainly consisted of the modernisation of the local state or was restricted to administrative aspects, but the centralist heritage remained strong (OECD, 2017). Decentralisation in Mexico and Brazil led to greater changes to the intergovernmental balance of power than those of Argentina and Peru (Montero, 2001; Falleti, 2003).

In most countries in the world, administrative decentralisation has seen major public services such as education and health transferred to subnational governments, following the subsidiarity principle in the public sector which proposes that if a particular service or administrative function can be carried out by local government just as well as by a higher level it should be assigned to the former (Wilson, Ward & Spink, 2012). Also in Latin America local arenas became the new spaces for the provision of public goods and services (Moscovich, 2015). Local authorities became responsible for delivering public services from security to transport, and in some instances healthcare and education. Political and administrative decentralisation advocated intense transfer of competencies to municipalities, cantons or communes, depending on the country, whereas fiscal decentralisation was more limited. In the multilevel distribution of responsibilities for public service provision, municipalities play differing roles with varying levels of intensity. Municipal powers are defined in the respective national or political constitutions and in municipal and state laws, regulations, ordinances and agreements. The range of services provided by local government is broad and includes common tasks such as the provision of drinking water, sanitation, transportation, cleaning, cultural activities and recreation and the maintenance of streets, avenues, parks and monuments. Responsibility for more complex services such as education, health and urban planning are usually shared with other levels of government (Mascareño, Balbi & Cunill, 1995).

The Political Constitution of Peru establishes, in Article 192, that municipalities have the power to approve their own internal organisation and budget; manage their own assets and revenue and organise, regulate and administer local public services. In Mexico, Article 115 of the Constitution declares that municipalities must provide the following services: drinking water and sewerage, public lighting, cleaning, markets and supply centres, cemeteries, streets, parks and gardens, public safety and traffic. Article 311 of the Constitution of Colombia stipulates that municipalities are responsible for providing basic services, Article 2 of Law 60 establishing that municipalities, directly or through decentralised municipal entities, must provide preschool, basic, secondary and middle education, finance urban investments and infrastructure, and supervise and evaluate educational services; promote public health, prevent disease, finance the provision of first-level treatment and rehabilitation services and second- and third-level services if they have the scientific, technological, financial and administrative capacity; supply drinking water, sewerage, water treatment and disposal, urban cleaning and basic sanitation and provide housing for the low-income population (ibid). The local functions in Chile, as established in Article 3 of the Organic Law of Municipalities, elaborate, approve and modify communal development plans; plan and regulate communes and prepare regulatory plans; promote development and provide public transport, investment in urbanisation, and public cleaning. In addition, Article 4 of the Organic Law of Municipalities establishes various functions that municipalities may carry out directly or with other state administration organs (i.e. education, public health, social assistance and training and promotion of employment) (Pacheco, Sánchez & Villena, 2013). The national Constitutions of Brazil (Article 30) and Venezuela (Article 30) specify similar municipal functions. National Constitutions in Argentina, El Salvador and Cuba do not directly allude to municipal powers, but in Argentina each province has its respective organic laws that specify municipal powers (Mascareño, Balbi & Cunill, 1995) because decentralisation in Argentina favours provincial governments over municipalities (Moscovich, 2015).

Moscovich (2015) highlights that when local governments assume more responsibilities, they also need more resources. Yet functions devolved to subnational levels in this region have not always been accompanied by more resources from central government or by a greater capacity to collect local taxes. Falleti (2005) argues that when administrative decentralisation advances without a transfer of fiscal authority, the autonomy of subnational officials is affected and local governments become more dependent on national fiscal transfers or subnational debt for the delivery of public social services.

Latin America's growing fiscal imbalance is double that of Eastern Europe and three times that of Asia. Using fiscal data for 2002–2009 in ten Latin

American countries, Moscovich (2015) shows that subnational financing depends upon transfers from central governments and that this dependence has been increasing, mainly due to higher levels of expenditure not accompanied by higher own local revenues. According to Wilson, Ward and Spink (2012), city and metropolitan authorities in Latin American have to deal with reductions to public budgets and local and metropolitan adequate tax systems remain a work in progress.

Summing up, the local governments and mayors in most countries in the region have been made legally autonomous so that they can take on more of their local administration. However, this reallocation of powers and spending overwhelmed most of them because they had been unable to develop adequate capacity for management under the historically strongly centralised structure of political power. In many cases, local governments found themselves in critical situations due to limitations to their use of their powers, finance, management of citizen participation and fostering of participatory governance. The complex framework of municipal powers and functions has put them under permanent strain with an urgent need to improve their overall performance (Mascareño, Balbi & Cunill, 1995; Moscovich, 2015).

The key lessons here are that without an extensive program to build local institutional and financial capacity, decentralisation usually fails (Simon & Sweigart, 2020); and that decentralisation does not necessarily increase the power of governors and mayors (Falleti, 2005). Furthermore, Andersson (2017) argues that the recent Latin American experience of decentralisation is contradictory, because it was driven more by a desire to improve policy efficiency than the intention of increasing citizen participation and democracy. However, as a region Latin America is regarded as being in a better position than before, because in most of its countries democracy and the rule of law are stronger than in the 1990s and early 2000s. In addition, local governments have access to new tools to promote transparency, train civil servants and strengthen institutions (Simon & Sweigart, 2020).

Urban politics is an important decentralisation issue that has often been overlooked (Moscovich, 2015). Besides the usual urban problems of crime, public transport, housing, pollution, poverty, etcetera, local governments in metropolitan areas face political and administrative fragmentation and coordination failures. On the other hand, they usually have more informed voters, more mobilised civil societies and higher tax revenues. These big cities are bastions of political opposition, which is why central government is reluctant to decentralise them and unleash a metropolitan level of political power.

The state of metropolitan governance in a decentralised environment

Cities in the geographic region of Latin America, unlike those in Europe or North America, and with the exclusion of a few cases such as Quito, whose metropolitan district is constituted by law and has a metropolitan political-administrative structure of popular election, lack a tradition of establishing metropolitan governments and have little experience of developing metropolitan institutions (Rodríguez & Oviedo, 2001; Andersson, 2017). As in most of the world, the main governance problem is that Latin America's metropolitan areas are not recognised as political entities, and so lack political legitimacy and depend on the legal and political force of their municipalities. Moreover, metropolitan arrangements and conventions are often ambiguous or non-compulsory (Lanfranchi & Bidart, 2016). Even where metropolitan agencies are created, they seldom have the legal status and finance necessary to address fundamental urban problems such as how land is to be used and the need for investment in infrastructure, housing and mobility (Mashini, 2020).

Brazil's constitution allows the creation of metropolitan regions; once the responsibility of the federal government, this has now been devolved to state governments. The states do not need to consult their municipalities about creating metropolitan regions and other types of municipal agglomerations to facilitate the shared organisation, planning and implementation of public functions in the common interest. Once a metropolitan region has been created, municipalities' participation is mandatory. However, there is still the political difficulty of establishing formal metropolitan government: states, municipalities and the federal government may prefer to enter into "cooperation agreements" on providing common services and sharing the costs. Local authorities can form a public consortium, which is more formal than a cooperation agreement but has as a disadvantage the fact that participation is voluntary and members are required to negotiate a cost-sharing agreement defining the size and types of financial contribution that they are willing to make. São Paulo provides examples such as its intermunicipal consortium to manage shared water resources through improvements to waste collection and disposal, and its consortium created to address the problem of slum urbanisation (Slack, 2019).

In part, the slow progress in metropolitan matters has been due to efforts to strengthen decentralisation (Souza, 2006). According to Rodriguez-Acosta and Rosenbaum (2005), the movement towards decentralising government authority and enhancing local governments has worked against the development of metropolitan governments and governance within the region. Decentralisation implies that any attempt to establish a new level of government involves a loss of power for local governments that must hand over part of their power and resources (Rodríguez & Oviedo, 2001). With decentralisation, municipalities slowly began to acquire some degree of independence in policymaking and became reluctant to cede any of their authority to either comprehensive or highly specific metropolitan-wide governing bodies (Rodriguez-Acosta & Rosenbaum, 2005).

Wilson, Ward and Spink (2012) argue that there are two important differences between federal and unitary systems in Latin American countries: first, if the key to metropolitan management is the creation of an independent metropolitan government, it is probably easier to achieve this in a unitary state, since central government can legislate to create a new tier of government, as in Quito; and second, while it may be difficult for federal systems to make constitutional changes that would create a new tier of government, they can allow state and local governments to formally engage in intergovernmental relations and collaborative arrangements that offer viable means of constructing some level of metropolitan governance.

Even facing these two political realities, one of the main challenges is to define coordination, planning and implementation processes that maximise economic and social efficiency across the metropolitan area. According to the collective action approach, in the absence of a metropolitan government coordination is an excellent test of governance. Where there is no metropolitan body, developing associations of local authorities can be explored as a strategy for governance and urban development and planning in Latin America (Rodríguez & Oviedo, 2001; Rodriguez-Acosta & Rosenbaum, 2005; Lanfranchi & Bidart, 2016; Slack, 2019). Because local governments' coordination among themselves and with regional and national authorities in each country is determined by the political will, legal framework, and structure of the different levels of government, metropolitan realities are highly heterogeneous. Different political regimes that establish competencies and degrees of autonomy for local government coexist (Lanfranchi & Bidart, 2016).

While the analysis of metropolitan issues and governance in Latin America and the Caribbean has not been as systematic and abundant as that of Europe and North America, Lanfranchi and Bidart (2016) survey the forms of metropolitan governance, financing, legal framework and planning in 64 metropolitan areas with more than a million inhabitants in 2010 in Latin America and the Caribbean. More than half of these are in Brazil and Mexico, and all of the national capital cities are included. Combined these metropolises contained 205 million inhabitants, spread across 21 countries and involved 1000 local governments. Each is governed by from 1 to 75 local governments, with the average 15.6. Some of the largest metropolitan areas – Buenos Aires, Santiago, Mexico City, Lima and San Juan de Puerto Rico – present highly fragmented scenarios covering more than 20 municipalities.

Many of these 64 metropolises had a metropolitan plan – understood as a metropolitan-wide strategic, sectoral or territorial programme – and some form of regulation or legal framework to guide metropolitan relations. But the existence of a plan and/or regulations does not determine the formation of a governing metropolitan body. Most of the metropolitan bodies are in Brazil and Colombia and were created either via an agreement between local or provincial governments or by an ad hoc authority.

The types of representatives of these metropolitan organisations vary depending on the country and legal framework, but in the main they are unelected. In the absence of metropolitan bodies, coordination mechanisms are a pressing necessity. The sectors with the greatest potential for coordination in these metropolises are urban planning, followed by water, sanitation and transport. Lastly, they find evidence of the great financial dependence of local governments facing increasing allocation of responsibilities and problems. Their revenue consists mostly of transfers from local, provincial or national governments, and their budgets vary widely.

Even if effective governance has not been achieved, different forms of metropolitan organisation are in operation in the region (Mashini, 2020), and the experiences of metropolitan management are diverse. The fairly successful institutionalisation of a metropolitan wide area can be found in the Metropolitan District of Quito, established by the Metropolitan Regime Law of December 1993. The law gave the metropolitan district new powers in land management, environmental control, transport administration, administrative deconcentration and citizen participation. Although the new metropolitan regime has supported some effective economic and industrial development in Quito, further challenges in meeting both old and new needs – environmental sustainability, economic efficiency, interinstitutional coordination, systematic citizen participation, the modernisation of the municipal administration and sustainable municipal finances – have had to be addressed. In Buenos Aires, attempts at sectoral and in some cases general coordination have included numerous public and private actors, although in most such attempts the federal government has been responsible for metropolitan management, guided by a clearly centralising model. On the other hand, institutional alternatives based on interjurisdictional agreements established in the National Constitution have not been applied (Rodríguez & Oviedo, 2001).

Metropolitan issues are especially hard to deal with in some countries such as Chile. Steps toward metropolitan governance have involved fundamental changes to the organic constitutional laws, reconsideration of the transfer of powers from central to regional governments and the creation of a new service division. In Santiago, all levels of government have tended to intervene in metropolitan matters, from the municipalities to regional government, national ministries, sectoral bodies, the police and deputies (Rodríguez & Oviedo, 2001). According to Grin, Hernández Bonivento and Abrucio (2017), central government still strongly intervenes in the city's cross-cutting issues. Mashini (2020) argues that the institutional construction of metropolitan governance in Chile has raised questions that other countries have already tried to solve: what role must central government play in delivering political legitimacy to the metropolitan authorities? How should responsibilities be established to allow metropolitan authorities to implement their own policies and finance their own projects? How should coordination between the different actors in metropolitan areas be promoted?

In most metropolitan areas in Latin America political conflict between municipal, provincial and national officials is neither unusual nor infrequent.

In the face of reluctance to form metropolitan governmental bodies, many of the region's metropolitan areas slowly began to advance various forms of voluntary cooperative efforts to address their problems. There are permanent coordination units or other light governance structures that can be catalysts for joint initiatives addressing a variety of metropolitan subjects, often in the form of associations that evolve into more comprehensive coordination entities, such as the Council of Mayors of the Metropolitan Area of San Salvador (Andersson, 2017). In most cases, however, these efforts at coordination are relatively limited or at an early stage.

Article 115 of Mexico's National Constitution allows municipalities, with the approval of their assemblies, to coordinate and associate with one another to deliver better services and solve common problems. Argentina's National Constitution allows provinces to create 'regions' to promote economic and social development, and its provincial legislation allows municipalities to create consortiums amongst themselves or together with national government or another province. But the implementation of coordinated action is always challenging. Lima's efforts to coordinate different municipalities' service provision have not been very successful. Coordination and common policies for urban development in Colombia, and especially in the metropolitan area of Bogotá, have been difficult to achieve due to the lack of an appropriate institutional and legal framework and of a national law on territorial organisation, as also administrative fragmentation, and overlapping competencies across different administrative levels (Rodriguez-Acosta & Rosenbaum, 2005). In Mexico City, some efforts to create metropolitan coordination via commissions and committees for the delivery of strategic public services have neither been successful nor induced the coordination of local governments, as governance of the metropolitan area is most influenced intermediate governments (ibid; Trejo Nieto, 2020).

Although alliances and institutional cooperation between local jurisdictions are important in promoting effective metropolitan governance, coordination failures are still the norm in Latin America's metropolises. Extensive fragmentation, as in Mexico City, is a constraint as the cooperation of many actors, agencies or jurisdictions imposes the problems of collective action by a large group, which involves high costs and requires consensus across different levels of government (Trejo Nieto, 2020). In countries such as Brazil and Mexico, party conflicts and rigid intergovernmental relations are powerful obstacles to metropolitan integration and coordination. The absence of permanent financing mechanisms is another common problem that limits and challenges metropolitan management (Clementino & Almeida, 2015; Trejo Nieto, 2020).

Local conflict overrides metropolitan consensus, making these areas unmanageable. This can originate from different situations of uncertainty about the financing of projects, infrastructure and service provision, mistrust, aversion to municipalities' possible loss of autonomy, the possibility of needing more public resources and bureaucracy. An institutional vacuum persists with respect not only to integrated governance but also to shared governance based on collective action, in which several actors decide to cooperate in a territory to produce common benefits (ibid). Metropolitan areas can suffer from significant institutional weaknesses that mechanisms of governance to solve existing urban problems are difficult to implement. Weak governance can also be explained by the absence of a metropolitan identity, coupled with the lack of a civic culture that encourages citizens to participate. Even in the presence of opportunities for self-governance, metropolitan residents usually identify themselves with somewhere outside the metropolitan area: "It is not unusual for residents and natives born of metropolitan areas to identify with that city or region – as *chilangos* in the Federal District of Mexico, *porteños* in Buenos Aires, *cariocas* in Rio de Janeiro, *caraqueños* in Caracas" (Wilson, Ward & Spink, 2012, p. 18). This hinders collective action that could guarantee governability and hampers social mobilisation. The lack of an organised society and its mobilisation to solve common problems makes it difficult to build collective solutions (Souza, 2006).

Sectoral experiences with cooperation mechanisms and specific objectives can be established between municipalities, despite the lack of global institutional coordination at the supramunicipal level. This occurs in situations where institutional collective action leads the signatories of power to cooperative action, based on trust and inclusive participation. On the other hand, there are instances where centralised structures and top-down approaches enforced by national or intermediate authorities lead to metropolitan-wide projects or service provision (Trejo Nieto, Niño Amézquita & Vasquez, 2018). Some of these experiences are identified in the case studies in this book.

While the problems of metropolitan governance in Latin America are both pressing and widespread, in virtually no instance has it been possible to overcome all the complexities of multiple jurisdictions, high levels of inequality and extensive political conflict (Rodriguez-Acosta & Rosenbaum, 2005). There is no universal equation for the institutional construction of metropolitan governance (Rodríguez & Oviedo, 2001). Slack (2019) argues that it is very difficult to suggest one governance model for all of the Latin American or any other context because the appropriate governance structure for a metropolitan area depends on its legal context, the roles and responsibilities of its local governments, its sources of revenue, its intergovernmental relations, the political strength and will of its local leaders, the capacity of its civil service and further factors. However, good practice in similar contexts can be very informative for implementing metropolitan reforms, good governance in metropolitan policies and the provision of strategic services.

Metropolitan service delivery and spatial inequality

While metropolitan areas are exposed and increasingly vulnerable to threats such as natural challenges, including earthquakes, hurricanes and other extreme climatic events, socio-economic disparities and public service provision remain as strong sources of vulnerability. In urban centres in the developing world, poor and informal settlers in particular tend to lack adequate urban services (Wilson, Ward & Spink, 2012). Around one in seven of the world's population lives in poverty in urban areas, most in overcrowded, poor-quality homes in informal settlements lacking basic infrastructure and services (UCLG, 2012). One strategic area for action by urban governments is therefore the equitable provision of public services (Slack, 2007). In Latin America metropolitan expansion has been taking place in a context of insufficient normative, technical and financial capacity to attend to critical items on the urban agenda. The local governments of several metropolises in the region have reported tremendous difficulties, particularly in providing efficient public services (Blanco-Ochoa, Osorio-Lara & Gómez-Álvarez, 2017). Insufficient networks for the provision of and access to services have been associated in general terms with the urban territories – usually the peripheries – where the poorest live (Rojas, 2005).

There are few studies such as Trejo Nieto, Niño Amézquita & Vasquez's (2018) paper on the provision of urban services in Latin America's metropolitan areas. But the delivery of urban services in general has been studied more systematically. Pírez (2013) argues that the provision of urban services in the region has been sustained by common structural features and analogous historical processes, and that such provision has generally followed approaches based on various social, political, technical and economic criteria. Before their decentralisation, Latin American states administered and managed a set of urban services through their national apparatus (Pírez, 2000; Antúnez & Galilea, 2003). Nation-states played a powerful role in the production and management of urban services and revealed their economic and above all their political capacity to produce goods and services and to allocate fiscal resources (Antúnez & Galilea, 2003; Pírez, 2016). The centrally managed system intended universal coverage via the provision of free services or the use of explicit or implicit subsidies to create wide access (Pírez, 2000, 2016). For example, Venezuela provided free education and health services and subsidies for water, electricity, gas and telephone services (Pírez, 2000). Seeking to create conditions conducive to long-term development covering all segments of the population, the state introduced such redistribution principles. Moreover, urban management was predominantly modernist and regulatory, with the state the producer of standards and responsible, particularly financially, for the production of city services (Pírez, 2013).

Despite the expansion of coverage and certain vindication for universal access, a considerable part of the population remained excluded from service provision (Pírez, 2012, 2013). General evidence from the centralised management model indicates that the coverage network did not reach the poorest population due to limited finance for the expansion of the infrastructure networks (Rojas, 2005), and that part of the population could not afford services even at a low price. Informal housing and labour precarity have explained the lack of their incorporation into formal services (Pírez, 2000).

Besides the limited coverage and inability to keep up with the expansion of cities, the central state management of urban services was of low quality, largely due to the prevalent institutional arrangements and lack of efficient management, with financing deficits and reduced investment growing central issues. These factors explain the continuous degradation of services, which were exacerbated by Latin America's rampant urbanisation (Pírez, 2000). The low-income population, many of whom accessed land and housing via invasion and irregular and informal urbanisation, managed their access to services directly, either by self-production or by demands from state agencies. In most cases the absence of formal networks forced them to pay for more expensive, lower-quality services (Pírez, 2013, 2016).

With decentralisation, the municipalities became responsible for providing services such as drinking water, sewerage, sanitation, cemeteries, civil registries, markets, citizen security and the collection and processing of solid waste. The potential incorporation of non-governmental actors in the delivery of services initiated debates about public responsibility and private participation, regulatory frameworks and the growing transition towards new management models (Antúnez & Galilea, 2003). Over the decades the reduction of central governments' participation in the management of urban public services was followed by the increasing incorporation of private companies as service producers and co-producers. This gave rise to different management models according to the type of actors involved and their relationships. These management models also incorporated, although often in a relatively subordinate way, community players (Pírez, 2000; Antúnez & Galilea, 2003).

In the 1990s, different forms of private and social agents' participation were promoted in what had traditionally been strictly public service provision. With decentralisation not yet complete, four types of urban management could be distinguished: state management, decentralised management, private management and mixed management. In this context, the privatisation of basic services was framed in a complex political and ideological debate (ibid).

As discussed, decentralisation caused increasing difficulties for subnational governments that were not equipped to take on the management of services. The weakness of Latin America's municipalities is particularly significant in view of the region's serious and growing urban problems with cities' administrative, financial, technical and political capacities. The participation of private firms in service supply was linked to local governments' difficulties with implementing policies for financing services autonomously. Mixed management basically involved government contracting one or more private companies to carry out, for instance, tasks such as water and sanitation services and the collection and disposal of solid waste in Mexico City and Santiago. Other methods included social management and self-management schemes, which played a marginal role in service provision. In some cases, the transition from state to private production brought improvement, at least in the quality of services and management, as for instance in Buenos Aires, where telephone, water and sanitation, electricity, gas and urban railway and subway services were privatised at the beginning of the 1990s. However, private provision had differential social significance depending on economic conditions in the implementing country. In Latin American societies, characterised by precariousness in the labour markets and a large number of inhabitants below the poverty line, the privatisation of urban services signified exclusion for the latter (Pírez, 2000).

The evidence does not provide clear results regarding decentralised service management compared to centralised provision. Decentralised state management and all its emerging modalities have exhibited similar problems that had been identified in central state management. In addition, the outcomes vary depending on the type of urban service, and the country and the cities within it in each case. The variation could depend on technical-economic factors and subordination to local processes of political accumulation, often based on clientelism (Pírez, 2000, 2013).

Antúnez and Galilea (2003) discuss the main challenges to urban service provision prevalent at the onset of the twenty-first century. First, they note that service delivery has faced a complex set of historical deficits that had accumulated over time with regard to both access to services and the quality with which they have been delivered to the public. There is significant inequality in the supply of health, education, drinking water and sanitation, waste treatment, public safety, urban transport, and local services in general, with lack of access mostly affecting a significant proportion of the poor. In Latin American cities access and quality problems require huge governmental and social attention. Even though some deficits have reduced, these are exceptional instances, as in the case of Chile's housing. Actually, housing is the most-cited example of the reduction of the service gap in the region's cities.

Second, social heterogeneity is expressed in a striking socio-spatial segregation that manifests as varied configurations of public services in Latin American cities. There are usually areas or neighbourhoods with wide deficits in coverage and quality.

Third, the provision of public services is structurally underfunded. Lack of knowledge about financing structures, the allocation of social costs and benefits and adequate targeting of public budgets at different territorial scales seem to prevail. The financing problems depend on the tax structure and the systems for paying for public services and related gratuities and subsidies predominate. This is accompanied by the citizens' unwillingness to pay for public services. As a result of subsidies and unpaid services, the state and its respective agencies, including municipal government, accumulate extraordinary amounts of debt.

Fourth, forms of citizen participation are highly insufficient. While in developed countries society and community organisations play an important role in the control and assessment of service delivery, in Latin America, such systems are precarious and generally focus on demanding that the state satisfies their immediate needs.

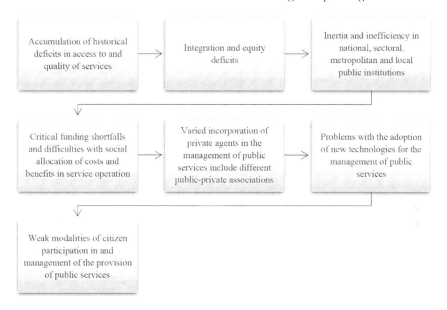

Figure 1.3 The challenges for delivering public services in Latin American cities

Source: Based on Antúnez and Galilea (2003).

The technological orientation from which services are provided is another area of concern. In only a few areas of public services technological options are more "open", but it is possible to appreciate a remarkable technological evolution, as in the case of solid waste collection and treatment, where new technologies have substantially modified traditional systems. However, there is inefficient routinisation of processes and a strong resistance to change in many sectors. Figure 1.3 summarises the main problems of public services in Latin American cities over the last decades. Additionally, Pírez (2016) calls attention to politicisation in the provision of services: some governments have developed compensatory social policies targeting certain population groups for electoral gain.

The question is how problems of local service provision are expressed at the metropolitan scale in cities such as Santiago where the urban area doubled in the 1980s expanding into unstructured neighbourhoods that continue deficient in services (Antúnez & Galilea, 2003). Moreover, how the delivery of services throughout an entire metropolitan area alters the pattern of spatial inequality. In the face of differential service provision, citizens with higher incomes tend to move to areas with better services and a better quality of life, while the ability to move of the poorest is limited, increasing social inequality (Sellers & Hoffmann-Martinot, 2008) and affecting competitiveness and social cohesion.

In metropolitan areas, the type of governance can be an essential determinant of the quantity, quality and efficiency of the services provided, and of how fairly and efficiently the costs are shared by local governments throughout the metropolis. An effective system of governance covering an entire metropolitan region might be needed to ensure that transportation, water, solid waste treatment, policing, health and education are delivered efficiently and the costs are shared equitably (Slack, 2007; Lanfranchi & Bidart, 2016).

Final remarks

As the world becomes increasingly urbanised, the accelerated expansion of metropolitan regions becomes more visible. The urban expansion of the previous decades and the resulting economic, social, political and environmental transformations have introduced profound territorial reorganisation processes, ranging from new patterns for the location of urban activities to significant changes to the territorial level deemed appropriate for designing and implementing public policies and managing the provision of public goods and services. In this context, the challenges of cities exist on the regional and metropolitan scales as well as locally. High urbanisation and the trend towards the emergence of large cities and metropolitan areas are prominent features of Latin American societies. But because accelerated urban growth, urban biases and excessive primacy preceded Latin America's urbanisation the latter is seriously flawed, with most of the population experiencing social, economic and environmental shortcomings. Among all of the urban challenges, the delivery of public services is outstanding.

With decentralisation reforms triggered under different arrangements in the 1980s, education, health, transport, and urban services increasingly became the responsibility of local or regional governments. Varied approaches to local service supply have been implemented across the region including public provision schemes, public–private systems and coproduction arrangements, with the increasing involvement of non-public actors in the delivery of different services. While the mixture of social, public and private participation has allowed greater flexibility, long-lasting problems including historical deficits in access to and the quality of services, unequal distribution, funding shortfalls, problems with the adoption of new technologies and weak citizen participation have all prevailed after decentralisation.

Allowing for metropolisation, if service provision is decentralised, its management is important because the territorial distribution of services does not necessarily follow the logic in the distribution of urban populations. Because urban sprawl in metropolitan areas crosses municipal borders, the one urban area is subject to different municipal legal frameworks and technical and financial capacities. Differentiated endowments of services across the territory result in such circumstances. The question of spatial variation in public goods and service allocation as a reflection of differing local conditions is particularly important in decentralised contexts. Decentralisation and metropolisation can be powerful causes of spatial inequality in public service provision because metropolitan governance is deeply affected by existing systems of intergovernmental relations that generally do not include metropolitan governments. Moreover, uneven urban service delivery and infrastructure may reproduce income inequality by providing fewer and poorer-quality services to low-income inhabitants; or alternatively they may contribute to reducing disparities via integrated policies and planning.

In metropolitan areas, while most urban issues transcend political–administrative limits they can be addressed more efficiently through metropolitan coordination than at the municipal level. Effective metropolitan coordination can contribute to not only urban productivity and efficiency but also inclusiveness and equality. Pressing issues regarding the effective delivery of services and metropolitan governance require discussion and analysis: political legitimation, intersectoral and multilevel coordination based on political and institutional support, fiscal autonomy and responsibility, technical capacity, the comprehensive geographic delimitation of services areas and representation and participation in decision-making processes. Some of these are discussed in the remaining chapters of this book with relevant case studies from the region.

References

Andersson, M. (2017). 'Metropolitan Governance: The New Normal for Improved Quality of Life'. In Gómez-Álvarez D. et al., *Steering the Metropolis Metropolitan Governance for Sustainable Urban Development*. Washington, DC: Inter-American Development Bank, pp. 73–85. At: https://unhabitat.org/sites/default/files/download-manager-files/Steering_the_Metropolis.pdf

Angotti, T. (1995). 'The Latin American Metropolis and the Growth of Inequality'. *NACLA Report on the Americas*, 28(4), 13–18. At: http://dx.doi.org/10.1080/10714839.1995.11722946

Angotti, T. (1996). 'Latin American Urbanization and Planning: Inequality and Unsustainability in North and South'. *Latin American Perspectives*, 23(4), 12–34.

Antúnez, I. & Galilea, S. (2003). *Servicios públicos urbanos y gestión local en América Latina y el Caribe: problemas, metodologías y políticas*. Serie Medio ambiente y desarrollo, No. 69. Santiago: CEPAL/ECLAC. At: https://repositorio.cepal.org/bitstream/handle/11362/5770/1/S039607_es.pdf

Blanco-Ochoa, K., Osorio-Lara, E. & Gómez-Álvarez, D. (2017). 'Guadalajara, Mexico's Metropolitan Governance Laboratory'. In Gómez-Álvarez, D. et al., *Steering the Metropolis Metropolitan Governance for Sustainable Urban Development*. Washington, DC: Inter-American Development Bank, pp. 290–298.

Cerrutti, M. & Bertoncello, R. (2003). 'Urbanization and internal migration patterns in Latin America'. *Paper prepared for Conference on African Migration in Comparative Perspective*, Johannesburg, South Africa, 4–7 June 2003.

Clementino, M. L. M. & Almeida, L. S. B. (2015). 'Construção técnico-política de governança metropolitana'. *Cadernos Metrópole*, 17(33), 201–224. At: https://doi.org/10.1590/2236-9996.2015-3309

Falleti, T. G. (2003). 'Governing Governors: Coalitions and Sequences of Decentralization in Argentina, Colombia, and Mexico'. PhD dissertation, Northwestern University.

Falleti, T. G. (2005). 'A Sequential Theory of Decentralization: Latin American Cases in Comparative Perspective'. *American Political Science Review*, 99(3), 327–346. DOI:10.1017/S0003055405051695

Firebaugh, G. (1979). 'Structural Determinants of Urbanization in Asia and Latin America, 1950-1970'. *American Sociological Review*, 44, 199–215.

Grin, E. J., Hernández Bonivento, J. & Abrucio, F. (eds.) (2017). *El Gobierno de las grandes ciudades: Gobernanza y Descentralización en las Metrópolis de América Latina*. CLAD Centro Latinoamericano de Administración para el Desarrollo and Universidad Autónoma de Chile, Santiago.

Hardoy, J. E. (1982). 'The Building of the Latin American Cities'. In Gilbert, A., Hardoy, J. E. & Ramirez, R. (eds.) *Urbanization in Contemporary Latin America: Critical Approaches to the Analysis of Urban Issues*. Chichester: John Wiley, pp. 19–33.

Lanfranchi, G. & Bidart, M. (2016). *Gobernanza metropolitana en América Latina y el Caribe*. Documento de Trabajo No. 151. CIPPEC.

Lattes, A. E. (1995). *Urbanización, crecimiento urbano y migraciones en América Latina*. Notas de Población. Santiago: CEPAL, pp. 211–260. At: https://repositorio.cepal.org/bitstream/handle/11362/38594/NP6206_es.pdf?sequence=1&isAllowed=y

Lattes, A. E. (2000). 'Población urbana y urbanización en América Latina'. In Carrión, F., (ed.) *La ciudad construida: urbanismo en América Latina. II Jornadas Iberoamericanas de Urbanismo sobre las Nuevas Tendencias de la Urbanización en América Latina*. Quito: FLACSO-Ecuador, pp. 49–76. At: https://biblio.flacsoandes.edu.ec/catalog/resGet.php?resId=19146

Mascareño, C., Balbi, G. & Cunill, N. (1995). 'Descentralización y municipios en América Latina: Necesidades de información de los gobiernos locales'. Caracas: Centro Latinoamericano de Administración para el Desarrollo (CLAD). At: https://idl-bnc-idrc.dspacedirect.org/bitstream/handle/10625/28148/IDL-28148%20.pdf?sequ

Mashini, D. (2020). Metropolitan Dialogues: Steps towards the Institutional Construction of Metropolitan Governance. Blog Post Ciudades Sostenibles. At: https://blogs.iadb.org/ciudades-sostenibles/en/metropolitan-dialogues-steps-towards-the-institutional-construction-of-metropolitan-governance/

Montero, A. P. (2001). 'After Decentralization: Patterns of Intergovernmental Conflict in Argentina, Brazil, Spain, and Mexico'. *Publius: The Journal of Federalism*, 31 (4), 43–64.

Moscovich, L. (2015). 'Decentralization and Local Government in Latin America'. In Millett, R. L., Holmes, J. S. & Pérez, O. J. (eds.) *Latin American Democracy: Emerging Reality or Endangered Species?* Abingdon: Routledge, pp. 134–152.

OECD (2017). *Making Decentralisation Work in Chile: Towards Stronger Municipalities*. Paris: OECD Publishing. At: https://doi.org/10.1787/9789264279049-en

Pacheco, F., Sánchez, R. & Villena, M. (2013). *Eficiencia de los Gobiernos Locales y sus Determinantes. Un análisis de Fronteras estocásticas en datos de Panel Para Municipalidades Chilenas*. Santiago: Dirección de Presupuestos del Ministerio de Hacienda. At: https://www.dipres.gob.cl/598/articles-114713_doc_pdf.pdf

Parilla, J., Leal, J. & Berube, A. (2015). 'Latin America's Stagnating Global Cities' [Online]. At: https://www.brookings.edu/blog/the-avenue/2015/03/05/latin-americas-stagnatingglobal-cities/

Pinto da Cunha, J. M. (2002). *Urbanización, redistribución espacial de la población y transformaciones socioeconómicas en América Latina*. Serie Población y Desarrollo. Santiago: UN, CEPAL, CELADE. At: www.cepal.org/es/publicaciones/7168-urbanizacion-redistribucion-espacial-la-poblacion-transformaciones

Pírez, P. (2000). *Servicios urbanos y equidad en América Latina. Un panorama con base en algunos casos*. Serie Medio ambiente y desarrollo, No. 26. Santiago: CEPAL/ECLAC.

Pírez, P. (2012). 'Urban Services and Urbanization in Latin America: The Guidance between Welfare and Restructuring'. *Geo Uerj, Universidade do Estado do Rio de Janeiro-Uerj*, 573–573. At: https://go.gale.com/ps/anonymous?id=GALE%7CA372693032&sid=googleScholar&v=2.1&it=r&linkaccess=abs&issn=14157543&p=IFME&sw=w

Pírez, P. (2013). 'La urbanización y la política de los servicios urbanos en América Latina'. *Andamios: Revista de Investigacion Social*, 10(22), 45–67. DOI: 10.29092/uacm.v10i22.266

Pírez, P. (2016). 'Las heterogeneidades en la producción de la urbanización y los servicios urbanos en América Latina'. *Territorios* (34), 87–112. At: http://www.scielo.org.co/pdf/terri/n34/n34a05.pdf

Portes, A. (1971). 'Urbanization and Politics in Latin America'. *Social Science Quarterly*, 52 (3), 697–720.

Rodgers, D., Beall, J. & Kanbur, R. (2011). 'Latin American Urban Development into the 21st Century: Towards a Renewed Perspective on the City'. WIDER Working Paper 2011/05, Helsinki: WIDER. At: http://hdl.handle.net/10419/54165

Rodríguez, A. & Oviedo, E. (2001). 'Gestión urbana y gobierno de áreas metropolitanas'. *CEPAL, Serie Medio Ambiente y Desarrollo*, No. 34. Santiago: CEPAL.

Rodriguez-Acosta, C. A. & Rosenbaum, A. (2005). 'Local Government and the Governance of Metropolitan Areas in Latin America'. *Public Administration and Development*, 25(4), 295–306. At: https://doi.org/10.1002/pad.387

Rojas, E. (2005). 'Las regiones metropolitanas de América Latina. Problemas de gobierno y desarrollo'. In Rojas, E., Cuadrado-Roura, J. R. & Fernández Güell, J. M. (eds.) *Gobernar las metrópolis*. Washington, DC: Inter-American Development Bank, pp. 35–62. At: http://site.ebrary.com/id/10201140

Rondinelli, D. A. (1981). 'Government Decentralization in Comparative Perspective: Theory and Practice in Developing Countries'. *International Review of Administrative Sciences*, 47(2), 133–145. At: https://doi.org/10.1177/002085238004700205

Rondinelli, D. A., Nellis, J. R. & Shabbir Cheema, G. (1983). 'Decentralization in Developing Countries. A Review of Recent Experience'. World Bank Staff Working Papers No. 581. New York: World Bank. At: http://documents1.worldbank.org/curated/en/868391468740679709/pdf/multi0page.pdf

Simon, R. & Sweigart, E. (2020). 'Why Latin America's Bet on Local Government Is Ambitious and Risky'. *Americas Quarterly*, January 13. 2020. At: https://www.americasquarterly.org/article/why-latin-americas-bet-on-local-government-is-ambitious-and-risky/

Sellers, J. & Hoffmann-Martinot, V. (2008). Metropolitan Governance. United Cities and Local Governments, *World Report on Decentralization and Local Democracy*, 255–279. Washington, DC: World Bank.

Slack, E. (2007). 'Managing the Coordination of Service Delivery in Metropolitan Cities: The Role of Metropolitan Governance'. Policy Research Working Papers No. 4317. Washington, DC: World Bank. At: https://openknowledge.worldbank.org/handle/10986/7264

Slack, E. (2019). *Metropolitan Governance. Principles and Practice*. Working Paper IDB-DP-659. Washington, DC: Inter-American Development Bank.

Souza, C. (2006). 'Condições Institucionais de cooperação na Região Metropolitana de Salvador'. In Carvalho, I. & Pereira, G. C. (coords.), *Como anda Salvador*. Salvador: Edufba.

Trejo Nieto, A. (2017). *Localización manufacturera, apertura comercial y disparidades regionales en México*. México, D F: El Colegio de México. At: www.jstor.org/stable/j.ctv1fxg2x.

Trejo Nieto, A. (2020). *Metropolitan Economic Development. The Political Economy of Urbanisation in Mexico*. London: Routledge, At: https://doi.org/10.4324/9780429456053

Trejo Nieto, A. B., Niño Amézquita, J. L. & Vasquez, M. L. (2018). 'Governance of metropolitan areas for delivery of public services in Latin America'. *Region*, 5(3), 49–73. DOI: 10.18335/region.v5i3.224

UCLG (2012). *Who Can Address Urban Inequality? The Often Forgotten Roles of Local Government*. United Cities and Local Governments. At: https://www.uclg.org/sites/default/files/UCLG%20Possition%20paper_local%20government%20and%20urban%20inequality_0.pdf

UN (2016). *Latin America and the Caribbean Challenges: Dilemmas and Commitments of a Common Urban Agenda*. MINURVI, ECLAC and UNHabitat/ROLAC. United Nations: Santiago. At: https://www.cepal.org/en/publications/40657-latin-america-and-caribbean-challenges-dilemmas-and-commitments-common-urban

UN-Habitat (2012). *State of Latin American and Caribbean Cities 2012: Towards a New Urban Transition*. Nairobi: UN-HABITAT. At: https://unhabitat.org/state-of-latin-american-and-caribbean-cities-2

Vargas et al. (2017). RED 2017. *Urban Growth and Access to Opportunities: A Challenge for Latin America*. Bogota: Banco de Desarrollo de América Latina, CAF. At: http://scioteca.caf.com/handle/123456789/1091

Wilson, R., Ward, P. & Spink, P. K. (2012). 'The Challenge of Metropolitan Governance in the Federal Americas'. In Spink, P. K., Ward, P. & Wilson, R., *Metropolitan Governance in the Federalist Americas: Strategies for Equitable and Integrated Development*. Notre Dame: University of Notre Dame Press, pp. 1–43.

Zarate Martín, A. (1989). 'Notas sobre el modelo urbano latinoamericano'. *Espacio, Tiempo y Forma, Serie VI, Geografía*, t. 2, 267–290. At: http://revistas.uned.es/index.php/ETFVI/article/view/2465/2338

Part II

2 Metropolitan centralism, governance and service delivery in Bogotá

Jose L. Niño Amézquita

Introduction

Urban growth and expansion are not only phenomena of the Global North, they are also occurring intensely in the Global South. High urbanisation, expansion and urban macrocephaly became dominant features in Latin America at the end of the twentieth century, creating an urban landscape that would have been unthinkable just half a century earlier. This urban reality has forced us to seek to understand cities' urban dynamics and the new challenges that various actors face within these urbanised environments.

Demographic and territorial dynamics transformed Colombia's urban and national economic activities and social realities in the second half of the twentieth century. Although many of its municipalities became the recipients of large flows of goods, people and capital, local governments did not fulfil population demands in the new territorial and social realities. Rapid urbanisation and the geographic concentration of population produced challenges of great relevance. Bogotá, the Colombian capital, is one of the cities in Latin America where urban macrocephaly developed. The city experienced exponential population growth and urban escalation distinctive in the Latin American region. Colombia faced these urban changes in the context of its territory's geographical fragmentation by its three mountain ranges. But the country's serious difficulties with territorial integration meant that the primacy of its capital city was not as strong as in the other countries of Latin America, with important intermediate cities such as Medellin, Cali, Barranquilla and Bucaramanga developing to concentrate more than a quarter of Colombia's overall economic activity.

Bogotá attempted to establish different mechanisms to leverage its urban growth. It was the target of national government centralisation and was given the special status of Capital District (CD). The annexation of municipalities was seen as a form of amalgamation to allow the integration of urban processes in the capital city. However, planning efforts and centralisation were not enough to control the rapid urban evolution, relocation of activities and intermunicipal dynamics. With the rigid prevailing administrative-political structure and neighbouring municipalities increasing in demographic relevance, Bogotá faced growing pressures.

DOI: 10.4324/9781003105541-5

By the end of the twentieth century, Bogotá was struggling to provide public services across the whole of its urban functional territory. This raised significant concerns about urban management, and more specifically about its metropolitan efficiency, which has not been a priority for the CD's authorities. Similarly since the 1990s the national government has been slow to implement metropolitan integration mechanisms.

This chapter calls attention to the necessity of understanding the interaction between Bogotá as a Capital District and the Bogota metropolitan area (hereafter BMA). While the CD concentrates a large part of the nation's wealth and population, its functional links with its peripheries is undeniable. Today this interrelationship generates both positive and adverse effects for both the different territorial jurisdictions and metropolitan inhabitants' well-being. For this reason, adequate governance is required to strengthen metropolitan institutionalisation, whose implementation has been fragile since its beginnings in the 1950s.

Bogotá's diverse functional links with its metropolitan area give rise to complex requirements in terms of public services, and an assessment of the state of public service provision is urgently needed. In this chapter, I evaluate the metropolitan governance of three specific public services: water and sewerage, waste collection, and transport. This evaluation is based on three pillars of governance: coordination, coverage/quality and financial sustainability, in the BMA, covering Bogotá CD and three rings of its neighbouring municipalities.

Urban consolidation in Bogotá's metropolitan area

Between 1819 and 1910, following Colombia's independence, Bogotá transitioned from a colonial town to a bourgeois city. During this time, colonial powers vanished and the consolidation of Colombia as a nation-state began (Niño Amézquita & Niño-Molina, 2020). The city of Bogotá accumulated political and economic power and centrality, generating social and economic interactions with the jurisdictions surrounding it.

As a consequence, during the first half of the century, the Sabana of Bogotá became the nucleus of a broad historical region. The Sabana is a high plateau in the Cundinamarca department that includes the city of Bogotá, the towns of Soacha, Fontibón, Engativá, Serrezuela, Funza, Bojacá, Facatativá, the Funza River, the eastern hills, the Juan Amarillo River basin, and the hamlets of Usaquén and Chapinero. The metropolis and the broader Sabana have shared close relations in the supply of consumer products. However in time Bogotá began to separate from the rest of the Sabana socially, politically and economically due to its rapid urban densification and the agile division of real estate in the second half of the century (Mejía Pavony, 1999).

Later, the beginning of the second half of the twentieth century was the starting point for Bogotá's current urban challenges, including its delimitation that has transgressed the Capital District's borders, the definition of municipal and other levels' functions and the implementation of mechanism for achieving the best performance of the entire metropolitan area.

From border redefinition to decentralisation

Bogotá's current official jurisdiction was determined mainly by the annexation of adjacent municipalities due to the city's rapid urban growth, the need for good-quality public and social services, and a number of institutional arrangements motivated by the Colombia's conflict with migration from rural areas. In 1954 Gustavo Rojas Pinilla's national government annexed the first six municipalities surrounding Bogotá, i.e. Usaquén, Suba, Engativá, Fontibón, Bosa and Usme, to create Bogotá Special District (Cortés Díaz, 2005).

One of the primary purposes for the annexation of these municipalities was to integrate the planning of infrastructure, residential development and public services with that of Bogota. However, fast urbanisation and uncontrolled growth resulting from a lack of long-term planning led to the emergence of informal developers, who built low-cost housing in peripheral areas with little or no public service provision. As a result of this lack of planning, Bogotá became one of the nation's densest cities. In the 1950s, the city engaged famous planners such as Le Corbusier and Wiener and Sert to design urban planning programmes; however, the implementation of many of these programmes failed. For example only 60 per cent of the street plan has been implemented, and other projects such as a metro system are still pending (Guzman, Oviedo & Bocarejo, 2017).

The vibrant growth of the city and the annexation of the six neighbouring municipalities made it necessary to modernise local administrations, and decentralisation became crucial. These processes have passed through several stages, including the new 1991 national constitution and the city's Organic Statute (Botero-Ospina & Suárez Espinosa, 2010).

In the 1950s Le Corbusier was contracted to carry out an urban plan for Bogotá, based on the 1933 Athens Charter, in two phases: a pilot plan and a regulatory plan. This responded to the 1954 reform to consolidate Bogotá as the national capital and as a modern and international city. A different phase of the regulatory plan, proposed by Wiener and Sert, was never approved. One reason for not adopting this later regulatory plan was the conflicting economic interests of legal and illegal developers (Cortés Díaz, 2005). As a result, the city was expanded by all kinds of developers with no urban planning.

Following the urban pilot plan carried out after 1954, four areas experienced significant expansion: first, to the south of the new historic centre; later the municipality of Bosa to the south-west; then the former municipality of Fontibón in the south-west and last the area between Calle 68 and Avenida Ciudad de Quito in the west. In this way the government boosted the construction of residential complexes on the urban periphery, and especially in the annexed territories, leading to rapid growth of that periphery (ibid.).

The second half of the twentieth century began with the annexation of municipalities neighbouring Bogotá with the ultimate aim of integrating the functional city in the face of the enormous increase in the urban population. Most of the population growth was due to Colombians fleeing violence at the hands of various illegal armed groups in other parts of the country.

That population migrating to Bogotá was also suffering unprecedented state neglect. In addition to ordering the annexation of municipalities to the capital, Decree 3640 of 1954 divided the city into zones, each administered by a local mayor under the authority of the superior mayor (Figure 2.1). The

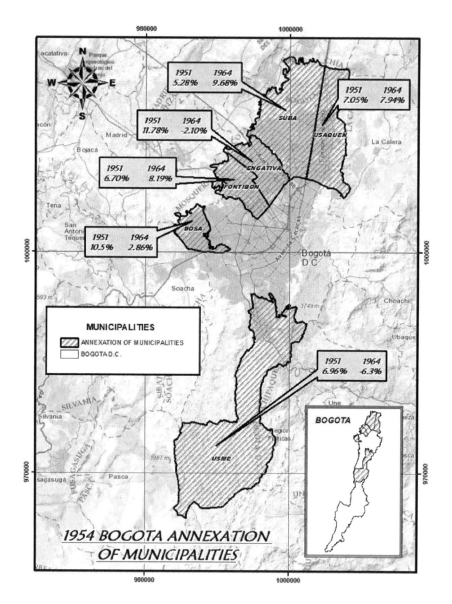

Figure 2.1 Bogotá, annexed municipalities and administrative division by zones after decree 3640 of 1954

Source: Author's elaboration.

Table 2.1 Decentralisation reforms from 1954 to 1987: Main changes

Decree 3640 of 1954
Orders the annexation of municipalities to Bogotá, dividing Bogotá into areas administered by local mayors that depend on the district's mayor. Initiates decentralisation and attempts to order the city.

Agreement 26 of 1972
Territorial demarcation of 16 local mayoralties, aiming to strengthen local governments. Local mayors became responsible for contracting public works, licensing concessions and managing projects and public works.

Agreement 8 of 1977, repealed by Decree 2621 of 1982
Denominates zonal mayoralties to the previous local mayoralties. It defines the new zonal mayoralties.

Agreement 8 of 1987
Divides Bogotá into 20 zones to increase the efficiency. Seeks solutions to citizens' needs, and awards interventions in planning; oversees and controls the provision of public services, and its administration and budget.

Source: Author's elaboration.

incipient decentralisation was weak because it responded more to an attempt to order the territory than to a desire to empower local governments. Table 2.1 summarises the decentralisation regulations from 1954 to 1987.

Soacha, which was not annexed in 1954, stands out among all the metropolitan municipalities because its population has increased very fast since 1973, sometimes in illegal and unplanned ways. Its growth is related to Bogotá's demographic dynamics, and internal industrialisation processes and the national armed conflict that displaced hundreds of vulnerable people. Although citizens' amenities and recreational and service provision were improving in Bogotá, Soacha faced increasing residential demand. It was an attractive location with its proximity to Bogotá, lower cost of living and low-cost public services and land. It became a dormitory town with growing connections to Bogotá in terms of commuting, public services, infrastructure and land occupation (Duque-Duque, Trejos-Ballesteros & Moreno-Obando, 2020). After an economic downturn in the 1990s, several industries in Bogotá migrated to neighbouring municipalities such as Soacha, attracted by its lower cost of land, low road traffic and environmental congestion, municipal tax exemptions and proximity to large markets. However, the quality of life in these locations remained less attractive (ibid.).

The provision of public services became and continues to be an important issue in Bogotá's expansion. Between 1960 and 1980 public infrastructure agencies boasted a rapid increase in the capacity and coverage of water, sewerage and electricity services. However, administrative regulations limited this expansion, generating an imbalance between the centre and the urban periphery (Gilbert & Varley, 1990).

Importantly, reforms between 1954 and 1972 focused on increasing citizen participation and local autonomy. They pursued the functional deconcentration of the CD towards smaller localities. However, in practice Bogotá's superior mayor's initiatives were implemented and effective decentralisation was not implemented. In the 1990s a redefinition of responsibilities and municipal strengthening was sought (Botero-Ospina & Suárez Espinosa, 2010).

Municipalised decentralisation

Bogotá's expansion and its annexation of six neighbouring municipalities made the modernisation of the city's administration necessary and territorial decentralisation important. The 1991 Constitution and the city's Organic Statute were used as the basis of wide decentralisation (Botero-Ospina & Suárez Espinosa, 2010), although steps had already been taken in this direction. The fiscal decentralisation of Colombia had begun in 1960, but it was not until 1980 that political, fiscal and administrative decentralisation were broadened (Falleti, 2010) with the strengthening of subnational governments and their increased autonomy with the transfer of financial resources and responsibilities. They were given powers of management but not of response capacity or operational ability. In many instances, the functions across levels of government were duplicated, creating inefficient use of resources.

The 1991 Constitution, Law 1 of 1992 and the 1993 Organic Statute of Bogotá contained specific steps for Bogotá's decentralisation and the modernisation of local administrations. They endowed the CD with a legal framework within which to adapt decentralisation according to the needs of the moment and set out a decentralising thinking. They created a specific device such as the special district for the capital city. The aim was to strengthen subnational governments, including those of departments and municipalities.

Law 1 of 1992 specifically sought to optimise Bogotá's development, public spending and citizen participation and to strengthen localities based on subsidiarity, complementarity, efficiency and harmony. It granted the direct election of local assemblies, establishing the duration of their period of government and their autonomy of resources (Botero-Ospina & Suárez Espinosa, 2010). It also has specified functions such as development planning and the managing of budgets allocated by the central administration (Skinner, 2004). However, the 1992 law generated corruption and inefficient service delivery and did not improve local administration. This led to the creation of the Organic Statute of Bogotá (Decree-Law 1421 of 1993), which recentralised financial functions, decentralised specific responsibilities and empowered the superior mayor to appoint local mayors. Thus, some decentralisation was possible only through establishing very well-defined functions and efficient tools to local authorities (Botero-Ospina & Suárez Espinosa, 2010).

Local assemblies, planned in 1986 but implemented in 1991, were a clear outcome of Bogotá's decentralisation. Between 1995 and 1998 the CD's administration was strengthened with more qualified officials in local administration and by participatory processes that continued during the following administration (Skinner, 2004).

By delegating duties through decentralisation, laws passed in the 1980s and '90s empowered the provision of public services by local authorities (Alvarez, 1997, cited in Skinner, 2004). This provision had reached a crisis point due to population increase and required administrative, structural and functional modernisation (Botero-Ospina & Suárez Espinosa, 2010). District and municipal institutions in the metropolis also acquired some functions and initiated the implementation of social programmes between 1987 and 1993.

Although decentralisation was accepted nationally, Skinner (2004) confirms that in practice Bogotá CD continued to govern centrally in some ways, as it neither devolved many competencies to its localities nor supported their assumption of other tasks. Local mayors did not acquire decisive power in critical areas in their communities such as health, education and other public services.

Still, decentralisation strengthened some powers granted to mayors' offices, including the employment of workers and the management of expenditures financed by means of local development funds (Decree 533 of 1993); permission to employ personnel with payments for up to 2,000 minimum wages (Decrees 698 of 1993 and 50 of 1994); the creation of administrative units to centralise expenditure (Decree 176 of 1998); judicial and extrajudicial representation of local development funds (Decree 367 of 2001); and the performance of management functions in municipal development programmes and sub-programmes using development funds (Decree 421 of 2004).

To sum up, following the decentralisation process, local administrations within the CD enjoyed greater autonomy. But the influence on political or investment decisions of municipalities that had become jurisdictions of Bogotá by annexation were negatively affected because they depended in many ways on the CD's government (Guzman, Oviedo & Bocarejo, 2017). The urban area of Bogotá continued to expand, but the CD remained reluctant to annex poor and informal municipalities, which would not make a significant economic contribution to the whole.

Bogotá's metropolitan rings

Metropolitan definition is important in this analysis. Bogotá CD includes the surrounding municipalities annexed to its administrative division in the 1950s (Buelvas Ramírez, 2014). Their representative bodies are local assemblies without fiscal autonomy. Bogota CD is a separate jurisdiction of the department of Cundinamarca, with fiscal and political autonomy and popular election of its mayor and district councils.

Altogether 20 municipalities have been incorporated into Bogotá's metropolitan area. They are distributed across three rings: in the first ring are Soacha, Cota, Chía, Mosquera, Funza, Cajicá, Madrid and La Calera; in the second, Tocancipá, Tenjo, Sibaté, Sopó, Tabio, El Rosal, Bojacá, Subachoque and Gachancipá and the third ring contains Facatativá, Zipaquirá and Fusagasugá, as Figure 2.2 illustrates. All of these municipalities have fiscal, political and

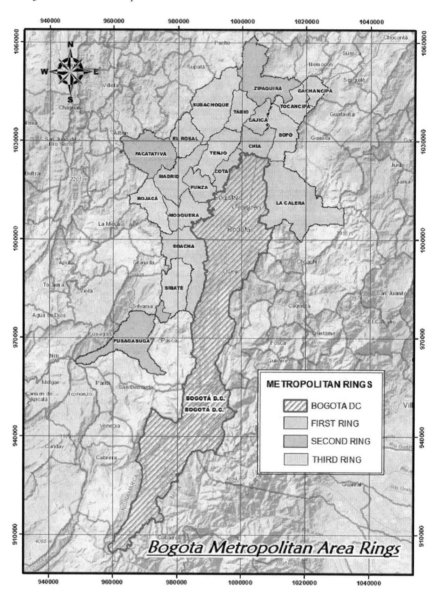

Figure 2.2 Bogotá's metropolitan rings

Source: Alcaldía de Bogotá (2019).

administrative autonomy, with only some operational and financial restrictions. Municipalities with more than 10 per cent of their population working or studying in the CD – Zipaquirá, Soacha, Chía, Facatativá, La Calera and Tabio, all with large populations – usually have stronger relationships

Table 2.2 Population by municipality, 2021

	Municipality	Population	Percentage
First ring	Bogotá, DC	7,834,167	77.90%
	Soacha	783,632	7.79%
	Cota	38,469	0.38%
	Chía	155,541	1.55%
	Mosquera	156,680	1.56%
	Funza	109,281	1.09%
	Cajicá	96,678	0.96%
	Madrid	132,214	1.31%
	La Calera	34,224	0.34%
Second ring	Tocancipá	47,539	0.47%
	Tenjo	25,053	0.25%
	Sibaté	38,114	0.38%
	Sopó	30,157	0.30%
	Tabio	25,172	0.25%
	El Rosal	25,757	0.26%
	Bojacá	11,535	0.11%
	Subachoque	17,408	0.17%
	Gachancipá	20,150	0.20%
Third ring	Facatativá	162,205	1.61%
	Zipaquirá	152,195	1.51%
	Fusagasugá	160,296	1.59%
	TOTAL	**10,056,467**	

Source: Departamento Administrativo Nacional de Estadística (DANE) (2021).

and dependency with the CD. The less-dependent municipalities are Tenjo, Tocancipá, Sibaté, Madrid, Sopó, Cajicá and Cota.

Total population in the metropolitan area has exceeded the 10-million mark. Regarding its geographic distribution, 78 per cent of the metropolitan inhabitants locates in the CD, while the remaining portion is distributed across the other 20 municipalities. Soacha is the largest municipality after the CD with 8 per cent of population, followed by Facatativá and Fusagasugá. These last two municipalities belong to the third ring. The second ring has the lowest population percentage (2.4 per cent), whereas the third ring concentrates on 4.7 per cent of population (Table 2.2).

Urban consolidation has followed the socio-spatial segregation of Bogotá's central municipality since the nineteenth century. These segregation patterns have been replicated over the entire Sabana, dividing the region into the prosperous north with a high-income population, the intermediate west with a middle-income population and the impoverished south (Alfonso, 2001).

Employment in the CD can be separated into three main types of concentrations: the first, with 150,000 jobs in Centro Histórico-Centro Internacional, Calle 72-Calle 100 and Salitre-Zona Industrial; the second in Aeropuerto el Dorado-Fontibón (west), Usaquén-Santa Bárbara (north) and Delicias-Ensueño (south-west) with 50–100,000 jobs and the third with 30–50,000 jobs in Chapinero, Siete de Agosto and Restrepo. In addition the BMA contains two

Table 2.3 Interdependence index

	Municipality	Interdependence index
First ring	Bogotá, DC	100
	Soacha	16.2
	Cota	15.5
	Chía	14.68
	Mosquera	14.16
	Funza	14.14
	Cajicá	13.65
	Madrid	13.02
	La Calera	13.01
Second ring	Tocancipá	13.7
	Tenjo	13.62
	Sibaté	13.41
	Sopo	12.46
	Tabio	11.33
	El Rosal	9.98
	Bojacá	9.94
	Subachoque	9.84
	Gachancipá	9.47
Third ring	Facatativá	11.99
	Zipaquirá	11.59
	Fusagasugá	9.59

Source: Alcaldía de Bogotá (2019).

further concentrations of more than 100,000 jobs in Funza-Madrid-Mosquera (south-west) and Soacha (south) (Alcaldía de Bogotá, 2019).

Defining a dependency marker for economic and housing relocation requires knowledge and understanding of economic autonomy and movement between people's places of work and homes. Table 2.3 shows that Bogotá is 100 per cent dependent on itself: the most dependent municipality is Gachancipá (9.47 per cent), and the least dependent, Soacha (16.2 per cent) (ibid.). This means that Soacha have strong functional links with Bogotá CD, but among all municipalities, it depends more on itself than the rest.

Metropolitan service provision

This section analyses metropolitan governance regarding the provision of water and sewerage, solid waste collection and transport services in the BMA. Governance refers here to horizontal and vertical articulation and coordination between metropolitan actors. It is strongly linked to the idea of the power to carry out policies to meet population and territorial needs (Osmont, 1998; Lefèvre, 2005; Galvis Gómez, 2020). Public and private actors participate in the provision of public services within each municipal administration, but municipal arrangements differ in each jurisdiction and across public services (Table 2.4). Private operators are predominantly present in the delivery of public transport.

Table 2.4 Type of provision by municipality and service

	Municipality	Water and sewerage	Transport	Waste collection
First ring	Bogotá DC	Public	Public	Private
	Soacha	Public and private	Public	Private
	Cota	Public	Private	Public
	Chía	Public	Private	Public
	Mosquera	Public	Private	Public
	Funza	Public	Private	Public
	Cajicá	Public	Private	Public
	Madrid	Public	Private	Public
	La Calera	Public	Private	Public
Second ring	Tocancipá	Public	Private	Public
	Tenjo	Public	Private	Public
	Sibaté	Public	NA	Public
	Sopo	Public	Private	Public
	Tabio	Public	Private	Public
	El Rosal	Public	Private	Public
	Bojacá	NA	Private	NA
	Subachoque	Public	Private	Public
	Gachancipá	Public	Private	NA
Third ring	Facatativá	Public	NA	Public
	Zipaquirá	Public	Private	Public
	Fusagasugá	Public	Private	Public

Note: NA = no data available.

Source: Alcaldía de Bogotá (2019).

Water and sewerage provision

Water is a human right that dignifies life, and its provision must favour people's realities, be sufficient, healthy, acceptable, physically accessible and affordable (UN, 2002). In Colombia each administrative entity must provide it according to its capacities. The Aqueduct and Sewerage Company (Empresa de Acueducto y Alcantarillado de Bogotá, hereafter EAAB) provides water to Bogotá CD and several municipalities in the Sabana, while the other municipalities deliver the service autonomously (Buelvas Ramírez, 2014). Water is a publicly provided service in all municipalities except Soacha, whose water and sewerage service is supplied by a private company. EAAB can provide the service in other municipalities according to its capacities. In so doing, it helps to articulate the metropolitan delivery of services by expanding its operation as a private company. Soacha depends on EAAB water provision and has unattended demand. Tocancipá, Cajicá, Chía, Sopó, La Calera and Gachancipá are also dependent on EAAB, which covers most demand; Funza, Madrid and Mosquera are partially dependent on EAAB and have limited resources; Cota, Tabio, Tenjo and Sibaté are partially dependent with sustainable resources and Facatativá, Subachoque, Bojacá and El Rosal are autonomous.

Table 2.5 summarises the results of my research on Bogotá's metropolitan provision of services. Classifications are based on the following criteria. If

Table 2.5 Governance aspects for water provision

	Municipality	Coordination	Coverage/quality	Financial sustainability
First ring	Bogotá DC	Incipient	High/good	Sufficient
	Soacha	Incipient	High/good	Sufficient
	Cota	Non-existent	High/medium	Sufficient
	Chía	Incipient	High/good	Sufficient
	Mosquera	Non-existent	High/good	Sufficient
	Funza	Non-existent	High/good	Sufficient
	Cajicá	Incipient	High/good	Sufficient
	Madrid	Non-existent	Medium/good	Acceptable
	La Calera	Incipient	High/good	Deficient
Second ring	Tocancipá	Incipient	High/good	Deficient
	Tenjo	Non-existent	High/good	Acceptable
	Sibaté	Non-existent	High/medium	Sufficient
	Sopo	Incipient	High/medium	Sufficient
	Tabio	Non-existent	Medium/medium	Deficient
	El Rosal	Non-existent	High/good	Deficient
	Bojacá	Non-existent	Low/good	NA
	Subachoque	Non-existent	Medium/good	Acceptable
	Gachancipá	Incipient	Medium/good	Acceptable
Third ring	Facatativá	Non-existent	High/good	Deficient
	Zipaquirá	Non-existent	High/good	NA
	Fusagasugá	Non-existent	High/good	Sufficient

Source: Author's elaboration.

there is no shared provision with other municipality, coordination is catego-rised as "Non-existent"; if less than 25 per cent of provision is shared with other municipality then coordination is "Incipient" (Superintendencia de Servicios Públicos Domiciliarios, 2015, 2017b). If the local provider covers around 30 per cent of population, coverage is "Low", around 60 per cent is classified as "Intermediate" and closer to 100 is "High" (Superintendencia de Servicios Públicos Domiciliarios, 2017a). If the water quality risk index is less than 3 per cent, the quality is "Good", an index above 13 per cent is "Poor" and values in between refer to "Intermediate" quality (National Institute for Health, 2017). Financial sustainability is "Deficient" if net income and Earnings Before Interest, Taxes, Depreciation and Amortisation (EBITDA) are negative, "Sufficient" if net income is positive and EBITDA is negative, and "Acceptable" if both are positive (EMIS, 2021). If there is no data, the rating is "NA" (not available).

Bogotá, Soacha, Chía, Cajicá, La calera, Tocancipá, Sopo and Gachancipá show incipient capacities for coordination due to the scarce intermunicipal mechanisms for collaboration. Cota, Mosquera, Funza, Madrid, Tenjo, Sibaté, Tabio, El Rosal, Bojacá, Subachoque, Facatativá, Zipaquirá and Fusagasugá operate autonomously without collaborating with other municipalities.

In terms of financial sustainability, demographically small munici-palities with lower demand for providing the service, such as Madrid, Tenjo, Subachoque and Gachancipá, show acceptable financial conditions. Meanwhile, the demographically large city Bogota CD, supported by its economic and technical capacity, displays sufficient resources as most municipalities within the fort ring. A few municipalities have deficient financial conditions for providing water.

The so-called Superintendency of Services evaluates the coverage of water services by considering the proportion of residential units receiving the service in relation to the total number of such units. Coverage in BMA is high at over 70 per cent, the lowest coverage observed in the second ring, where public companies do not meet the needs of the population. According to the Water Quality Risk Index (IRCA) and decree 1575 of 2007, Cota, Sibaté, Sopo and Tabio receive intermediate quality services and the rest of the metropolitan area receives good quality water.

Overall the municipalities with high ratings for governance parameters in water delivery services are Bogotá, Soacha, Chía, Mosquera, Funza, Cajicá and Sopó, all with high coverage and good quality, sufficient resources, with lack of coordination for Mosquera and Funza, and incipient coordination for the rest. The municipalities with low ratings are El Rosal and Bojacá, both with no coordination with other municipalities, low coverage, and good quality and deficient financial resources. Cota, Madrid, La Calera, Tocancipá, Tenjo, Sibaté, Tabio, Subachoque, Gachancipá, Facatativá, Zipaquirá and Fusagasugá have intermediate ratings. The first ring has municipalities with high or intermediate ratings, the second ring has some municipalities with low ratings, whereas the municipalities in the third ring all have intermediate ratings.

Public transport

In Bogotá CD, public transport is the responsibility of the public bus rapid transit company Transmilenio and the Bogotá Urban Transport System (SITP). In the first ring, transport services are provided by private outsourced companies, excepting in Soacha. In the second and third rings, transport services are supplied by private companies which have stronger links to the corresponding municipal administrations.

Again, coordination is "Incipient" if there are attempts of intermunicipal collaboration and "Non-existent" if coordination is absent. According to intermunicipal and internal routes, there is "Low" coverage if the percentage is 30 per cent and "High" if it is close to 100% per cent. Secondary information was not available to assess quality but according to fieldwork carried out in 2016, services were regarded as low quality in transport systems other than Transmilenio. Financial sustainability, "Deficient" if net income and EBITDA are negative, "Sufficient" if net income is positive and EBITDA is negative and "Acceptable" if both are positive (EMIS, 2021). If there is no data, the classification is "NA" (not available).

Table 2.6 shows that there is no coordination on transport service provision between most municipalities with the exception of Bogotá and Soacha, where some coordination is being needed due to their geographical proximity. Yet their intermunicipal interaction has been problematic.

Table 2.6 Governance aspects for transport provision

	Municipality	Coordination	Coverage/quality	Financial sustainability
First ring	Bogotá, DC	Incipient	Consolidated	Acceptable
	Soacha	Incipient	Incipient	Acceptable
	Cota	Non-existent	Incipient	Sufficient
	Chía	Non-existent	Incipient	Acceptable
	Mosquera	Non-existent	Incipient	Sufficient
	Funza	Non-existent	Incipient	Sufficient
	Cajicá	Non-existent	Incipient	Sufficient
	Madrid	Non-existent	Incipient	NA
	La Calera	Non-existent	Incipient	Acceptable
Second ring	Tocancipá	Non-existent	Incipient	Sufficient
	Tenjo	Non-existent	Incipient	Acceptable
	Sibaté	Non-existent	Incipient	NA
	Sopo	Non-existent	Incipient	Deficient
	Tabio	Non-existent	Incipient	Acceptable
	El Rosal	Non-existent	Incipient	Acceptable
	Bojacá	Non-existent	Incipient	Acceptable
	Subachoque	Non-existent	Incipient	Acceptable
	Gachancipá	Non-existent	Incipient	Deficient
Third ring	Facatativá	Non-existent	Incipient	Deficient
	Zipaquirá	Non-existent	Incipient	Deficient
	Fusagasugá	Non-existent	Incipient	Acceptable

Source: Author's elaboration.

Financial sustainability, understood as the degree of compatibility between existing financial resources and the sufficiency of those resources to offer the service, is heterogeneous across the metropolitan area. In 10 out of the 21 municipalities, financial sustainability is rated as acceptable. These include Bogotá, Soacha, Chía, La Calera, Tenjo, Tabio, El Rosal, Bojacá, Subachoque and Fusagasugá. In four municipalities, sustainability is rated as Sufficient, and in five, deficient. According to these ratings, most municipalities are able to sustain financially the provision of transport.

This confirms the results reported by Trejo Nieto, Niño Amézquita and Vasquez (2018), who found public transport's financial sustainability dependent on the extent that the companies that provide the service have the freedom to operate with profits. Market and economic orientation have been the solutions to financial feasibility for the vast majority of private transport operators.

In terms of coverage and quality, Bogotá CD is in the best position while other municipalities offer low formal coverage. This is because Bogotá CD's transport system is more integrated: Transmilenio offers a medium- and long-distance public transport service and SITP covers short and medium distances. The capital also offers a variety of alternatives such as taxis, motorbikes, bikes and scooters in addition to informal transport services using unlicensed private vehicles.

Waste collection

Until the 2016–2019 administration, Bogotá CD's solid waste system was managed by EAAB, which also provides water and sewerage services. There are currently five areas under concession to private waste service providers: Bogotá Limpia, Ciudad Limpia, Área Limpia, Promoambiental and Limpieza Metropolitana (LIME). They provide services to the south and west, south-west, northwest and east of the CD, respectively, but exclude the rest of the metropolitan municipalities. They simultaneously manage the collection, transport and separation of solid waste for reuse, recycling, and burning to generate energy, compost or any other health, environmental, social or economic benefit. The CD's municipal planning instrument is called Integrated Solid Waste Management.

In the other municipalities, the service is provided by public companies except in Soacha, which is served by a private company, Aseo Internacional. No private company operates simultaneously in more than one municipality; moreover, few municipal administrations have been willing to outsource these services to private companies. In contrast, the large size of Bogotá CD has forced the district administration to delegate the delivery of waste management to private companies.

As with other services coordination is "Non-existent" if there is not coordinated shared provision with other municipality or incipient if there are some attempts at coordinated provision (Superintendencia de Servicios Públicos Domiciliarios, 2015, 2017b). A coverage around 30 per cent is "Low", around 60 per cent is "Intermediate" and close to 100 per cent is "High" (Superintendencia de Servicios Públicos Domiciliarios, 2017a). If the operational and quality index is Rank III, the quality is "poor"; Rank II is "medium" and Rank I is "good" (Superintendencia de Servicios Públicos Domiciliarios, 2015). Finally, in financial sustainability, "Deficient" if net income and EBITDA are negative, "Sufficient" if net income is positive and EBITDA is negative and "Acceptable" if both are positive (EMIS, 2021). If there is no data, the rating is "NA" (not available).

Table 2.7 shows that most municipalities do not collaborate with other municipalities on service provision. The exception is Gachancipá, the only municipality (with a public company in charge of providing the service) that has technical links to another municipal provider.

The first ring has the highest number of municipalities with acceptable financial sustainability, Bogotá, DC, included. In contrast, five municipalities – most of them in the second ring – have deficient sustainability. In this case, the ratings show that financially most municipalities can bear the provision of the service.

Regarding coverage of service delivery, 12 of the 21 municipalities have high coverage, 3 have intermediate access and 6 have low coverage. Overall, there is good coverage in the CD and adjacent municipalities, but peripheral

Table 2.7 Governance aspects for waste collection provision

	Municipality	*Coordination*	*Coverage/quality*	*Financial sustainability*
First ring	Bogotá, DC	Non-existent	High/good	Acceptable
	Soacha	Non-existent	High/good	Acceptable
	Cota	Non-existent	High/good	Acceptable
	Chía	Non-existent	High/good	Acceptable
	Mosquera	Non-existent	High/good	Acceptable
	Funza	Non-existent	High/good	Acceptable
	Cajicá	Non-existent	High/good	Acceptable
	Madrid	Non-existent	Intermediate/good	Sufficient
	La Calera	Non-existent	Low/good	Deficient
Second ring	Tocancipá	Non-existent	High/NA	Deficient
	Tenjo	Non-existent	High/poor	Sufficient
	Sibaté	Non-existent	Intermediate/NA	Acceptable
	Sopo	Non-existent	High/good	Acceptable
	Tabio	Non-existent	Low/poor	Deficient
	El Rosal	Non-existent	Intermediate/poor	Deficient
	Bojacá	Non-existent	Low/NA	NA
	Subachoque	Non-existent	Low/poor	Sufficient
	Gachancipá	Incipient	Low/NA	Sufficient
Third ring	Facatativá	Non-existent	High/poor	Deficient
	Zipaquirá	Non-existent	High/NA	NA
	Fusagasugá	Non-existent	Low/good	Acceptable

Note: Quality measured according to the Operational and Aggregate Quality Indicator (IOCA) implemented after resolution 315 of 2005.

Source: Author's elaboration.

municipalities tend to have lower coverage. In terms of quality, according to the criteria of the Operational and Aggregate Quality Indicator (IOCA) implemented after resolution 315 of 2005, the first ring provides high-quality services. Only three municipalities in the second and two in the third provide good-quality services, while the rest are poor quality or data was unavailable.

Towards genuine and inclusive metropolitan governance

The previous section has shown the deficiencies in the supply of public services in BMA, particularly in water, waste management and public transport. This is related to the current development of territorial expansion and sectoral organisation which creates important differences based on the location of municipalities in relation to the CD. Municipalities in the second and third rings usually face more difficulties in providing services. This makes metropolitan governance a fundamental issue as it strongly impacts on the proper functioning of the municipalities affected (López-Moreno et al., 2019).

Due to the concentration of population and economic activities in the CD, which is in part explained by the annexation of municipalities in the 1950s, the delivery of services to the majority of the population of the metropolitan area is determined by how the district government functions. However, the metropolisation process also continues in areas outside Bogotá CD and may be accelerating. Bogotá+13 (Bogotá CD plus 13 other municipalities) defined the metropolitan area at the beginning of the twenty-first century. This has now been redefined as Bogotá+20, which includes all of the municipalities in the first, second and third rings (Alcaldía de Bogotá, 2019). This is the definition I consider in this chapter.

Bogotá's evolving metropolitan configuration which results from productive and functional connections between municipalities is determining municipal problems, including service delivery (Roldán Alzate, 2017; Parrado Rodríguez, 2020). It also determines intra-urban inequalities that compel municipalities close to the main urban centre to focus on establishing a strategic alliance for intermunicipal cooperation and coordination, although such arrangements could affect, to some extent, their autonomy to respond to their specific population needs, especially in the face of their varying realities (Galvis Gómez, 2020). Thus the expansive nature of the metropolitan area forces municipal authorities to implement strategies to improve their level of development and respond to the individual and social requirements of their inhabitants (Bonnet & Alvarez Huwiler, 2020).

Despite a good degree of metropolitan consolidation in the CD, metropolitan governance has not necessarily been able to respond to the increasing service gaps between municipalities, both near to and further from Bogotá. Despite the housing expansion in the periphery, a similar relocation of economic activities has not yet been achieved. Most metropolitan municipalities outside the CD have not yet managed to establish a consolidated economic nucleus. At the most, some industrial activity locates in the second ring (Galvis Gómez, 2020).

My analysis indicates that depending on the sector, two trends delineate differential behaviours in managing municipalities and the overall metropolitan management of public services. One trend is defined by a similar behaviour in the water and the waste collection sectors, and the other is determined by the transport sector. Better provision of water/sewerage and waste collection services to citizens is linked to the service provider's capacity to develop better coverage in the CD. In addition, the provider of these two services in the CD (i.e. EAAB) is linked to other municipalities in the metropolitan area. But even where municipalities subcontract EAAB, they continue to regulate and control its services (Garzón Cevallos, 2020), retaining the responsibility for their delivery.

The transport sector exhibits a different rationale. Like other services, public transport is a municipal responsibility, and one of the key problems is the absence of an institutional framework for an integrated inter-municipal or metropolitan transport system. Only in 2020 did legislation begin to treat metropolitan transport differently from other types of provision. The transport system in Bogotá CD is strongly based on the Transmilenio monopoly which responds to the needs of the CD, although it has extended some of its lines into the municipality of Soacha. The transport system shows a more significant metropolitan disarticulation and does not recognise the commuting needs of people living across the whole metropolitan area.

From a general perspective, attempts at intermunicipal collaboration are scarce and fragile. A practical metropolitan solution, developed 70 years ago, may be to dissolve the administrative divisions by municipal annexation and centralise power in a single metropolitan core. This may serve to ensure the functional viability of different metropolitan projects (Roldán Alzate, 2017). However, it opposes the existing municipal autonomy and so other alternatives need to be considered. In any case, options are constrained since municipalities do not seem willing to give up some of their autonomy to strengthen intermunicipal cooperation mechanisms.

Although there is a generalised fiscal decentralisation in Colombia with some resources directed to municipal governments and an increase in transfers, this has not helped to develop the competencies and abilities of local authorities (Lozano Gómez, 2019). Frequently other government levels frame the relevant strategies and tools; for example the Superintendency of Residential Public Services establishes strategic mechanisms to provide water and sanitation services in Colombia.

Indicators of performance are fundamental parameters in making the need for integrated services visible. Colombia's Unique Information System, the Superintendency of Residential Public Services' quality and coverage indicators used in this chapter comply with national parameters that restrict the participation of municipal entities in generating indicators, making the design of measurement instruments the responsibility of national-level institutions. Therefore indicators are prone to inaccuracy. Furthermore, the absence of information on potential demand does not allow full definition of the local deficiencies in service delivery. Historically the national government has developed proposals focused on much broader regional projects that have not efficiently solved local or metropolitan problems. This significantly affects responses to pressing issues because national standardisation is often not based on municipalities' realities (Parrado Rodríguez, 2020). Technical and financial difficulties due to national regulations generate a level of dependence on central transfers to leverage parameters coming from the national level (Bonnet & Alvarez Huwiler, 2020).

The broad evaluation in service provision in BMA has shown the essential relevance of strengthening metropolitan-wide service provision, beginning with the design and implementation of information mechanisms that clearly characterise municipalities' supply and demand to ensure that metropolitan problems are addressed more efficiently. A central issue for consideration is the spatial inequality caused by inadequate provision of metropolitan services, which mirrors the prevalent segregation patterns in Bogotá and the entire Sabana region.

Final remarks

This exploratory analysis has revealed that public service delivery in BMA is dependent on the socio-political context determining its current conditions of governance and is not linked or sensitive to the actual metropolitan functionality. However, deficiencies in the provision of public services show similar governance behaviour in the water and waste collection sectors and a different pattern in the transport sector. Part of this differentiation is because transport remains a very municipally based service, but transport services often do not serve the actual flows of the metropolitan population. In any case, important differences are observed across the metropolitan area even if the aggregate performance indicators based on national standards often end up hiding differences in the quality and quantity of the provision of the three services analysed.

With a large population and economic activities concentrated in Bogotá CD, municipalities in the three metropolitan rings have failed to attract economic centres or provincial development poles, reducing their local capacity for improving the supply and financing of services.

The limited public service budgets and the variety of service delivery mechanisms (public, private and mixed) further restrain municipalities' capacity to provide adequate services. Technical and financial difficulties generate dependence on central transfers and guidelines, reducing local autonomy. Central government has developed service-oriented projects, but these are based on a broad regional vision and do not address specific local and metropolitan problems. Problematical governance is caused by a lack of governmental cooperation, institutional weakness and differential decentralisation. Despite its relatively consolidated territorial pattern, the expansive metropolisation of Bogotá has produced significant gaps between municipalities.

Even with decentralised governance, finances could be used and managed more efficiently to generate less fiscal imbalance and more benefits by metropolitan-wide provision of public services. Moreover, an inclusive metropolitan governance strategy could address the patterns of territorial inequality. The Colombian system already includes compensatory instruments to alleviate some socio-economic inequalities: a subsidy mechanism established in law uses a socio-economic stratification of dwellings as a targeting tool, assigning its implementation to municipal authorities. Dwellings are classified into six strata (*estratos*) based on their observable characteristics: *estrato* 1 comprises the dwellings identified as the poorest, while *estrato* 6 corresponds to those identified as the richest. According to law, the lowest *estratos* can receive subsidised public services while the highest *estratos* pay higher tariffs. This cross-subsidy system has helped to reduce differential economic access to public services (Meléndez, 2008). However, the geographic location of the BMA's population in the CD and the other municipalities still creates differential access to services, and thus other socio-spatial differences emerge.

Finally, metropolitan governance does not mean that there must be one government level or a single large company providing services: local authorities could coordinate and cooperate within the metropolitan area for better use of their resources. Territorial realities that are broken down by municipal boundaries do not have to obstruct the improvement of living conditions, access to different public services, and fairer, more competitive and developed territories.

References

Alcaldía de Bogotá (2019). Documento técnico de soporte para la constitución de un área metropolitana entre Bogotá y sus municipios. Bogotá. At: http://www.sdp.gov.co/sites/default/files/libro_dts_areametropolitana-bgtamunicipios.pdf.

Alfonso, Ó. A. (2001). 'Ciudad y Región en Colombia Nueve Ensayos de Análisis Socio-Económico y Espacial'. *Con-texto*, 11, 101–106.

Bonnet, A. & Alvarez Huwiler, L. (2020). 'Estado y políticas públicas desde una perspectiva crítica'. *Journal of Management & Primary Health Care*, 12, 1–9. DOI: 10.14295/jmphc.v12.981.

Botero-Ospina, M.-H. & Suárez Espinosa, C. (2010). 'Bogotá y la descentralización intraterritorial: crónica de una historia inconclusa'. *Repositorio Institucional EdocUR*. Bogota: Editorial Universidad del Rosario. At: https://repository.urosario.edu.co/handle/10336/3354.

Buelvas Ramírez, D. L. (2014). Gobernanza metropolitana: Urbanización y Organización Territorial en la Sabana de Bogotá. Master Thesis, Universidad Nacional de Colombia. At: https://repositorio.unal.edu.co/bitstream/handle/unal/47290/1016016932.2014.pdf?sequence=1&isAllowed=y.

Cortés Díaz, M. E. (2005). 'La anexión de los 6 municipios vecinos a BOGOTÁ en 1954'. *Bitácora Urbano Territorial*, 9(1), 122–127. At: https://revistas.unal.edu.co/index.php/bitacora/article/view/18743.

Duque-Duque, N., Trejos-Ballesteros, J. A. & Moreno-Obando, J. W. (2020). 'Los impactos de Bogotá sobre Soacha y su importancia frente a la conformación del Área Metropolitana'. *Cuadernos Latinoamericanos de Administración*, 16(30), 1–11. DOI: 10.18270/cuaderlam.v16i30.2849.

EMIS. (2021). *Emerging markets research, data and news*. London: EMIS. At: https://www.emis.com/.

Falleti, T. G. (2010). *Decentralization and subnational politics in Latin America*. Cambridge: Cambridge University Press. DOI: 10.1017/CBO9780511777813.

Galvis Gómez, C. F. (2020). 'Área metropolitana Bogotá-Cundinamarca: potencialidades, obstáculos, retos'. *Revista Ciudades, Estados y Política*, 7(3), 51–62. DOI: 10.15446/CEP.V7N3.86625.

Garzón Cevallos, D. M. (2020). La aplicación del impuesto de patente municipal para las empresas florícolas por parte de los Gobiernos Autónomos Descentralizados Municipales. Master Thesis, Universidad Andina Simón Bolívar. At: https://repositorio.uasb.edu.ec/bitstream/10644/7630/1/T3318-MDEM-Garzón-La aplicación.pdf.

Gilbert, A. & Varley, A. (1990). 'Renting a home in a third world city: Choice or constraint?' *International Journal of Urban and Regional Research*, 14(1), 89–108. DOI: 10.1111/j.1468-2427.1990.tb00822.x.

Guzman, L. A., Oviedo, D. & Bocarejo, J. P. (2017). 'City profile: The Bogotá Metropolitan Area that never was'. *Cities*, 60, 202–215. DOI: 10.1016/j.cities.2016.09.004.

Lefèvre, C. (2005). Gobernabilidad democrática de las áreas metropolitanas. Experiencias y lecciones internacionales para las ciudades latinoamericanas. In Rojas, E., Cuadrado-Roura, J. R. & Fernández Güel, J. M. (eds.) *Gobernar las metrópolis*. Washington, DC: Banco Interamericano de Desarrollo, pp. 195–262. At: https://publications.iadb.org/publications/spanish/document/Gobernar-las-metrópolis.pdf.

López-Moreno, D. G. et al. (2019). *Gobernanza Metropolitana: El gobierno de las metrópolis para el desarrollo urbano sostenible*. Washington: Banco Interamericano de Desarrollo. At: https://publications.iadb.org/publications/spanish/document/Gobernanza_Metropolitana_El_gobierno_de_las_metrópolis_para_el_desarrollo_urbano_sostenible.pdf.

Lozano Gómez, J. D. (2019). 'Medellín tiene norte. La planeación urbana como una producción estratégica del espacio'. Universidad Nacional de Colombia. At: https://repositorio.unal.edu.co/bitstream/handle/unal/77548/1152208536.2020.pdf?sequence=7&isAllowed=y.

Mejía Pavony, G. R. (1999). *Los años del cambio: historia urbana de Bogotá, 1820–1910*. Bogotá: Centro Editorial Javeriano.

Meléndez, M. (2008). 'Subsidios al consumo de los servicios públicos: reflexiones a partir del caso colombiano'. CAF Working Papers No. 2008/02. At: https://scioteca.caf.com/bitstream/handle/123456789/216/200802Melendez.pdf?sequence=1.

National Institute for Health. (2017). *Estado de la vigilancia de la calidad del agua para consumo humano en Colombia*. Bogotá: Instituto Nacional de Salud, Dirección de Redes en Salud Pública. At: https://www.ins.gov.co/sivicap/Documentacin%20SIVICAP/Informe%20Nacional%20de%20Calidad%20del%20Agua%202016.pdf.

Niño Amézquita, J. L. & Niño-Molina, D. (2020). Bolivar and Liberation from Spain: The historical development of the public servant in Colombia. In Sullivan, H., Dickinson, H. & Henderson, H. (eds.) *The Palgrave handbook of the public servant*. Cham: Palgrave Macmillan, pp. 1–23.

Osmont, A. (1998). 'La "governance": Concept mou, politique ferme'. *Les Annales de la recherche urbaine*, 80(1), 19–26. DOI: 10.3406/aru.1998.2193.

Parrado Rodríguez, C. (2020). 'La accesibilidad en debate: ¿localizar vivienda social en áreas centrales de Bogotá?' *Cuadernos de Vivienda y Urbanismo*, 13, 1–18.

Roldán Alzate, L. M. (2017). 'Instituciones formales de la gobernanza metropolitana en Colombia: un análisis de elección racional', *Opera*, 21, 113–132. At: https://revistas.uexternado.edu.co/index.php/opera/article/view/5132/6200.

Skinner, R. (2004). 'Bogotá', *Cities*, 21(1), 73–81. DOI: 10.1016/j.cities.2003.10.003.

Superintendencia de Servicios Públicos Domiciliarios. (2015). *Nivel de riesgo servicio de aseo*. Bogotá: Superservicios. Superintendencia de Servicios Públicos Domiciliarios. At: https://www.superservicios.gov.co/sites/default/archivos/Acueducto%2Calcantilladoyaseo/Aseo/2018/Oct/nivelderiesgoserviciodeaseomayoresa2.500.2015.pdf.

Superintendencia de Servicios Públicos Domiciliarios. (2017a). *Coberturas de Acueducto, institutoAlcantarillado y Aseo*. Bogotá: Superservicios, Superintendencia de Servicios Públicos Domiciliarios. At: http://www.sui.gov.co/suibase/html/estratificacion/estratificacionSUI.htm.

Superintendencia de Servicios Públicos Domiciliarios. (2017b). *Evaluaciones integrales*. Bogotá: Superservicios. Superintendencia de Servicios Públicos Domiciliarios.

Trejo Nieto, A. B., Niño Amézquita, J. L. & Vasquez, M. L. (2018). 'Governance of metropolitan areas for delivery of public services in Latin America: The cases of Bogota, Lima and Mexico City'. *Region*, 5(3), 49–73. DOI: 10.18335/REGION.V5I3.224.

UN. (2002). *Cuestiones sustantivas que se plantean en la aplicación del pacto internacional de derechos económicos, sociales y culturales.* New York: United Nations. Consejo Económico y Social. Comité de derechos económicos, sociales y culturales. At: https://www.acnur.org/fileadmin/Documentos/BDL/2012/8789.pdf.

3 Governance structures and the unequal provision of services in metropolitan Lima

Matteo Stiglich and María Luisa Vásquez

Introduction

The Lima Metropolitan Area (LMA), as defined by the National Institute for Statistics and Informatics (Instituto Nacional de Estadística e Informática – INEI), includes the provinces of Lima and Callao. Its population grew rapidly since the mid-twentieth century and today, over nine million people live in this metropolitan area which concentrates around 30 per cent of the total population in Peru. Between 2000 and 2018, the urbanised area has grown by almost 40 per cent, and 90 per cent of this growth has been in informal or illegal settlements (Espinoza & Fort, 2020).

Poverty incidence in LMA is low compared to other regions in Peru; however, an important percentage of Peruvians living below the poverty line reside in this metropolitan area. Poverty in LMA decreased between 2005 and 2015, when it reached its lowest point at 11 per cent (INEI, 2018). But it increased slightly in 2017 and more during the COVID-19 pandemic. LMA has a large central zone with low levels of poverty and vulnerability and several areas in the periphery with higher levels of socio-economic vulnerabilities (Pereyra, 2006; Fernández de Córdova, Fernández-Maldonado & Del Pozo, 2016; Bensús Talavera, 2018; Talavera, 2019). Moreover, most of the population living in land that has been urbanised in the last two decades is from lower socio-economic sectors (Espinoza & Fort, 2020). Figure 3.1 shows this spatial distribution according to socio-economic levels.

Many of the shortcomings affecting the provision of local public services in LMA became more evident during the COVID-19 pandemic. The deficient access to water and sanitation made it difficult for households to follow the most basic hygiene recommendations, while the lack of an integrated transport system made it harder to preserve social distance in public transport. An evident inability to deal with the health crisis led to a public discussion about new models for metropolitan governance. The result was that two mayors announced proposals to reorganise the city's government (Pereyra Colchado, 2020).

Although there is extensive literature that addresses Lima public services' failures on water (Coto Zevallos & Romero Pariachi, 2010; Huamaní, 2017), housing (Calderón, 2015), transport (Poole Fuller, 2017) and waste

DOI: 10.4324/9781003105541-6

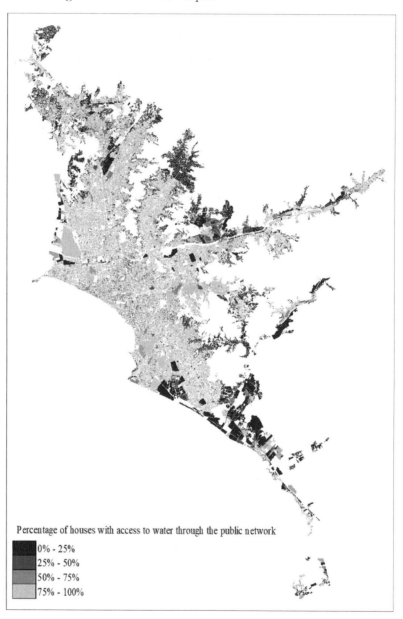

Percentage of houses with access to water through the public network

- 0% - 25%
- 25% - 50%
- 50% - 75%
- 75% - 100%

Figure 3.1 Income per capita per households at block level

Source: INEI (2020).

management (Riofrío, Olivera Cárdenas & Callirgos, 1994; Durand & Metzger, 2009; Riofrío & Cabrera, 2012), the number of studies that focus on more than one service and on metropolitan governance is limited (e.g.

Fernández-Maldonado, 2008; Criqui, 2013). This chapter analyses metropolitan governance in LMA, identifying common issues and particularities in the governance of solid waste management, water and transport services and how these factors shape inequalities in service provision. Our analysis of metropolitan governance focuses on the institutional set up of each sector, including the network of actors involved, their roles, coordination dynamics at the metropolitan level and financial resources. While we acknowledge that governance includes state and non-state actors (De Mattos, 2004; Swyngedouw, 2005), in this chapter we focus mostly on arrangements within the state. The analysis is based on a review of secondary sources and includes results from the field research conducted in Lima as part of the project "Intra-Metropolitan Dynamics in Latin America, Challenges and Problems of Cooperation and Coordination". To discuss inequality in service provision, we use different measurements of access and quality of service provision in each sector, based on the information available.

The chapter is organised as follows. In the first section, we describe the institutional arrangements of LMA and we expound the cases of solid waste management, water and transport services. In the second section, we compare the three cases and analyse the implications of metropolitan governance dynamics in service provision. Section three presents the conclusions.

The provision of public services in Lima

In LMA all four levels of government are involved in the provision of public services: the central, regional, provincial and district level. As shown in Figure 3.2, the province of Callao is governed by both, the regional government and by the provincial municipality. The province of Lima is governed by the Metropolitan Municipality of Lima (MML), which also performs the responsibilities of a regional government. Within Lima and Callao there are 50 districts in total. The capital districts of Callao and Lima are governed by

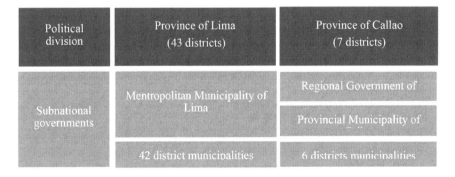

Figure 3.2 Subnational-level governments in LMA

Source: Authors' elaboration.

the provincial municipality of Callao and the MML, respectively. The other 48 districts are governed by district municipalities.

The distribution of responsibilities between these governmental actors is unclear in some aspects and there are frequent overlaps (Bensa, 2015; Barco, Chavez & Olivas, 2020). The scenario is further complicated because the decentralisation that started in 2001 has been slower to transfer responsibilities to the MML (PCM, 2020). While most local responsibilities have been already decentralised to the regional government of Callao, the central government remains a main provider of several public services in Lima, including education and health.

The fragmented and intricate institutional set up has hindered coordination at the metropolitan level (Fuentes & Durán, 2018), and there are no instances of metropolitan coordination with the institutional strength to serve as a connecting bridge between the multiple metropolitan actors (Bensa, 2015; Fuentes & Durán, 2018). We next discuss in detail the metropolitan governance in the three services selected.

Public transport

In Peru national laws divide transport-related responsibilities in three areas: roads, traffic and transport. Specific responsibilities within these three sub-sectors, in turn, are given to distinct public entities. Roads cover everything related to road infrastructure, including capital investments and maintenance. Traffic deals with traffic control and regulation. Lastly, public transport (including infrastructure) and taxis pertain to the transport area. In the LMA, responsibilities within each of these three areas are shared by different levels of government. Depending on the road hierarchy, road construction and maintenance are either the responsibility of the provincial or the district municipality. The provincial governments manage highways, but toll roads are outsourced. The national government, in turn, is planning a new highway, which would fall under its responsibility because it is considered to be a national rather than a metropolitan road.

The national government manages traffic regulation, but some responsibilities are shared with other levels. Traffic signals are maintained by different levels of government according to road hierarchy. The national police, in turn, enforces traffic rules, which are also established at the national level, while provincial and district governments can pass ordinances complementing them. Lastly, the national government, in charge of issuing driving licenses, has outsourced this process to private operators.

Provincial municipalities are in charge of delivering road-based public transport. But given that it has been outsourced to private operators, their actual role is to supervise and regulate. The urban rail, which is also outsourced, is the responsibility of the national government. Taxis are regulated by the provincial governments, while districts regulate jitneys, which also provide taxi service.

Most of the daily trips in LMA are done by public transport, which is highly fragmented. The most used system is composed of a large number of loosely regulated and fully privately operated buses. In 2018, around 59 per cent of people in LMA reported using this system as their main transport mode (Lima Cómo Vamos, 2019). Private companies own the right to serve one or more bus routes. These firms lease that right to the owner of a vehicle, who in turn rents their vehicle to a driver and a fare collector. In some cases, a single company integrates two or all of these roles. The Urban Transport Offices are the municipal agencies that have been in charge of overseeing this system (Gerencia de Transporte Urbano, GTU) of Lima and Callao. But in a system like this, there is no opportunity for fare integration, so each transfer forces the passenger to pay a new ticket. Moreover, fares rise with distance. The system also produces a low quality and dangerous service, with few incentives for investing in renovating the vehicles. As drivers earn their income according to the number of passengers, competition induces reckless driving (Bielich, 2009).

Three other systems are operated by private consortia under long-term contracts with the government. A metro line accounted for 550,000 daily trips in 2019 (Línea Uno, 2020). In 2018, 3 per cent of population in LMA reported this as their main transport mode to their job or school (Lima Cómo Vamos, 2019). The national government administers and subsidises metro operations. A 2015 study estimated the farebox recovery ratio at 63 per cent (Kohon, 2015).

A Bus Rapid Transit (BRT) system, called Metropolitano, which operates one main line and feeder buses, concentrated 7,00,000 daily trips in 2018 (Agencia Andina, 2019). In LMA, 3 per cent reported using Metropolitano as their main mode to work or study (Lima Cómo Vamos, 2019). The third bus system is called Corredores Complementarios and is composed of four mixed-traffic bus corridors with a few routes each. In 2018, 1.5 per cent of population in LMA reported them as their main transport mode (ibid.). The Metropolitano and the Corredores Complementarios are overseen by Protransporte, a Lima municipal agency that is separate from the GTU. Metropolitano and Corredores Complementarios share a fare collection system, but transfers are not free. In each line fares are flat, that is, their cost does not increase with distance. By design, all operations must be covered by farebox revenues, and consequently Metropolitano fares are considerably higher than Metro fares. All three systems operate within the limits of Lima and do not cover Callao.

Lastly, three other services complete the transport system. The implementation of Corredores Complementarios resulted in some service gaps that are being served by *colectivos*, which are unlicensed small vehicles, usually sedans or vans. In 2018, 3 per cent of people in LMA reported using colectivos as their main transport mode, and 6 per cent used it along their trip (Lima Cómo Vamos, 2019). Jitneys (*mototaxis*) operate mostly in peripheral districts, and are intensely used for the "last mile" of trips. In LMA,

4 per cent of respondents reported them as their main mode of transport to their job or school, while 14 per cent reported that they used them somewhere along their trip. Taxis in turn, are relatively non-expensive because of the high informal supply. In LMA, 5 per cent of respondents reported using taxis regularly somewhere along their trip as one of their modes to work or school (ibid.).

Transport access and quality are highly unequal. Average travel times to work by public transport are somewhere between 50 per cent (MTC-JICA, 2013) and 87 per cent (Vargas et al., 2017) higher than trips done by automobile. Inequalities in travel times become more striking when considering that, compared to around two-thirds of the trips to work or school done mainly by public transport, only 11 per cent are done by private vehicles. Moreover, the vast majority of population makes considerably longer daily trips than a privileged minority.

Transport inequalities also reflect income and spatial inequalities. Automobile ownership and use are concentrated in the central area of the city, where a large share of job opportunities is located. In LMA, 19 per cent of the population in the A/B sectors and 21 per cent of those living in central LMA drove to their workplace or school, compared to 11 per cent in the city as a whole (Lima Cómo Vamos, 2019). The farther one lives from central LMA, the more likely one is to use public transport. Furthermore, the longer the trip, the more likely that transfers are needed to reach your destination, or that you need to pay higher fares based on distance. In the far peripheries, not reached by regular transport services, people usually need to take jitneys, which adds to the cost of travel. Spatially, then, distance from the central area makes mobility more expensive and more time consuming. This spatial inequality, in turn, mimics income inequalities, as the peripheries are considerably poorer than the central area. In fact, while the opening of the BRT line in 2010 improved travel times and access to jobs, those benefits have not been directed to the poorest sectors of the population (Oviedo et al., 2019).

In this respect, transport governance can contribute to reproduce metropolitan inequalities. The inexistence of a centralised fare collection system has hampered the establishment of a progressive fare structure that does not penalise those who have to travel longer distances or need to transfer. Furthermore, the different levels of technical and financial capacity among levels of government have meant that some segments of the transport system do achieve relatively affordable fares. But without integrating the whole system, benefits are limited to those that only use those segments. In addition, the separation of responsibilities has led to poor coordination. For instance, in 2012, when the national government announced the construction of a second metro line, the MML was forced to cancel a project for a second BRT line.

In 2018, the Urban Transport Authority (Autoridad de Transporte Urbano – ATU) was created in order to advance the consolidation of transport services within one entity and under the Ministry of Transport and Communications (MTC). ATU is an example of efforts towards metropolitan centralisation in two senses. On the one hand, it centralised the responsibility of providing and regulating nearly all transport services (except jitneys, which remain the responsibility of district governments). On the other hand, it transferred responsibilities previously held by the provincial governments toward an agency in which the national government plays an important role.

However, ATU faces three major challenges for reducing inequalities in transport access. First, ATU centralises transport services, but can do little to de-incentivise automobile use or to transfer resources from automobile use to public transport. Second, ATU has to face political issues. When Corredores Complementarios were planned in the early 2010s, the MML announced that the first line would run on segregated routes. A major artery, Arequipa avenue, would be converted into a semi-exclusive public transport corridor. Wealthy residents of San Isidro protested with the support of their district government. The MML cancelled its plans and run the buses on mixed-traffic. Powerful local interests remain a barrier to implementing transport policies that reduce inequalities. Third, there are several political economy factors. The whole transport system of LMA depends heavily on private providers. As every transport route is operated by a different consortium, changes require constant renegotiations between the local governments and several consortia. With the fare collection system in the integrated Metropolitano – Corredores Complementarios network also outsourced to a private company, there is another actor in the renegotiation, potentially increasing costs for the public (cf. Sclar, 2001, 16–19). In renegotiations, private actors have much less to lose than the government. While they do not have a public responsibility to deliver good services, only a responsibility according to contract, the government has urgency to accept costly changes in order to fulfil its obligations. This is not just a theoretical assertion. During the 2020 pandemic, the MML repeatedly accepted new terms demanded by the consortia operating the BRT system in order to continue operations. At all times, these decisions were made while the operators threatened to suspend the service (Gestión, 2020a, 2020b, 2020c).

Despite the challenges mentioned above, there are two reasons why ATU might help reducing the fragmentation in transport provision. First, it will eliminate the division of responsibilities by levels of government, at least regarding transport services. Regular public transport, BRT, Corredores Complementarios and metro lines will all operate under ATU. Second, given that the national government will be closely involved, the imbalances of power between the public and the private sector mentioned above might be diminished. The national government might have more technical capacity and financial resources to negotiate in less unequal terms with private providers.

Water and sanitation

Water and sanitation service in the metropolitan area is provided by the Service of Drinking Water and Sewage of Lima (Servicio de Agua Potable y

Alcantarillado de Lima – SEDAPAL), a government-owned company that operates under a private legal regime. Currently, the company is under the Ministry of Housing, Construction and Sanitation (Ministerio de Vivienda, Construcción y Saneamiento – MVCS). SEDAPAL is regulated by the National Superintendence of Sanitation Services (Superintendencia Nacional de Servicios de Saneamiento – SUNASS). SUNASS is a national agency that regulates and supervises water and sanitation provision in Peru and establishes water rates.

There has not been effective metropolitan coordination between SEDAPAL, the provincial and district municipalities to plan for the expansion of the public network and to close service gaps. The main task of the district municipalities is limited to providing possession certificates and approve layout plans (Criqui, 2013) that allow neighbourhoods to be part of the infrastructure projects that extend the public network.

SEDAPAL has been subject to a market-oriented reform since the 1990s (Ioris, 2013). This reform was part of a global trend that sought to "insulate" water and sanitation services, avoiding political pressures against cost recovery measures, and to allow managers to focus on quality and coverage issues in the medium and long run (Herrera & Post, 2014). As we can see in Figure 3.3, SEDAPAL has been able to increase the percentage of micro-measurement while decreasing the water not billed in the last decade. Compared to smaller, decentralised, municipal water services companies in Peru, SEDAPAL has a better performance in these indicators and a healthier financial status (MVCS, 2017).

SEDAPAL has also increased the average rate in the last decade (Corporación FONAFE, 2009, 2020). An important modification in the fees structure was

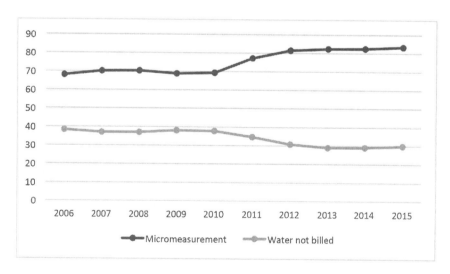

Figure 3.3 Micro-measurement and water not billed (2006–2017)

Source: SEDAPAL Annual reports 2006–2017.

implemented in 2017, when progressivity, based on level of consumption, was complemented by one based on socio-economic status. The aim was to reduce the gap between cost and price for non-subsidized households, and to protect access to subsistence consumption for population below the poverty line (SUNASS, 2015; SEDAPAL, 2018). However, rate increases approved by SUNASS have been consistently lower than what SEDAPAL has suggested (Cueva López, Powzén Reaño & Ramos Taipe, 2019) and insufficient to cover the investment needed to close the access gap. SEDAPAL (2019) recognises that resources are needed to close the coverage gap.

Unlike other large cities in Latin America, SEDAPAL provides the service to the whole metropolitan area. Furthermore, SEDAPAL serves areas beyond Lima and Callao when there is territorial continuity and provision is technically feasible, such as in parts of the province of Huarochirí. To serve the growing metropolitan area, in the last 20 years SEDAPAL expanded its water network by 65.5 per cent and its sanitation network by 68.5 per cent (Figure 3.4). The main programs to expand access have been Project of Coverage Expansion (Proyecto de Ampliación de Cobertura), Water for All (Agua para Todos), Programme of Safe Water for Lima and Callao (Programa de Agua Segura para Lima y Callao – PASLC). Most of this expansion has taken place after the occupation of land (Criqui, 2013).

The MVCS plays a crucial role in expanding coverage. A substantial share of the investment projects executed by SEDAPAL has been funded by central public resources. Since 2011, 25 per cent of the resources for investment projects came from transfers from the MVCS (Figure 3.5). SEDAPAL (2019) recognizes that to close the coverage gap in LMA the central government will need to continue to provide resources. The role of the MVCS was further enhanced in 2018 when it created PASLC to accelerate the execution of

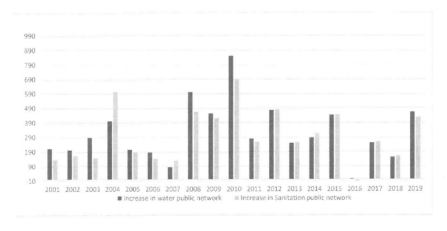

Figure 3.4 Increase in the water and sanitation network, 2001–2019 (km)

Source: SEDAPAL Annual Reports 2001–2019.

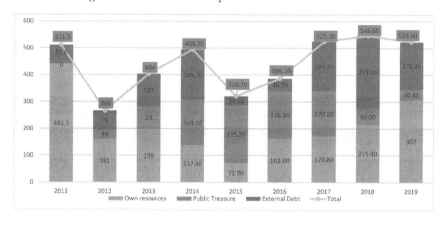

Figure 3.5 SEDAPAL Investment program by source 2011–2019

Source: SEDAPAL Annual reports 2011–2019.

projects which was considered to be slow under SEDAPAL. Only between 2018 and 2020, the program has executed PEN 853 million in projects (MEF, 2021).

In the case of water and sanitation, we use access to water through the public network as a measure of coverage. The coverage has increased from 74.4 per cent of houses with access to water through the public network and 72 per cent to sanitation in 1993 to 88.4 and 89.5 per cent, respectively, in 2017. Although there are challenges on quality of the service, this is better than the services provided by companies outside the LMA. In 2019, the average continuity of the services was more than 21 hours, with most of the areas of the city having a service continuity above 17 hours (SUNASS, 2019). Water rates for households are, on average, low compared to rates in other Latin American cities (SEDAPAL, 2019). Huamaní (2017) estimates that households with incomes less than PEN 750 spend, on average, 1.72 per cent of their income in water if they are connected to the public network of SEDAPAL.

As the service coverage has increased and rates remain low, the main challenges for access to water and sanitation in Lima are found outside the limits of the public network, in the periphery of the city. Figure 3.6 shows that blocks with low coverage are concentrated in the borders of the south, east and north of the city. There, households pay higher fees and water is usually bought from tanker trucks that, in turn, buy the water from SEDAPAL (Huamaní, 2017). According to a survey conducted for SUNASS in 2015, households not connected to the public network paid almost seven times more for the same level of consumption than households connected to the public network (ibid.). Moreover, they consume on average 5.44 cubic meters per month, a little lower than the minimum consumption recommended by the World Health Organization (WHO, 2013) and 6.5 times lower than the average consumption per person of SEDAPAL users (Iagua, 2015).

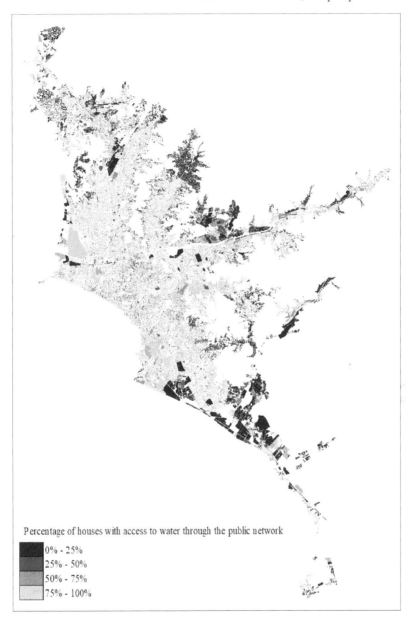

Percentage of houses with access to water through the public network

- 0% - 25%
- 25% - 50%
- 50% - 75%
- 75% - 100%

Figure 3.6 Percentage of houses with access to water through the public network at the block level

Source: INEI (2017).

Achieving full water and sanitation provision becomes increasingly difficult and the costs of expanding the network increase as Lima expands to areas of difficult access (SEDAPAL, 2019). The projects included in SEDAPAL investment program for 2015–2020 have an average cost of PEN 12,000 per connection (Huamaní, 2017) which is considerably higher than the PEN 2,000 estimate of governmental investment per lot to provide basic services across Peru (Espinoza & Fort, 2020). In some projects the cost per connection is as high as PEN 28,000 (Huamaní, 2017).

Problems with water access in LMA cannot be understood without looking at geography and the urbanisation process. Historically, for a large portion of LMA, services have followed housing construction. Since the mid twentieth century, collective processes of urbanisation have paralleled the developments of the private housing market. As the latter was urbanising flat areas close to the city centre and with all the services available from the outset, low-income residents were left with no option but to occupy farther away areas. Initially these were also in relatively flat areas, but as land became scarcer hilly spaces were occupied.

Since the 1990s, what was once a collective urbanisation process has become more and more subject to private land markets, albeit almost always informal (Fernández-Maldonado, 2014). Land traffickers with ties to local governments occupy hilly areas in order to sell plots. Both sellers and buyers are often confident that they will be able to remain in the site, as the national government periodically grants land ownership to residents living in these areas.

It is highly unlikely that this mode of urban production will change in the near future. Demand for low-cost housing remains, and the supply for it is almost non-existent. The only means for many low-income families to access housing is by engaging in this market. It is a highly irrational and inefficient system that can be explained in part by a lack of coordination between the MVCS, SEDAPAL and the governments at the local level. In a different scenario, the resources needed to deliver urban services to these areas could be transferred to a public housing program that guarantees the supply of low-income housing, limiting the expansion of the city into the hills. But there is no public housing program in Peru. Instead, since the 2000s the government has provided subsidies to help families buy houses in the private market or improve their houses (Fernández-Maldonado, 2014), a system that has clearly been insufficient to cover the housing deficit.

Waste management

Public cleaning services include the collection, transport and final disposal of solid waste. These services are regulated and overseen by the central government. The Ministry of Environment (Ministerio del Medio Ambiente – MINAM) regulates solid waste management, including infrastructure, reutilisation, recuperation and valorisation, among other aspects. The Agency of Environmental Evaluation and Supervision (Oficina de Evaluación y Fiscalización Ambiental – OEFA) oversees local governments, supervise the implementation of provincial and district solid waste management plans, and supervises the management of solid waste in facilities managed by local governments or operating companies.

At the subnational level, district municipalities are responsible for cleaning, collection and transport of waste, as well as its final disposal. District municipalities also regulate waste management services in their jurisdiction and can sign cooperation agreements with other municipalities to integrate service provision to trigger economies of scale and efficiency. In the case of the capital districts, the provincial municipalities are in charge of these functions. Provincial municipalities regulate and supervise waste management, identify the location of infrastructure, authorise public and private investment projects and supervise solid waste management services in their jurisdictions. However, supervision is weak. A 2019 report from Defensoría del Pueblo recommends the MML to improve the supervision of district municipalities to reduce the accumulation of waste on critical points in the city (Defensoría del Pueblo, 2019).

Solid waste management services can be provided directly by the municipalities, by contractor companies or through mixed schemes. In 2018, 49 per cent of the municipalities in Lima contracted out the collection services, 21 per cent used a mixed scheme, and 30 per cent provided the service directly (Ministerio del Ambiente, MINAM, 2018a). On the other hand, all of the four metropolitan landfills in Lima and Callao are managed by private companies. Innova Ambiental S.A. (also called ReLima) and Petramás are companies that control all four metropolitan landfills in Lima and Callao (Innova: Portillo Grande and Zapallal; Petramás: Huaycoloro and Callao), and most municipal-level collection services. This small number of private providers configure an oligopolistic market in both collection and disposal. Both markets are controlled by the same two companies. The dependence on a small number of private providers to establish PPPs is questionable since public-private partnerships in Peru present opportunities for rent-seeking (Takano, 2017), and can distort the public interest through the influence of private providers, especially in cases where the state does not have financial or administrative capacities (Stiglich, 2019).

To finance the service, municipalities establish and collect fees. However, compliance varies greatly across municipalities in LMA. The Integral Plan for Environmental Management of Solid Waste of the Lima Province (2015–2025) (Plan Integral de Gestión Ambiental de Residuos Sólidos de la Provincia de Lima – PIGARS) reported that non-compliance was over 60 per cent in the districts from the south and north of Lima, as high as 82 per cent in San Juan de Lurigancho, 44 per cent in the east, and 37 per cent in the centre of Lima, and as low as 11 per cent in San Isidro (MML, 2014). Although municipalities can sign agreements with local utilities companies to entrust them with the payment collection, this mechanism has not been used in LMA.

Revenues collected for cleaning fees have been increasing in Lima, including the districts in the periphery. Among them, San Juan de Miraflores, Villa el

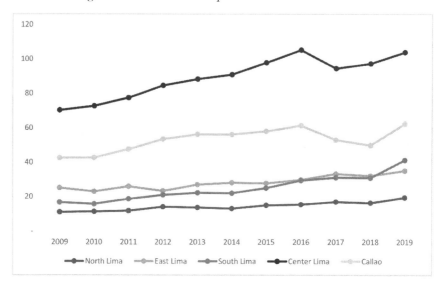

Figure 3.7 Revenue per capita for public cleaning services by city area, 2009–2019 (PEN)
Source: MEF (2021).

Salvador, Santa Anita and Independencia have more than tripled their revenues per capita. However, about half of the municipalities outside the centre of the city collected less than PEN 30 per capita in 2019. Furthermore, as the Figure 3.7 shows, the gaps between revenues collected by municipalities in the centre of Lima and the rest of areas are significant and have broadened in the last decade.

The variation in revenue collection capacity is reflected in the percentage of waste management expenditures that municipalities are able to cover with their own resources. Between 2015 and 2019, some municipalities were not able to cover practically none of the expenditures while other municipalities were able to cover 100 per cent of their expenditures. Municipalities that are not able to cover the expenditures with these resources, usually rely on the Fondo de Compensación Municipal (FONCOMUN), a transfer from the central government (MEF, 2021). Although these transfers support municipalities, they are clearly insufficient. Annual expenditure per capita varies highly. In 2019, Punta Negra spent as little as PEN 3, and La Punta as much as PEN 447 (ibid.). Not surprisingly, the lack of resources is identified as one of the main constraints for municipalities in the peripheries to provide adequate service. Limited resources lead to difficulties in service provision due to underinvestment in equipment and infrastructure; and even to discontinuity of services due to debts to companies and staff.

Measuring the access and the quality of waste management services is challenging. Overall indicators depict a positive perspective in Lima and Callao relative to other areas in the country. A 100 per cent of households in Callao and 98.9 per cent in Lima reported to receive the services in 2018 (INEI, 2019). Furthermore, all of the municipalities in Lima and Callao report disposing of the waste to one of the four sanitary landfills near the city (Contraloría General de la República, 2019), while in the rest of the country most municipalities leave the solid waste on dump sites (Defensoría del Pueblo, 2019).

The quality of collection services is usually lower in the districts in the periphery (Durand & Metzger, 2009). High expenditure central districts have few points of waste accumulation, in contrast with lower expenditure districts in the periphery, as seen in Figure 3.8. Gaps in quality are reflected in lower satisfaction with waste collection services outside of central Lima.

□ Between 0 and 11
▩ Between 11 and 16
■ Between 16 and 135

□ Less than S/46
▩ Between S/46 and S/90
■ Between S/90 and S/447

Figure 3.8 Number of points of waste accumulation identified in districts of Metropolitan Lima and Expenditure per capita on waste management in Metropolitan Lima, 2019

Source: MEF (2020, 2021).

The dissatisfaction with waste collection services is consistently higher outside central Lima, and especially in Southern Lima and among households from lower socio-economic status. For instance, in 2019 the dissatisfaction with the waste collection service was 45 per cent in central Lima and 50 per cent among the higher socio-economic sectors; while it was 73 per cent in Southern Lima and 66 per cent among the lowest socioeconomic sectors (Lima Cómo Vamos, 2020).

An extreme case that illustrates the kind of constraints faced by districts in the periphery is Villa María de Triunfo where waste management was declared in emergency in 2018 by MINAM, with 135 points of waste accumulation. That year, the municipality only collected PEN 10.72 per capita, which covered just 46.5 per cent of the estimated cost of the service (MEF, 2021). The service collapsed when the contractor in charge of transferring waste to the landfill refused to continue receiving the waste due to an outstanding debt by the municipality. Storage was not possible because the municipality did not have containers on public roads. Finally, the sweeping service was also paralysed as the workers went on strike to protest the lack of payment of their salaries (Ministerio del Ambiente, MINAM, 2018b).

The governance of three public services: institutional set up, metropolitan coordination and challenges

The service provision in each sector we analysed involves more or less actors according to levels of decentralisation and the distribution of responsibilities. These actors are accountable to the central government or to local elected officials, and follow different patterns of coordination at the metropolitan level. These distinct institutional arrangements face different challenges to deliver equal access to the services.

This institutional design of the water and sanitation sector in LMA affects the access of the population to the service provision in different ways. As the single water service provider in the metropolitan area, SEDAPAL has been able to expand service without having the provincial borders as barriers, a problem that is seen in other Latin-American cities. It has also implemented cross subsidies across the city. Service centralisation may have also contributed to implementing effective cost-recovery policies. Due to its size, SEDAPAL has the technical and operational capacity to implement these policies. Furthermore, because it is ascribed to the MVCS and not to a municipality, it faces less political pressure, compared to municipal public companies. However, the large size of the company and the development of cumbersome processes imposed difficulties to the timely execution of projects, which led to the creation of PASLC outside of SEDAPAL. Furthermore, as described in the previous section, the coordination at the metropolitan level regarding the planning of the city and the expansion of the public network is virtually non-existent and this absence contributes to an unplanned, reactive and inefficient mode of expanding the public network.

Waste management services also face particular challenges to ensure equal access by all population segments. The service is provided by each of the municipalities, there are no agreements between them to collaborate and gain economies of scale and the role of the provincial municipalities is limited. This creates significant differences in revenues between municipalities in the centre of Lima and the rest of the city. Although average revenues per capita have increased in the last ten years, and a few municipalities in the periphery have had large increases, the gaps across municipalities remain large and an important number of districts are being left behind. Lesser resources result in an important constraint to provide waste management services in the districts, as reflected by the distribution of critical points of waste accumulation in the city. The lower income levels in these districts are a major constraint to increase revenues. Lower technical capacity and political costs that mayors face to enforce payment seem to be another constraint to increase revenues. Further research exploring how some districts in the periphery have increased their revenues could shed light on this issue.

Finally, transport is a complex case in which service provision is fragmented in three ways. Different levels of government are responsible for different parts of the transport network, the network itself is fragmented, with different systems operated by private operators without an integrated fare system, and the whole transport system is divided in transport services, traffic, and road infrastructure, with different levels of government or jurisdictions responsible for each. The fragmentation of these services hinders even access to transport services because it makes it difficult to develop an integrated public network, to prioritise public transport over automobiles and to provide high quality access to the whole metropolitan area. The creation of ATU represents an opportunity to integrate the network. However, while ATU will centralise transport policy, it will not be directly in charge of road infrastructure and traffic management, which are key to ensuring the quality-of-service provision. Therefore, ATU will not have much power to influence policies related to automobile use, or to redistribute resources from automobiles to public transport.

Planning and housing policy

While each sector has particular challenges related to their institutional design, common issues emerge regarding planning and housing policy. The process of urbanisation in the fringes of the city, which occurs in hilly areas with difficult access, presents a major challenge for all three services covered in this chapter. The cost of delivering services to these areas is considerably higher than the cost of delivering them to flat areas near major transport corridors. The difference is especially acute for water and sewage services. This seemingly irrational urbanisation arrangement is explained by two interrelated factors: the lack of effective planning and the absence of housing policies that effectively supply affordable housing for low-income people.

The responsibility for urban planning is shared between the provincial and the district municipalities, but not all districts have active plans in place. The issue is not just the lack of actual plans, but of mechanisms to make them functional. In fact, the Peruvian planning framework lacks mechanisms to monitor plan implementation (Fernández-Maldonado, 2019). The result is scant planning with weak instruments to implement plans in practice, which results in market forces defining the expansion of the city into its hills.

The weakness around planning for urban growth is not the only pressing issue. The push for expanding the city would not be so strong if enough affordable housing was available. But the existing housing policy, based on subsidies to families to buy or improve homes, is critically insufficient. As mentioned above, the pattern of urban growth increases the cost of delivering key services, contributing to an unequal provision. A portion of those costs could be saved by directing those resources to an effective housing policy that allows low-income families to live in more accessible areas.

In the case of water provision, the scarcity of land in a city surrounded by hills means that with each new home the cost of connecting it to the network increases, as it is expensive to move water uphill. But costs are not the only issue. In the historic process of urbanisation, low-income people have gained access to a plot of land before getting services. Rather than buying plots on houses that already have services, people have obtained these plots either through collective action (land squats) or through informal land markets. This can leave a large portion of Limeños without access to water because the process of obtaining it after settling in their plots can take years. For SEDAPAL it is not easy to keep up with the pace at which urbanisation occurs. In fact, the age of an informal settlement is a good predictor of whether it has access to the network or not (Fernández-Maldonado, 2008).

The political economy of service provision

Two characteristics are found across all three sectors: first, a lack of resources; and the outsourcing of services to private operators. All three sectors are underfunded and this is particularly severe for waste management and transport. All of the public transport routes in Lima are operated by a diversity of private firms. The highway network of the city is operated by two concessionaires. Most of the district municipalities outsource garbage collection to two private operators. These two operators also manage the four landfills. Thus, waste management is in the hands of a few operators, but most of them outside the state. As a public enterprise, SEDAPAL is an exception, but still depends on the private sector to implement infrastructure projects to expand capacity.

In theory, there is nothing wrong with individually outsourcing certain services. The local state does not necessarily have the knowledge or the capacity to deliver all services. However, there are issues at stake when the state does not develop any capacity to deliver services and when there is an imbalance of knowledge and power between the state and private operators. If all the knowledge on how to deliver services lies within the latter, then the former negotiates under asymmetric information. Firms that operate in the borders between the public and the private sectors often capture a good portion of the knowledge needed to negotiate successfully. Furthermore, given that we are talking about services delivered to the public, the government has a responsibility that the private firms do not. The misalignment of interests can lead to principal-agent problems, especially when scenarios of crisis require urgent solutions.

Power imbalance is aggravated if we consider the availability of resources and the capacity to raise finance for infrastructure projects. Often, large corporations have the capacity of financing projects that the local government cannot. This deepens the imbalance of power from the beginning, especially when the lower levels of government are involved. A way of overcoming these issues would be for the state to develop the capacity to deliver itself these services, even if it keeps outsourcing some of them. Information asymmetries would be reduced and the state would have the capacity to take responsibility of services in critical situations.

Conclusions

In this chapter, we have analysed the governance of metropolitan service provision in three sectors in LMA and explored their relationship with the differences in service quality and coverage across the metropolitan area. First of all, we have found important variations in the governance of public services in LMA and provided insights about the different challenges that arise from the particularities in each sector. We also have found that the lack of urban planning and the difficult political economic dynamics with private companies are recurring issues across the sectors. Several of these problems are being publicly discussed, such as the lack of revenue capacity of district municipalities, the fragmentation of public transport between Lima and Callao, and the lack of urban planning. However, issues like the administrative fragmentation of transport policy, the consequences of the lack of public housing programs for service provision and the complex relation with private providers need more attention from policy makers.

Regarding water provision, the main issue is the large swaths of the metropolitan area that remain disconnected from the public network. These areas are in the peripheries and are mostly inhabited by people from the lower brackets of the income distribution. Furthermore, not being connected to the network carries huge costs for population because buying water from private providers is considerably more expensive than from SEDAPAL. The main explanations for the persistence of disconnected homes are related to the process of urbanisation. Homes in the fringes of the city are being built before services have been provided. That very fact means that there will always be a sector that is disconnected, at least while it waits for SEDAPAL to connect them. The issue is aggravated given that the wait might take years. Furthermore, a large portion of this process happens in hilly areas, where connecting each new home is more costly that the one before. A combination of poor planning and coordination, lack of affordable housing opportunities and cost of pumping water uphill explains why more than 10 per cent of homes in Lima and Callao do not have access to water and sanitation, despite considerable improvements in the last 20 years. The issue forward requires looking beyond water and sanitation but into urban planning to provide affordable housing opportunities in more accessible areas of the metropolitan area.

The most striking issue regarding waste management is the inequality in service quality across municipal borders. Such inequality is related to income inequality. Per capita expenditure in wealthy districts is considerably higher than in low-income districts. Similarly, most of the points where waste that has not been properly disposed accumulates is in the peripheral, low-income districts. There is still some variation in capacity among those districts per capita revenues and expenditure among low-income districts, which leads to some variation in service quality as well, but the main differences are still explained by structural reasons. While it is important to understand what can explain those differences, an issue that needs more research, a path forward cannot overlook the importance of income inequality between districts as a key factor driving the differences in resources available to deal with waste management. Devising ways of reducing or eliminating inequalities in resources among districts is critical in dealing with inequalities in service provision.

The transport network of LMA is highly fragmented. There are several systems in the metropolitan area, each with its own fare structure and with little to no integration between them. As a consequence, the system penalises those that live farther from employment centres, as they travel longer distances and tend to need more transfers, both of which come at a higher cost. Given that income levels in the peripheries tend to be lower, this reproduces already existing inequalities. The system is also unequal in that travel times by private transport are considerably lower on average than by public transport. This factor also reproduces income inequalities. Political economic dynamics explain a large part of these inequalities. Provincial governments, which until recently were in charge of most of the system, have little capacity to plan and deliver large investments in transport. As a consequence, they have turned to the private sector, producing a fragmented public transport system in the hands of several private operators and directing a considerable amount of resources to improving automobile traffic. The consolidation of responsibilities into a new public entity, ATU, might be a step towards integrating the system. Centralising it at the national level might bring much needed financial and technical capacity, while facilitating the integration of all systems under one entity. However, limitations remain, as ATU is only in charge of transport rather than the whole transport system, and consequently there is little it can do to curb automobile use or otherwise capture resources from it in order to redistribute it within the system.

References

Agencia, Andina. (2019). 'El Metropolitano tendrá más buses, mejor ventilación y señalética'. *Agencia Andina*, January 22. At: https://www.andina.pe/agencia/noticia-el-metropolitano-tendra-mas-buses-mejor-ventilacion-y-senaletica-740001.aspx.

Barco, D., Chavez, P. & Olivas, K. (2020). 'Promoviendo mayor eficacia y menor desigualdad a través de la descentralización'. In *Perú Debate 2021.*

Bensa, J. (2015). 'La gobernanza urbana en contextos de descentralización y fragmentación institucional. El caso de Lima Metropolitana'. In Grin, E.J., Bonivento, J.H. & Abrucio, F.L. (eds.) *El Gobierno de las grandes ciudades: Gobernanza y Descentralización en las Metrópolis de América Latina.* Santiago: CLAD Centro Latinoamericano de Administración para el Desarrollo, pp. 241–264.

Bensús Talavera, V. (2018). 'Densificación (no) planificada de una metrópoli. El caso del Área Metropolitana de Lima 2000–2014'. *Revista Invi*, 33(92), 9–51.

Bielich, C. (2009). *La Guerra Del Centavo. Una Mirada Actual al Transporte Público En Lima Metropolitana.* Lima: CIES, IEP.

Calderón, J. (2015). 'Programas de vivienda social nueva y mercados de suelo urbano en el Perú'. *EURE*, 41(122), 27–47.

Contraloría General de la República. (2019). *Informe Consolidado del Operativo "Por una Ciudad Limpia y Saludable" – A la prestación del servicio de limpieza pública a cargo de las municipalidades.* Lima: Gerencia de Control de Servicios Públicos Básicos.

Corporación FONAFE. (2009). *Evaluación Financiera y Presupuestal – 2008.* Lima: Corporación FONAFE.

Corporación FONAFE. (2020). *Evaluación Financiera y Presupuestal – 2019.* Lima: Corporación FONAFE.

Coto Zevallos, J. L. & Romero Pariachi, R. (2010). *Equidad en el acceso al agua en la ciudad de Lima: una mirada a partir del derecho humano al agua.* Thesis. Pontificia Universidad Católica del Perú. At: http://tesis.pucp.edu.pe/repositorio/handle/20.500.12404/1365.

Criqui, L. (2013). 'Pathways for progressive planning through extending water and electricity networks in the irregular settlements of Lima'. In Garland, A.M. (ed.) *Innovation in urban development: Incremental housing, big data, and gender.* Washington, DC: Woodrow Wilson International Center for Scholars, pp. 34–56.

Cueva López, R. F., Powzén Reaño, G. T. & Ramos Taipe, C. L. (2019). *Sostenibilidad financiera de Sedapal.* Master Thesis. Universidad del Pacífico.

De Mattos, C. A. (2004). 'De la planificación a la governance: implicancias para la gestión territorial y urbana'. *Revista Paranaense de Desenvolvimento*, 0(107), 9–23.

Defensoría del Pueblo. (2019). *¿Dónde va nuestra basura?: Recomendaciones para mejorar la gestión de los residuos sólidos municipales.* Lima: Defensoría del Pueblo.

Durand, M. & Metzger, P. (2009). 'Gestión de residuos y transferencia de vulnerabilidad en Lima/Callao'. *Bulletin de l'Institut Français d'Etudes Andines*, 38(3), 623–646.

Espinoza, A. & Fort, R. (2020). *Mapeo y tipología de la expansión urbana en el Perú.* Lima: Grupo de Análisis para el Desarrollo (GRADE).

Fernández de Córdova, G., Fernández-Maldonado, A. M. & Del Pozo, J. M. (2016). 'Recent changes in the patterns of socio-spatial segregation in Metropolitan Lima'. *Habitat International*, 54, 28–39.

Fernández-Maldonado, A. M. (2008). 'Expanding networks for the urban poor: Water and telecommunications services in Lima, Peru'. *Geoforum*, 39(6), 1884–1896.

Fernández-Maldonado, A. M. (2014). 'Planeamiento urbano y producción de vivienda en el Perú'. In Abramo P., Rodríguez Mancilla M. & Erazo Espinosa, J. (eds.) *Procesos Urbanos En Acción. ¿Desarrollo de Ciudades Para Todos?* Ciudades de la gente 3. Abya-Yala. Clacso: Universidade Federal do Rio de Janeiro, pp. 81–115.

Fernández-Maldonado, A. M. (2019). 'Unboxing the black box of Peruvian planning'. *Planning Practice & Research*, 34(4), 368–386.

Fuentes, L. & Durán, G. (2018). 'La institucionalidad metropolitana frente al desafío del desarrollo en Latinoamérica: Los modelos de gestión urbana de Bogotá, Lima, Quito y Santiago en cuestión'. *IX Congreso Internacional en Gobierno, Administración y Políticas Públicas GIGAPP*, Madrid, September 24–27, 2018.

Gestión. (2020a). 'Metropolitano: se necesita aprobación unánime de concesionarias para uso del fondo de contingencia, según MML'. *Gestión*, March 31.

Gestión. (2020b). 'Metropolitano: operadores anuncian paralización del servicio desde el miércoles 15 de julio'. *Gestión*, July 9.

Gestión. (2020c). 'Metropolitano: Lima Bus suspenderá sus operaciones si hasta el viernes 4 no recibe compensaciones'. *Gestión*, December 1.

Herrera, V. & Post A. (2014). 'Can developing countries both decentralize and depoliticize urban water services? Evaluating the legacy of the 1990s reform wave'. *World Development*, 64, 621–641.

Huamaní, S. (2017). *Estimación de la rentabilidad social de incrementar la cobertura de agua potable en Lima Metropolitana*. Master Thesis. Universidad del Pacífico.

Iagua. (2015). 'Los limeños sin acceso al agua potable pagan 6 veces más por el agua', *Iagua*, May 29. At: https://www.iagua.es/noticias/peru/sunass/15/05/29/limenos-acceso-al-agua-potable-pagan-6-veces-mas-agua.

INEI. (2018). *Evolución de la Pobreza Monetaria 2007–2017 Informe Técnico*. Lima: Instituto Nacional de Estadística e Informática.

INEI. (2019). *Encuesta Nacional de Programas Presupuestales 2011–2018*. Lima: Instituto Nacional de Estadística e Informática.

Ioris, A. A. R. (2013). 'The adaptive nature of the neoliberal state and the state-led neoliberalisation of nature: Unpacking the political economy of water in Lima, Peru'. *New Political Economy*, 18(6), 912–938.

Kohon, J. (2015). *Metro de Lima: el caso de la Línea 1*. Bogotá: CAF. At: https://scioteca.caf.com/handle/123456789/894.

Lima Cómo Vamos. (2019). *Encuesta Lima Cómo Vamos 2018*.

Lima Cómo Vamos. (2020). *Encuesta Lima Cómo Vamos 2019*.

Línea Uno. (2020). *Informe de sostenibilidad 2019*. Reporte Línea Uno.

MEF. (2020). *Meta 3 Cuadro de Actividades. Implementación de un sistema integrado de manejo de residuos sólidos municipales*. Lima: Ministerio de Economía y Finanzas, pp. 11–76.

MEF. (2021). *Consulta Amigable*. Lima: Ministerio de Economía y Finanzas. At: https://apps5.mineco.gob.pe/transparenciaingresos/Navegador/default.aspx.

Ministerio del Ambiente. (2018a). Sistema de información para la Gestión de Residuos Sólidos SIGERSOL. Electronic dataset. At: https://sigersol.minam.gob.pe/.

Ministerio del Ambiente. (2018b). INFORME N° 0005-2018-MINAM/VMGA/DGRS-DVHL.

MML. (2014). *Plan Integral de Gestión Ambiental de Residuos Sólidos de la Provincia de Lima*. Lima: Municipalidad Metropolitana de Lima.

MTC-JICA. (2013). *Encuesta de recolección de información básica del transporte urbano en el área metropolitana de Lima y Callao*.

MVCS. (2017). *Plan Nacional de Saneamiento 2017–2021*. Lima: Ministerio de Vivienda, Construcción y Saneamiento.

Oviedo, D., Scholl, L., Innao, M. & Pedraza, L. (2019). 'Do bus rapid transit systems improve accessibility to job opportunities for the poor? The case of Lima, Peru'. *Sustainability*, 11(10), 1–24.

PCM. (2020). *Informe Anual de Descentralización 2019*. Lima: Presidencia del Consejo de Ministros, Secretaría de Descentralización.

Pereyra, O. (2006). 'Forma urbana y segregación residencial en Lima'. *Debates En Sociología*, 31, 69–106.

Pereyra Colchado, G. (2020). '¿Cómo sería Lima con un Alcalde Mayor? La propuesta que busca cambiar el gobierno de la capital'. El Comercio. At: https://elcomercio. pe/lima/sucesos/un-alcalde-mayor-para-lima-en-que-consiste-la-propuesta-de-miraflores-para-cambiar-el-gobierno-de-la-capital-jorge-munoz-luis-molina-noticia/.

Poole Fuller, E. (2017). 'Towards Sustainable Mobility? Challenges of the public transportation reorganization policies in Latin America. The case of Lima'. *Letras Verdes*, 21, 4–31.

Riofrío, G. & Cabrera, T. (2012). *Trabajadoras Por La Ciudad. Aporte de Las Mujeres a La Gestión Ambiental de Los Residuos Sólidos En América Latina - LIBROS PERUANOS*. Lima: Desco.

Riofrío, G., Olivera Cárdenas, L. & Callirgos, J. C. (1994). *Basura o desechos?: el destino de lo que botamos en Lima*. Lima: Centro de Estudios y Promoción del Desarrollo.

Sclar, E. (2001). *You don't always get what you pay for: The economics of privatization*. A Century Foundation Book. Ithaca, NY: Cornell University Press.

SEDAPAL. (2001). *Annual report 2000*. Lima.

SEDAPAL. (2002). *Annual report 2001*. Lima.

SEDAPAL. (2003). *Annual report 2002*. Lima.

SEDAPAL. (2004). *Annual report 2003*. Lima.

SEDAPAL. (2005). *Annual report 2004*. Lima.

SEDAPAL. (2006). *Annual report 2005*. Lima.

SEDAPAL. (2007). *Annual report 2006*. Lima.

SEDAPAL. (2008). *Annual report 2007*. Lima.

SEDAPAL. (2009). *Annual report 2008*. Lima.

SEDAPAL. (2010). *Annual report 2009*. Lima.

SEDAPAL. (2011). *Annual report 2010*. Lima.

SEDAPAL. (2012). *Annual report 2011*. Lima.

SEDAPAL. (2013). *Annual report 2012*. Lima.

SEDAPAL. (2014). *Annual report 2013*. Lima.

SEDAPAL. (2015). *Annual report 2014*. Lima.

SEDAPAL. (2016). *Annual report 2015*. Lima.

SEDAPAL. (2017). *Annual report 2016*. Lima.

SEDAPAL. (2018). *Annual report 2017*. Lima.

SEDAPAL. (2019). *Annual report 2018*. Lima.

SEDAPAL. (2020). *Annual report 2019*. Lima.

Stiglich, M. (2019). *City unplanning: The techno-political economy of privately-financed highways in Lima*. PhD Dissertation. Columbia University.

SUNASS. (2015). *Metas de gestión, fórmula tarifaria y estructuras tarifarias en el quinquenio regulatorio 2015-2020, para los servicios de agua potable y alcantarillado que brinda SEDAPAL S.A.* Lima: El Peruano.

SUNASS. (2019). *Benchmarking regulatorio de las Empresas Prestadoras (EP)*. Superintendencia Nacional de Servicios de Saneamiento.

Swyngedouw, E. (2005). 'Governance innovation and the citizen: The Janus face of governance-beyond-the-state'. *Urban Studies*, 42(11), 1991–2006.

Takano, G. (2017). 'Public-private partnerships as rent-seeking opportunities: A case study on an unsolicited proposal in Lima, Peru'. *Utilities Policy*, 48, 184–194.

Talavera, G. (2019). *Segregación residencial en Lima Metropolitana. Autocorrelación espacial y aglomeración en la ciudad*. Master's Thesis. Universitat Autónoma de Barcelona.

Vargas et al. (2017). *RED 2017. Crecimiento urbano y acceso a oportunidades: un desafío para América Latina*. Bogotá: CAF.

WHO. (2013). *The right to water*. Geneva: World Health Organization.

4 Fragmented governance, service provision and inequality in Mexico City Metropolitan Area

Alejandra Trejo Nieto

Introduction

Mexico City is one of the biggest and most complex capital cities in the world. As a result of its accelerated expansion in the second half of the twentieth century it has become a large metropolitan area which is the most important demographic, political, economic, financial and cultural urban nucleus in Mexico's urban system (Trejo, 2020). It is the third largest metropolitan area within the OECD and the largest outside Asia (OECD, 2015), and as one of the largest urban centres in Latin America and the world it is sometimes categorised as a global metropolis (Parnreiter, 2012). Mexico City Metropolitan Area (MCMA) has often been depicted as a case of urban gigantism with chaotic urban development (Gilbert, Khosla & De Jong, 2016). Its dynamic expansion has disconnected some parts of the urban structure from others, and the metropolis has developed in a socially differentiated and administratively fragmented way (Trejo Nieto, 2020). The lack of long-term urban planning has made it unable to provide its inhabitants with adequate basic public goods and services, with inappropriate financial and institutional arrangements creating patches of wealth and of poverty (Meza, 2018).

MCMA is an emblematic case of population concentration and political-administrative fragmentation and complexity, which increase the difficulty of designing and implementing efficient and equitable approaches to public policy, management and development. Mexico's constitution does not legally recognise metropolitan areas, and most institutional stratagems attempting to improve the planning and management of these urban centres have not been successful. The need for well-organised metropolitan development has been in conflict with rigid decentralisation, problematic intergovernmental relations, strong political powers and constrained public finances.

This chapter evaluates the extent to which the governance of MCMA offers conditions for comprehensive development in general and adequate provision of basic urban services in particular. It also explores the link between metropolitan governance and urban inequality in public service delivery. The focus is on three specific conceptual aspects of metropolitan governance systems: institutional structure, coordination and financial capacity. I identify the arrangements

DOI: 10.4324/9781003105541-7

and organisations involved in the provision of public transport, water, and waste collection, the extent of governmental and institutional coordination in this, and their financial sustainability. Assessing the service coverage across the metropolitan area allows me to infer the relationship between governance and urban inequality. I employ both secondary data and primary information collected during fieldwork in Mexico City, which included three focus groups with actors from academia, civil society, the private sector and local government, three semi-structured interviews and two technical visits to the metropolitan periphery.

This diagnosis to identify the key governance constraints and challenges in addressing gaps in urban service delivery is necessary to inform policy and promote the implementation of responses to metropolitan-wide problems. Although adequate metropolitan governance is important in local service delivery, I find that MCMA faces a fundamental failure of governmental coordination to achieve the efficient, sustainable and inclusive distribution of public services.

The first section of this chapter explains the process of metropolisation in MCMA. Section II describes its governance system; Section III describes the functioning and challenges of metropolitan provision of public transport, water, and waste collection. Section IV deals with how metropolitan governance mediates urban service inequality. In my final remarks, I explore the usefulness of institutional collective action as a means of capturing the complexities of the metropolitan governance institutions that are involved in urban service delivery in MCMA.

The metropolisation of Mexico City

Mexico City exists on two different levels. The first is a jurisdiction which now bears officially the name of Mexico City, but was formerly known as the Federal District. Due to a political reform, in 2016 the capital of Mexico officially changed its name from Federal District to Mexico City (previously Mexico City was associated only with the historic downtown area). The second is MCMA used to denote the entire larger, functionally integrated urban area (Salinas-Arreortua, 2017). While Mexico City originated in the fourteenth century as the Aztec capital of Tenochtitlan, its metropolitan area is the result of spatial, economic and social processes that gathered speed in the second half of the twentieth century (Trejo Nieto, 2020).

With its increased urbanisation Mexico City experienced a significant expansion of its built-up area and rapid population growth (OECD, 2015). Its expansion followed the patterns of urban primacy and centralism that occurred in other Latin American capital cities. Mexico City had a central role in the most accelerated phase of the nation's urbanisation and industrialisation. Its expansion was largely linked to its economic centrality as the axis of the country's import substitution strategy from the 1940s to the 1970s. Economic and demographic concentration produced agglomeration economies that made this city an ideal enclave for the country's rapid industrial development (Gilbert, Khosla & De Jong, 2016; Trejo Nieto, 2020). From the 1940s onwards the city's conurbation and expansion included municipalities in the State of Mexico

(Sánchez Almanza, 2012; Unikel, 2016; Trejo Nieto, 2020), almost doubling its population from 1.6 to 2.9 million in the first ten years (Raich, 2006). Such expansion was directly linked to secular dynamics, giving rise to a continuous functional integration among different jurisdictions.

People and economic activities started to move to neighbouring municipalities in search of cheaper land and housing (Raich, 2006; Sánchez Almanza, 2012). In the 1950s, regulations and norms prohibiting new human settlements in Mexico City were introduced, stimulating the occupation of land for housing purposes, mostly in an informal manner. The regulations furthered the city's metropolisation through the conurbation of an increasing number of municipalities in which such land occupation rules did not apply. Metropolitan expansion took place under different forms of land occupation and housing production towards the urban periphery (Legorreta, 1991; Sánchez Almanza, 2012; Gilbert, Khosla & De Jong, 2016).

Initially, the city's expansion took place through increasing land occupation and the construction of mainly houses by the low-income sector or *sectores populares*. Land invasion, illegal occupation and the uncontrolled sale of land, in most cases for self-constructed housing, made up a significant part of this expansion. Some higher-income groups started to move to the south and west of the city, while the poor moved to the north and east, where land was available and cheap (Gilbert, Khosla & De Jong, 2016). New housing policies and the deregulation of the financial and housing markets in the 1990s changed the characteristics of metropolitan expansion. From the early 2000s, housing policy focused on market-driven housing provision, displacing the poor to ever-more peripheral locations in the north and east. The new locations were characterised by small, low-quality housing units typically lacking sufficient infrastructure and urban services for their residents' basic needs (Trejo Nieto, 2020). This history of metropolitan expansion reveals the coexistence of informal and formal urbanisation with the most recent unparalleled state-driven housing development boom in the peripheries (Gilbert, Khosla & De Jong, 2016).

Further public policies targeting the densification of central areas of the city also contributed to peripheral expansion after 2000. A strategy for land use regulation known as 'Bando 2' prohibited the construction of new housing and commercial developments in the fringe boroughs of Mexico City. However, the high price of land in the central boroughs forced people to move outwards to the periphery (Raich, 2006). In this way 'Urban growth was not only the product of rapid industrialisation and demographic growth, it was also the product of competing urban policies and political struggles in and between the capital city and surrounding municipalities of the State of Mexico' (Gilbert, Khosla & De Jong, 2016, p. 16).

According to the federal government's latest delimitation of MCMA (SEDATU, CONAPO & INEGI, 2018), today it exists as a de facto functional unit spreading across fifty-nine municipalities in the State of Mexico, one municipality in the state of Hidalgo and the sixteen boroughs (territorial units similar to municipalities but without full autonomy) of Mexico City (Figure 4.1). According to the OECD (2015), while in 1950 the MCMA (using the current delimitation) had fewer than 5 million residents, by 2010

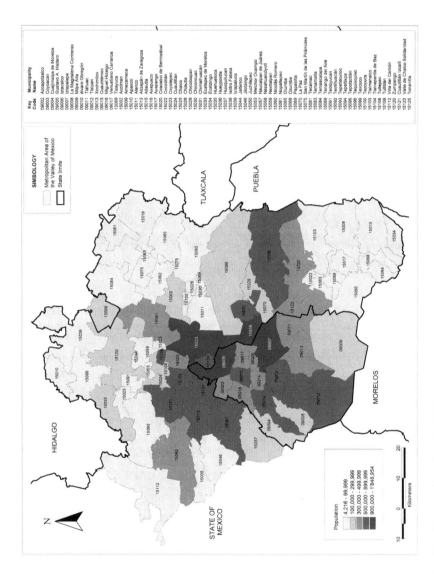

Figure 4.1 Mexico City Metropolitan Area in 2015

Source: Based on SEDATU, CONAPO & INEGI (2018).

this number had quadrupled. The strongest increase occurred between 1950 and 1980, when population growth was exponential. Between 1980 and 1990, the metropolitan area grew very little, but its expansion continued from 1990 onwards. In 2015, Mexico City had nearly 9 million inhabitants and the total metropolitan area had 21.5 million. Most (57 per cent) residents of the metropolis live in the built-up area expanding predominantly northwards and eastwards into the metropolitan municipalities in the State of Mexico (SEDATU, CONAPO & INEGI, 2018).

The functional interaction among the jurisdictions that comprise MCMA involve important urban sectors such as environmental management, public security, transportation, housing, water, solid waste management and the labour market, amongst others. Urban integration is engendered by the high degree of mobility, commuting and economic interaction. Because its urban expansion quickly outpaced the city's fiscal and administrative capacity for basic urban services, creating many problems (Gilbert, Khosla & De Jong, 2016), MCMA has been exceedingly slow and inefficient in dealing with these. So far, the evidence shows that attempts to create metropolitan policies have been insufficient, and that administrative and political structures have prevented efficient governance (Raich, 2006).

Administrative and governmental organisation in MCMA

While MCMA is a single spatial continuum in which a number of socioeconomic activities take place, it comprises a series of very different local and state jurisdictions that vary in their legal, administrative, political, economic and demographic characteristics. The multijurisdictional and multilevel nature of this metropolis makes it a particularly complex setting for governance (Ziccardi, 2016). Mexico is a federal republic with three levels of government: federal, state and local governments. There is no general law in the Constitution allowing the creation of other intermediate governments. The state and municipal governments are responsible for the territorial planning of their jurisdictions in accordance with the Constitution and with general regulations such as the General Law for Human Settlements. Article 115 of the Constitution establishes the municipalities' functions and capacities including urban development planning, local finance and the provision of public services, whereas Article 122 defines the governmental functions of Mexico City, which has special status as the capital city (Salinas-Arreortua, 2017). For instance, Mexico City's boroughs, known as *alcaldías*, are similar to municipalities but do not have full autonomy. Whereas political and administrative decentralisation made an impact on the autonomy of Mexico's states and municipalities, the policymakers ignored metropolitan areas in this process. Despite their de facto existence, Mexican legislation does not recognise the functional operation of these territories as integrated political and administrative entities. Formally, they represent geographic delimitations that help with mapping and analysing urban expansion (Raich, 2006).

MCMA's political powers include the federal government, due to Mexico City's status as the nation's capital and the home of the federal powers; the governorship and congresses of the State of Mexico and Hidalgo and the Mayor and Legislative Assembly of Mexico City; and the 16 local boroughs and 59 metropolitan municipalities of the State of Mexico, and single municipality in the state of Hidalgo. The fiscal structure is similarly intricate: Mexico City has the fiscal faculties of a federal state and centralises all the revenue functions of its boroughs. Metropolitan municipalities have more restricted fiscal powers but collect their own property taxes as their primary source of own revenue. Moreover, the 76 local governments have different types of political representation (Raich, 2006). In this context, MCMA should be largely understood as a collection of self-ruling state and local governments with no overall governing body administration or financing (Raich, 2006; Salinas-Arreortua, 2017).

Following Perlman and De Dios Pineda Guadarrama (2011), improved metropolitan governance entails the provision of good-quality public services in coordination with state, municipal and federal governments and requires institutional reform. In Mexico, federal and subnational laws provide the legal framework that allows some forms of integrated metropolitan management by means of coordination and associations via either agreements and contracts or commissions to collaborate in joint projects. However, intergovernmental associations as mechanisms of metropolitan management have scarcely been used, and the potential for municipal voluntary cooperation usually clash with several political and economic interests. The volunteer nature of intergovernmental associations does not favour formally integrated metropolitan governance. Intermunicipal coordination meets special resistance due to the competition of political parties at the municipal and state levels. Moreover, the lack of firmly established rules leaves room for ad hoc decisions at the expense of metropolitan planning and coordination (Raich, 2006; Salinas-Arreortua, 2017; Aguilar & López, 2018; Díaz Aldret, 2018). The legal constraints to the recognition of Mexico's metropolitan areas and the accompanying administrative and political fragmentation create significant challenges for governing the city and providing public services and adequate opportunities for development (OECD, 2015).

The country's mechanisms to solve problems involving multiple jurisdictions have been largely reduced to the formation of collective bodies or commissions and to narrow agreements. During the 1990s, following reforms to Article 122 of the Constitution, the federal government, the government of Mexico City and the government of the State of Mexico created six metropolitan commissions: the Water and Sewage Commission, the Commission on Roads and Transportation and the Public Safety Commission in 1994; the Commission for Human Settlements in 1995; the Environmental Commission in 1996 and the Civil Protection Commission in 2000 (Raich, 2006; Sánchez Almanza, 2012; Cenizal, 2015; Trejo Nieto, 2020). These commissions became strongly dependent on the federal and state governments, while autonomous municipalities operated with minimal attempts to interact in an integrated or coordinated fashion. Although the metropolitan commissions were created to evaluate, coordinate and promote metropolitan projects, their activities ended up as mere diagnostic reports. With the exception of the Environmental Commission their projects lacked enforceability and lacked enough funding and political support (Raich, 2006; Salinas-Arreortua, 2017; Trejo Nieto, 2020). Although there is no general agreement on the extent to which political plurality has impeded the formation of a metropolitan agenda, Raich (2006) argues that it is one of the main reasons for the absence of interjurisdictional coordination. Gilbert, Khosla and De Jong (2016) explain the issues and shortcomings of metropolitan governance in terms of not only local planning constraints and administrative deficiencies but also limited infrastructure planning and financing, legacies of authoritarian regimes and the clientelistic relations and regulatory oversights, political culture, widespread cronyism and other patronage arrangements that have long been central to Mexico's urbanisation process.

The latest effort to promote integrated metropolitan governance in MCMA culminated in February 2020, when the Metropolitan Development Law was approved with the objective of creating a coordination framework for the local governments. The open question is if this will result in better government relations and more efficient service delivery.

The delivery of public services and governance

According to Perlman and De Dios Pineda Guadarrama (2011) MCMA faces two fundamental and interrelated challenges due to its size and importance: delivering basic urban services to its numerous residents, and the lack of authorities and adequate organisation to provide these. The municipalities belonging to the metropolitan area face decentralised government and a widening gap between the availability of financial resources and necessary expenditure (Trejo Nieto, 2020), and often lack the technical capacity to deliver services to mitigate the rapidly increasing social and spatial divides (Gilbert, Khosla & De Jong, 2016). The challenge is one of organising, providing and financing services in a huge urban functional area that is administratively fragmented.

However, warnings about the limitations of MCMA's governance arrangements for delivering public services in a high quality, adequate and cost-efficient manner are often unaccompanied by substantiation or evidence of the extent and nature of the problem. In this section, I discuss governance issues related to organisation, coordination and financial sustainability in service delivery. These are expressed in two different domains of metropolitan governance – political/administrative and financial – as shown in Figure 4.2. In line with most of the empirical cases given in this book, I focus on water, waste collection and public transport.

DOMAIN		VARIABLES

DOMAIN
• Administrative/political

• Fiscal/financial

VARIABLES
• Institutional organisation and structure

Coordination

• Financial sustainability

Figure 4.2 Governance domains for analysing service delivery

Source: Author.

Water services

The current management of water delivery in MCMA is defined largely by the fragmented structure of government. In Mexico, the federal government is involved in water management through the National Water Commission (CONAGUA), which is in charge of authorising the use of national water and the bulk supply of water, constructing and operating the infrastructure and monitoring the preservation of aquifers. Municipalities have the right to manage and operate their own water systems through decentralised public bodies responsible for administering and providing potable water and drainage. One of the purposes of a public operator is to achieve efficiency and financial self-sufficiency. The exception to this decentralisation is Mexico City, where the Mexico City Water System (Sistema de Aguas de la Ciudad de Mexico, or SACMEX) centralises water provision for the 16 boroughs (Rosales, 2015). SACMEX operates as a deconcentrated public agency and entered into operation by decree in 2003. The same year the Water Law came into force to regulate the management of water resources and the provision of public drinking water, drainage and sewerage services. SACMEX operates most water services and the maintenance and construction of the infrastructure, but contracts four private companies to attend some areas of service provision. Because SACMEX is formally under the responsibility of Mexico City's Ministry of the Environment, the boroughs are left without any control, planning or design of the water management (ibid).

Municipalities in the State of Mexico should provide the service directly or through their own decentralised agencies. But the water provision organisation also involves the presence of other supply schemes in which different actors participate. There are three main supply schemes: decentralised public bodies, direct provision by local government and mixed provision (state, municipal or communal). Nongovernmental provision derives from historical authorisation for water extraction given by the federal government to communities or individuals who continue to use their permits to access water. Most (48 per cent) of the municipalities operate under a mixed scheme, and 28 per cent have their own decentralised providers (ibid).

The State of Mexico Water Commission (CAEM) intervenes in water management. There is also the Federal Basin Agency for the Valley of México (Aguas del Valle de Mexico) and the previously mentioned Water and Sewerage Metropolitan Commission. Thus a multiplicity of actors are involved in formal water provision, planning and regulation: the federal government, three state governments, a deconcentrated public body dependent on Mexico City's government, numerous decentralised municipal public bodies, municipal governments, community and neighbourhood bodies and private companies. In addition to formal water supply, informal access to water involves illegal connections to water pipes and reselling.

The multiplicity of actors providing the service and the intricate institutional structures complicate cooperation and dialogue in this fragmented metropolitan framework. Despite the establishment of the Metropolitan Commission, the metropolis has not developed coordination schemes geared towards improving the technical, financial and economic operation of the water supply. Only some horizontal coordination has emerged between the national and state governments regarding the infrastructure for wastewater, treated water systems and drainage. Far from being provided within an integrated framework, water services in the MCMA have caused conflicts between governments. Incentives for coordination are not developed and there are very few examples of intermunicipal cooperation in the provision of water services.

The financial organisation of the water sector demonstrates the intricate operational reality of governance in this service. The main characteristics of financial sustainability can be identified in relation to aspects of the funding, tariff and costs systems. Mexico's water rates are set differently across subnational governments, resulting in substantial tariff heterogeneity. In Hidalgo and the State of Mexico, decentralised public providers have the power to establish tariffs according to their state laws which are approved and published annually. Typically, charges depend on consumption levels, but the criteria and formulas vary from state to state and municipality and municipality. In Mexico City the rates are published in the city's Tax Code and apply to the population of the 16 boroughs (CONAGUA, 2013). Some users with and some users without water meters means that not all charges are based on micro-measurement of consumption levels (World Bank, 2013). A set of problems emerges with the issue of subsidies for consumption in Mexico City. SACMEX divides the city according to socioeconomic levels and tariffs differ depending on location. This division can be misleading and arbitrary, because there are neighbourhoods with a mixture of low and high-income households connected to the same water network. Due to financial weaknesses in the supply water system, there are subsidies from the city government to the service delivery.

In a study based on a sample of six water operators including SACMEX and the decentralised bodies of some of the largest municipalities in MCMA, the World Bank found that the water-delivery operation is not self-sustainable, as the tariffs cover only 64 per cent of operating costs. Subsidies are used not only to finance investment but also to cover the deficit in the operating cost. Decentralised providers depend heavily on central, state and local government financial resources. SACMEX has better finances than most municipalities, but financial balances are among the most acute challenges in metropolitan water management, the biggest being that operating costs exceed own revenues (World Bank, 2013).

Investment costs increase due to the old, inadequate and insufficient infrastructure, high water losses, electricity-intensive provision, and inefficient administration and operations. On the other hand, tariffs and charges are not based on real cost and consumption patterns; an average tariff of 3.5 Mexican pesos per cubic meter can cost 13.5 pesos (World Bank, 2013, CONAGUA, 2014). Furthermore, tariff collection rate is only 53 per cent. Current over-consumption negatively impacts the financial sustainability of water delivery: daily per capita consumption is 125 litres in Sao Paulo, and more than twice this amount at 300 litres per day in MCMA (World Bank, 2013). The estimates in the World Bank report do not include the numerous municipalities that provide services based on management schemes other than those of decentralised operators. These are mainly the smaller and poorer municipalities that have weak capacity for tariff collection and do not receive federal financial aid which is only provided to local water operators.

Solid waste collection

In Mexico urban solid waste (USW) is defined as (1) the waste generated in households resulting from the disposal of materials used in domestic activities; (2) waste from any other activity within economic units or on public roads; and (3) waste resulting from the cleaning of roads and public spaces such as markets and schools (Government of the State of Mexico, 2009). Collection continues to be at the core of USW management, although disposal and treatment are becoming increasingly critical. USW collection includes transportation of the waste to a processing facility, a transfer station or a landfill site (SEDESOL, NA). In 2000, Mexico City alone produced 11,674 tons of waste daily, more than 50 per cent of the total metropolitan area. In the early 2010s MCMA as a whole generated 21,000 tons of waste per day, more than 15,000 tons of which were collected from Mexico City (Navarro, 2012). MCMA produces a significant proportion of the nation's USW, including industrial and commercial waste, and the largest amount per capita in the country (Lámbarri et al., 2014).

USW management (collection, transportation, treatment and disposal), as stated in Article 115 of the constitution, is the responsibility of municipal authorities, which have the power to provide the service directly or employ sub-contract private companies. They provide the service via three schemes: local government supply, private supply, and public–private supply. In addition, as with other public services, municipalities can establish partnerships through intermunicipal or metropolitan agreements to collect USW (Navarro, 2012).

Boroughs in Mexico City are directly in charge of waste collection and public cleaning services. Various city government agencies are involved in USW management and regulation: the local Secretariat of the Interior, the Secretariat of Works and Services' General Board of Urban Services, the Secretariat of the Environment, and the Environmental Attorney of Land Management. Each of these includes a division that designs and implements the USW regulations, planning, control, operation, monitoring and coordination. In some boroughs that operate via participatory budgeting, citizens are directly involved in managing USW and prioritise efficient service provision.

The government of the State of Mexico formulates and conducts its own USW management policy and develops programmes. Collection and public cleaning services are performed by the municipalities, in some of which a Councilman (*regidor*) is in charge of managing collection services. In municipalities of greater organisational complexity a Director of Public Services is responsible for planning and managing USW services. Until the 1990s, most municipalities provided public cleaning and waste collection directly, but gradually they began to offer concessions. When the service delivery involves a concession to a private waste collector the state's Secretariat of Environment is responsible for monitoring its compliance with state regulations (Government of the State of Mexico, 2009). The wide range of technical and financial capacity across municipalities means that each organises and operates its USW collection in its own way. In a small municipality where I carried out fieldwork, the authorities mentioned that they did not have the financial capacity to provide the service directly and had only one small vehicle that collected waste from the municipal offices and some public spaces. The municipality provides permits to individuals who, without supervision, use their own waste collection trucks on routes designed by the local Office of Public Services. This municipality exemplifies the precarisation of services which, according to Bayón and Saraví (2013), is a mode of governance that normalises state' inaction and withdrawal from service delivery through a proliferating discourse of financial and administrative crisis.

Another dimension of this precarisation is the significant informality of USW collection. The informal sector includes individual or groups of waste pickers, *burreros* – pickers who carry the waste on donkeys – and *carretoneros* – pickers who use hand carts. The pickers also scavenge for recyclable materials (Trejo Nieto et al., 2018). The informal sector usually has strong workers' unions and powerful leaders (Lámbarri et al., 2014). Informality can also exist within formal USW collection: Mexico City's transport units belong to the borough administration, which hires drivers and some helpers; however, there are usually also voluntary workers or workers hired and paid directly by the driver. Therefore, a network of multiple actors is involved in the provision of waste collection services and USW collection has become an important source of local political power.

Different MCMA agencies intervene in the regulation, planning and implementation of waste management, creating institutional coordination issues. For instance, borough authorities and Mexico City's authorities for urban services should coordinate with the Secretariat of Environment on public cleaning activities and comply with environmental legislation and norms, but communication between these bodies is inadequate. Where municipalities in the State of Mexico grant permits and concessions for the provision of collection services there should be some set method of coordination between the local authorities and the private actors involved.

Despite the need to solve USW management problems using a coordinated metropolitan approach, the sector has received little attention. The absence of coordination has been linked to political factors that also affect other sectors. The Metropolitan Environmental Commission, created in 1992, focuses mainly on pollution, and does not include an explicit strategy for implementing coordinated USW policies, programmes and projects across jurisdictions. Although final disposal is a key problem requiring coordination and cooperation among municipalities, political, institutional, technical and financial issues have prevented the organisation of a metropolitan-wide waste management system that would help to reduce the constraints to the service's infrastructure and efficient implementation.

In Mexico, local government administrations do not charge fees for waste collection services as there are no official tariffs. Citizens give waste-disposal lorry drivers and their helpers discretionary tips. This means that local authorities must deliver the service but are not paid for it. The population perceive the service as free, and this weak user-provider link drives strong deficiencies and a fragile financial capacity for service delivery (Lámbarri et al., 2014). The tipping system has a number of perverse consequences: users do not understand the real cost of providing the service; provision and efficient operation are not encouraged; there is no policy on financial efficiency in the service provision; and there is limited investment in infrastructure improvement. Governments have to allocate their own financial resources to provide the service. Funding for investment and operating costs comes primarily from local scarce own revenue (Government of the State of Mexico, 2009). The direct providers' financial situations vary from jurisdiction to jurisdiction, especially in the State of Mexico. Whereas many municipalities find it convenient to grant permits and concessions, private concessionaires' profitability depends on the tips collected, making waste collection in low-income areas financially unattractive.

Public transport

MCMA's public transport sector is one of the largest in the world and comprises several systems. Mexico City has a Metro; Metrobus which is a bus rapid transit (BRT) system; the Electric Transport System providing trolleybuses and light rail; a buses network called Passenger Transport Network (known as RTP); and private bus and microbus concessions known as *colectivos o peseros*. The metropolitan municipalities in the State of Mexico have bus and microbus concessions, and in 2013 Mexibus, a BRT network, was introduced in some municipalities. Two underground lines operate in some of the metropolitan municipalities adjacent to Mexico City and a suburban train connecting Mexico City with several municipalities in the metropolitan area was introduced in 2008. Hence transport provision and whether it is supplied by government or concessions is variable. The government-run transport systems within Mexico City include the Metro, the Electric Transport System and Eco-bici, a public bicycle-sharing system. The concession service consists of *colectivos*. The Metrobus system combines government participation with a private concession (SEMOVI, NA). In the metropolitan municipalities in the State of Mexico and Hidalgo most demand is met by private concessions and Mexibus, which is also operated by private companies. About 47 per cent of everyday travel in Mexico City is on buses and minibuses run by concessions, with the Metro taking second place with 14 per cent of daily trips (LSE Cities, 2015). The BRT systems have seen the biggest expansion in recent years to replace of small-scale old microbuses.

Despite the very local nature of services, public transport is mostly planned and regulated by intermediate governments (Fernández, 2002). In Mexico City, the Secretariat of Mobility (SEMOVI) is responsible for this. In the municipalities of the State of Mexico public transport management and regulation involves two state agencies: the SEMOVI plans and regulates public transport concessions and the Secretariat of Communications regulates the Mexibus system. In the State of Hidalgo, regulation and planning are based on the state Transport Law and implemented by a decentralised agency under the Secretariat of the Interior (OECD, 2015). Some big municipal governments include a transport and transit agency responsible for regulating local traffic and managing road construction and maintenance. Apart from this most Mexican municipalities have limited or no input into the design and management of public transport and despite having the power to intervene in the public transport sector they have returned the task to state governments (IMCO, 2012).

The governance of public transport in MCMA thus involves a mixture of stakeholders including federal, state and local transport authorities, private national and international transport companies and an inoperative Metropolitan Transportation Commission. Informal transport services are also provided. As in other metropolitan issues, most attempts to coordinate public transport management and projects have provided poor outcomes. This limited capacity for coordination is a major constraint to the design and execution of coherent mobility policies and the development of an integrated metropolitan transport system. With institutions and jurisdictions handling public transport individually there is no common framework for planning, operation and funding. Differing funding and regulatory frameworks prevent the setting up of transport connections or corridors across the metropolitan area, and the separation of routes across administrative boundaries prohibits an integrated metropolitan transport system (OECD, 2015). Furthermore, each new local administration is likely to modify all previous plans and policies. These and other political factors are not favourable for long-term planning, with the lack of adequate funding schemes is another key issue (Raich, 2006).

Poor coordination is observed between different transport systems whose routes and schedules are not synchronised and which generally lack integrated tariffs. Only the Metro, Metrobus and Ecobici systems use a common ticketing and payment system. Many transport routes compete with rather than complement one another. The paucity of institutional communication between the mass transit services Metro and Metrobus poses a particular challenge. Other problematic issues for the governance of public transport include the political power of those holding concessions and the Balkanisation of the *colectivo* system because they hinder efficient operation. A wide proliferation of individual concessionaires does not follow the regulations and their operations are disorganised and uncoordinated. State and local governments exercise little coherent strategic oversight of the many private public transport concessions (OECD, 2015).

While there is practically no horizontal coordination, attempts at vertical coordination have depended heavily on political powers and partisanship in the different jurisdictions and levels of transport governance. Even though a number of metropolitan projects have been implemented, their governance has been enforced from the top down. Two examples are Metro Line B and the suburban train, two projects which were strongly implemented by national government rather than emerging from cooperative local governance. The federal government was keen to use its power to keep state and local institutions subordinates in decision-making. The suburban train involved foreign private participation and was exhibited as a major success of metropolitan planning. However, key technical issues in its operation such as overestimation of its demand and use, uncertain financial sustainability and lack of integration with other transport systems are symptomatic of the overarching difficulties that arise in metropolitan governance. The project was ultimately implemented as a federal initiative via a public-private partnership. The federal government not only played a convening role but shaped the project to suit its own requirements at the expense of its technical, financial and social effectiveness (Cenizal, 2015). Mexibus's Line 4, which established a corridor connecting the terminal of Metrobus Line 1 with Tecamac in the State of Mexico, is an ongoing attempt at integration. Metro Line A was the first public transportation project to run between Mexico City and the State of Mexico. However, it was conceived and treated as a separate transit system, requiring an additional payment to transfer between that line and the rest of the Metro system (ibid).

Persistent fragmentation has significant implications for users travelling across administrative jurisdictions and especially for those living in the periphery, whose commutes include a large number of transfers and high costs. The separation of services across systems and jurisdictions limits the efficient allocation of resources and compromises the financial sustainability of the entire transport sector. Rigorous financial assessment is limited by the lack of information on cost structuring. Funding schemes vary significantly between systems and jurisdictions because there are no common operating rules. Transport fares are fixed in each state, with fares in Mexico City significantly lower than those in the State of Mexico. Financial management and tariff fixing have been highly dependent on political conditions rather than on established formulas based on the technical assessment of cost and demand, as in Mexico City, where most transport systems are heavily subsidised. Tariffs are not fixed based on travel time and distance, and fares are not adjusted regularly according to variations in total costs. Systems operate under the assumption that affordable prices have to be granted, seeing public transportation in Mexico City as part of local social policy. The Metro system, for instance, grants students and the elderly free or discounted travel (OECD, 2015).

Generous subsidies affect financial capacity for infrastructure investment, maintenance and fleet renewal and the gap between real costs and actual fares has created huge financial losses. The government of Mexico City subsidises Metro by 50–60 per cent of its yearly budget. Even with this funding its operation is far from optimal. The financial capacity is further compromised because Metro covers the costs of running routes into the State of Mexico (ibid).

Metrobus has introduced a centralised fee collection system, and a private trust fund to collect and distribute revenues that pays operators on the basis of kilometres travelled. The Government of Mexico City invests in and manages the infrastructure, while private suppliers are in charge of operation and other investments, yet many of the conditions agreed upon when the first line was operationalised have imposed financial constraints on the overall system. The scheme based on operators' per-kilometre imbursement implies high payments that were initially made possible by cross-subsidisation. More recently, operational deficits and other financial requirements have been covered by general city funds (ibid).

The suburban train is more expensive than public transport within Mexico City but similar in price to other methods of transport in the State of Mexico. Tariff-setting in this system is more systematic and relates more closely to the actual cost of the service. However, the system is in financial difficulties due to the original overestimation of demand. During its first years, the private operator depended heavily on a contingency fund that included public resources and financial support from the federal government. To avoid bankruptcy, it was restructured in 2011 (SCT, 2012).

Mexibus does not have a centralised fee collection system. Passengers pay different fares on different lines and must buy a new ticket when they transfer between lines. The gap between expected and actual demand has necessitated financial support from the state government to maintain the system (OECD, 2015). *Colectivos* in both Mexico City and the State of Mexico are financially vulnerable, as they do not receive subsidies and must be self-financing. Maintaining and renewing their vehicles require private finance. They also deal with uncertainty about tariff adjustments which are negotiated with the city government.

Service provision and inequality

Socio-spatial inequality has been extensively researched as a distinctive problem in Mexico City and MCMA (e.g. Rubalcava & Schteingart, 2000; Parnreiter, 2005; Saraví, 2008; Ziccardi, 2016; Aguilar & López, 2018). According to Ziccardi (2016), the fast expansion and periurbanisation of MCMA has created a particular dynamic of socioeconomic and territorial inequality and strong segregation. These studies report strong contrasts in the urban landscape of the city and the inhabitants' living conditions. Generally, poorer citizens are found towards the east of the city and those on higher incomes in the northwest, the city centre and some southern areas. Yet the urban structure has been uncovered more complex and fragmented.

Inequality and segregation in Mexico's urban areas have largely been studied as a socioeconomic phenomenon (Meza, 2018). However, Bayón and Saraví (2013) consider that inequality needs more nuanced and complex understanding as a socially, spatially and politically produced phenomenon. Gilbert, Khosla and De Jong (2016) see inequality as a matter of not only income but also differentiated opportunities and vulnerabilities, concentration of social and infrastructural deficits, inherited disadvantages, and a range of other barriers that maintain and reinforce precarious living conditions such as the uneven spatial distribution of services. Meza (2018) sees inequality as a problem of systematic infrastructure distribution failure within cities, and considers that a more methodical view of inequality across the urban fabric is needed.

Furthermore, inequality is in no way an unfortunate or natural casualty of urbanisation: it is produced and sustained by governmental policies and structures (Gilbert, Khosla & De Jong, 2016). In other words, inequality is mediated by urban governance and has a political source (Meza, 2018). It is produced in systems where the urban development regime increasingly relies on the private sector and is deeply rooted in clientelist traditions that offer urban improvements in exchange for political support (Gilbert, Khosla & De Jong, 2016). Harris and Wild (2013) argue that the wider governance environment influences the delivery of basic services and helps to explain the heterogeneity and poor outcomes of service delivery.

Inequality can be addressed as a service provision problem in cities because citizens with poor access to and low coverage of basic services face excessive economic and social costs. Additionally, service provision is mediated by the governance arrangements described in the previous section. The extensive literature on MCMA's urban development highlights how the urban infrastructure, service provision and amenities have not kept pace with the rapid production of thousands of small houses on the peripheries, many of which are self-built, and the high inequality between the central city and the periphery, the highest percentages of homes lacking basic services being in the latter.

The fragmentation, lack of coordination and financial shortages in the provision of water, waste collection and public transport services are accompanied by heterogeneous coverage and access across MCMA. Official measures of coverage of and access to urban services are problematic in the context of the metropolis's high informality and presence of irregular settlements because the lack of available data. INEGI, Mexico's national office of statistics, provides some approximate measures of coverage by municipality and borough.

Water provision has historically been unequal. The western part of MCMA enjoys a better supply and the east suffers from continuous shortages. In some areas of Mexico City water delivery is intermittent due to low pressure. Residents in the east of the city also have to contend with significant water quality problems (Sánchez Almanza, 2012). Similar and worse problems extend to the metropolitan municipalities in the State of Mexico.

Connection to official piped water has been used as one criterion for measuring water service coverage. This implies a connection in a property-containing individual or multiple households and does not necessarily include a connection within each household. According to this indicator 95.5 per cent of the population of MCMA had piped water connection in 2010. On average, coverage reached 92.4 per cent across metropolitan municipalities and boroughs. The borough with the highest coverage surpassed 99.3 per cent. This is a misleading measure because a connection does not guarantee a flow of water. Some of these households have to buy water from water trucks or fetch it from communal connections, rivers, lakes or wells.

A better measure of coverage is daily availability. In MCMA, 72 per cent of the population is supplied with water daily, 14 per cent receive water every third day, 9 per cent once or twice a week, and the rest sporadically during the week. Some of those with daily access may only receive water for specific hours during the day. In the best-covered borough 98 per cent of the population has daily access, and some municipalities do not provide water daily at all. This explains the widespread use of devices such as water tanks and cisterns for storing water. The tendency is for most peripheral municipalities and boroughs to provide water less often, but there is no clear centre-periphery divide and an irregular spatial structure emerges (Figure 4.3).

Lower coverage is generally observed in irregular settlements, where formal operators incur an administrative liability if they provide the service.

Boroughs and Municipalities

Code	Name	Code	Name
09002	Azcapotzalco	15037	Huixquilucan
09003	Coyoacán	15038	Isidro Fabela
09004	Cuajimalpa de Morelos	15039	Ixtapaluca
09005	Gustavo A. Madero	15044	Jaltenco
09006	Iztacalco	15046	Jilotzingo
09007	Iztapalapa	15050	Juchitepec
09008	La Magdalena Contreras	15053	Melchor Ocampo
09009	Milpa Alta	15057	Naucalpan de Juárez
09010	Álvaro Obregón	15058	Nezahualcóyotl
09011	Tláhuac	15059	Nextlalpan
09012	Tlalpan	15060	Nicolás Romero
09013	Xochimilco	15061	Nopaltepec
09014	Benito Juárez	15065	Otumba
09015	Cuauhtémoc	15068	Ozumba
09016	Miguel Hidalgo	15069	Papalotla
09017	Venustiano Carranza	15070	La Paz
13069	Itzayuca	15075	San Martín de las Pirámides
15002	Acolman	15081	Tecámac
15009	Amecameca	15083	Temamatla
15010	Apaxco	15084	Temascalapa
15011	Atenco	15089	Tenango del Aire
15013	Atizapán de Zaragoza	15091	Teoloyucan
15015	Atlautla	15092	Teotihuacán
15016	Axapusco	15093	Tepetlaoxtoc
15017	Ayapango	15094	Tepetlixpa
15020	Coacalco de Berriozábal	15095	Tepotzotlán
15022	Cocotitlán	15096	Tequixquiac
15023	Coyotepec	15099	Texcoco
15024	Cuautitlán	15100	Tezoyuca
15025	Chalco	15103	Tlalmanalco
15028	Chiautla	15104	Tlalnepantla de Baz
15029	Chicoloapan	15108	Tultepec
15030	Chiconcuac	15109	Tultitlán
15031	Chimalhuacán	15112	Villa del Carbón
15033	Ecatepec de Morelos	15120	Zumpango
15034	Ecatzingo	15121	Cuautitlán Izcalli
15035	Huehuetoca	15122	Valle de Chalco Solidaridad
15036	Hueypoxtla	15125	Tonanitla

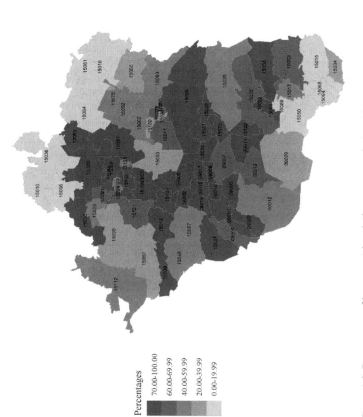

Percentages
- 70.00–100.00
- 60.00–69.99
- 40.00–59.99
- 20.00–39.99
- 0.00–19.99

Figure 4.3 Percentage of homes with a daily water supply in MCMA, 2010

Source: Based on INEGI (2010).

Although government authorities have started to intervene to supply irregular settlements with urban services, including water, these remain inadequate (National Research Council, 1995). Administrative, financial and technical deficiencies, particularly in the State of Mexico, poor water quality due to lack of maintenance, and lack of investment in infrastructure are also responsible for coverage problems.

According to official data, coverage of USW collection services, measured as the percentage of houses from which garbage is collected, is almost universal in MCMA. Between 88 and 98 per cent of households are covered by a waste collection service, the exception being some southern and northeastern and peripheral municipalities (Figure 4.4).

Figure 4.4 does not reflect the frequency and quality of waste collection services, which are highly inefficient due to their diffused financial status and organisation. Their poor infrastructure and lack of investment varies from one jurisdiction to another, with some neighbourhoods and areas receiving a more frequent service and equipped with better vehicles. The failure of the service is evident in the substantial presence of an informal sector operating predominately in low-income neighbourhoods of the metropolis.

INEGI's 2015 National Inventory of Housing includes one indicator quantifying the coverage of public transport in a municipality. It reports relatively better coverage in the central boroughs of Mexico City, with the exception of Benito Juarez, the richest jurisdiction in the metropolitan area whose inhabitants probably travel by car, and poor coverage in the northern and southern periphery. This data reveals a fairly well-defined divide in public transport coverage (Figure 4.5).

Prioritisation of road infrastructure and a focus on improving traffic speeds for private vehicles have resulted in severe limitations to the capacity and quality of public transport and deteriorating conditions (Paquette & Negrete, 2011). *Colectivos* are particularly inefficient in their schedules, quality, safety and environmental sustainability. The mass-transit services' capacity to meet demand has failed and their services are declining. The suburban train remains the best-rated service in terms of frequency, safety and quality (OECD, 2015).

Accordingly, data on water and public transport coverage exhibits the spatial inequalities across MCMA. They are critical services whose distribution contributes to overall inequality. In these sectors, the potential for better metropolitan governance to prevent and mitigate urban inequality through service provision is greater. Average metropolitan and municipal coverage figures in the official statistics can mask wider divides in the metropolitan area. While basic service coverage is almost universal in the city centre, it is very limited in some parts not only of the periphery but also right across the metropolis and even in some central neighbourhoods.

This lack of effective and equitable urban public service provision in MCMA reinforces inequality in different ways that merit detailed study. The

Boroughs and Municipalities

09002	Azcapotzalco	15037	Huixquilucan
09003	Coyoacán	15038	Isidro Fabela
09004	Cuajimalpa de Morelos	15039	Ixtapaluca
09005	Gustavo A. Madero	15044	Jaltenco
09006	Iztacalco	15046	Jilotzingo
09007	Iztapalapa	15050	Juchitepec
09008	La Magdalena Contreras	15053	Melchor Ocampo
09009	Milpa Alta	15057	Naucalpan de Juárez
09010	Álvaro Obregón	15058	Nezahualcóyotl
09011	Tláhuac	15059	Nextlalpan
09012	Tlalpan	15060	Nicolás Romero
09013	Xochimilco	15061	Nopaltepec
09014	Benito Juárez	15065	Otumba
09015	Cuauhtémoc	15068	Ozumba
09016	Miguel Hidalgo	15069	Papalotla
09017	Venustiano Carranza	15070	La Paz
13069	Tizayuca	15075	San Martín de las Pirámides
15002	Acolman	15081	Tecámac
15009	Amecameca	15083	Temamatla
15010	Apaxco	15084	Temascalapa
15011	Atenco	15089	Tenango del Aire
15013	Atizapán de Zaragoza	15091	Teoloyucán
15015	Atlautla	15092	Teotihuacán
15016	Axapusco	15093	Tepetlaoxtoc
15017	Ayapango	15094	Tepetlixpa
15020	Coacalco de Berriozábal	15095	Tepotzotlán
15022	Cocotitlán	15096	Tequixquiac
15023	Coyotepec	15099	Texcoco
15024	Cuautitlán	15100	Tezoyuca
15025	Chalco	15103	Tlalmanalco
15028	Chiautla	15104	Tlalnepantla de Baz
15029	Chicoloapan	15108	Tultepec
15030	Chiconcuac	15109	Tultitlán
15031	Chimalhuacán	15112	Villa del Carbón
15033	Ecatepec de Morelos	15120	Zumpango
15034	Ecatzingo	15121	Cuautitlán Izcalli
15035	Huehuetoca	15122	Valle de Chalco Solidaridad
15036	Hueypoxtla	15125	Tonanitla

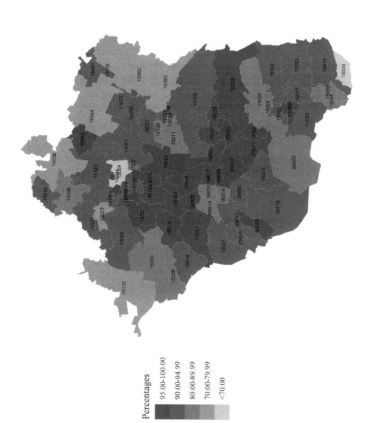

Percentages
- 95.00–100.00
- 90.00–94.99
- 80.00–89.99
- 70.00–79.99
- <70.00

Figure 4.4 Waste collection coverage in MCMA, 2010

Source: Based on INEGI (2010).

Boroughs and Municipalities

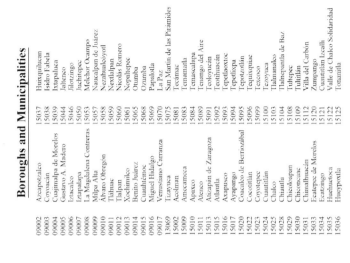

09002	Azcapotzalco	15037	Huixquilucan
09003	Coyoacán	15038	Isidro Fabela
09004	Cuajimalpa de Morelos	15039	Ixtapaluca
09005	Gustavo A. Madero	15044	Jaltenco
09006	Iztacalco	15046	Jilotzingo
09007	Iztapalapa	15050	Juchitepec
09008	La Magdalena Contreras	15053	Melchor Ocampo
09009	Milpa Alta	15057	Naucalpan de Juárez
09010	Álvaro Obregón	15058	Nezahualcóyotl
09011	Tláhuac	15059	Nextlalpan
09012	Tlalpan	15060	Nicolás Romero
09013	Xochimilco	15061	Nopaltepec
09014	Benito Juárez	15065	Otumba
09015	Cuauhtémoc	15068	Ozumba
09016	Miguel Hidalgo	15069	Papalotla
09017	Venustiano Carranza	15070	La Paz
13069	Tizayuca	15075	San Martín de las Pirámides
15002	Acolman	15081	Tecámac
15009	Amecameca	15083	Temamatla
15010	Apaxco	15084	Temascalapa
15011	Atenco	15089	Tenango del Aire
15013	Atizapán de Zaragoza	15091	Teoloyucan
15015	Atlautla	15092	Teotihuacán
15016	Axapusco	15093	Tepetlaoxtoc
15017	Ayapango	15094	Tepetlixpa
15020	Coacalco de Berriozábal	15095	Tepotzotlán
15022	Cocotitlán	15096	Tequixquiac
15023	Coyotepec	15099	Texcoco
15024	Cuautitlán	15100	Tezoyuca
15025	Chalco	15103	Tlalmanalco
15028	Chiautla	15104	Tlalnepantla de Baz
15029	Chicoloapan	15108	Tultepec
15030	Chiconcuac	15109	Tultitlán
15031	Chimalhuacán	15112	Villa del Carbón
15033	Ecatepec de Morelos	15120	Zumpango
15034	Ecatzingo	15121	Cuautitlán Izcalli
15035	Huehuetoca	15122	Valle de Chalco Solidaridad
15036	Hueypoxtla	15125	Tonanitla

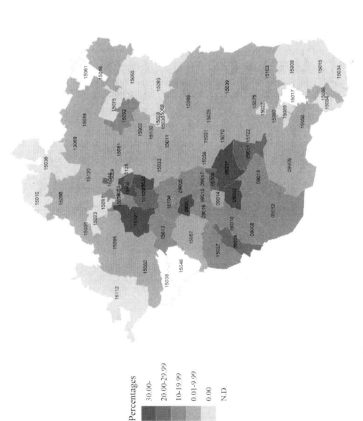

Percentages

- 30.00-
- 20.00–29.99
- 10–19.99
- 0.01–9.99
- 0.00
- N.D.

Figure 4.5 Public transport service coverage in MCMA, 2015

Source: Based on INEGI (2016).

extent to which low-income groups are systematically ignored in the distribution of public services must be measured and understood. Spatial patterns
emerging at the micro-scale need to be identified and the extent to which
inequality is more spatially diffused than polarised needs to be defined. In
MCMA there appears to be a strong link between spatial inequality and
service provision because Latin American metropolitan peripheries, unlike
suburbs in the United States and other developed countries, are populated
by a significant proportion of low-income residents and those who have long
been living in irregular, informal or poor neighbourhoods.

Final remarks

The metropolitan governance of Mexico City currently offers a bad scenario
for development and wellbeing. MCMA's local metropolitan governance and
service delivery are characterised by inefficient administration, fragmentation, poor coordination and inefficient rule enforcement, making collective
action by local administrations and between governments and other local
stakeholders difficult. The fragmented governance and sectoral approaches to
metropolitan problem-solving and policymaking have taken precedence over
equitable and efficient economic and social approaches. Institutional, administrative and political structures indicate that numerous uncoordinated and
sometimes unregulated suppliers of public services such as those discussed
above are disrupting integrated service delivery. This fragmented governance
regulates the formal and informal rules and practices of metropolitan service
management and delivery and shapes the incentives that drive the choices
and behaviours of local authorities and service providers, undermining their
will and ability to work together to improve public service delivery. The
weak and inflexible legal frameworks are symptomatic of governance failure
arising directly from deeply entrenched political and institutional structures
and from rigid intergovernmental relations. Decentralisation has added complexity to this setting, and the political turnover has made the situation even
less coordinated. This inability of governments and other local stakeholders
(communities, civic society, funders and private firms) to cooperate in ways
that produce, use and maintain effective public services confirms that current institutional arrangements are seriously flawed. Where institutions are
absent, contradictory, or used for political or economic ends at the expense
of the collective, few positive or even negative incentives to cooperate can
be found.

The lack of coordination may reflect failures of collective action driven
by local political and economic factors. Attempts to introduce operational
functions and resources in metropolitan organisations have not succeeded
in encouraging coordination or enforcing mandates to collaborate that are
compatible with the existing institutional framework. The metropolitan
commissions in particular do not function as institutional devices to develop
synergies across local jurisdictions. Local government associations are a rare

phenomenon. Due to the scarce and weak formal devices of integrated metropolitan policy and action (e.g. metropolitan commissions), self-organising mechanisms have not emerged among the various stakeholders participating in the delivery of water, public transport and waste collection. Collective organisation has been easily discouraged by political competition, the lack of incentives and self-interest. Mobile and sometimes polarised populations can further limit service delivery and collective action.

Dysfunctional institutions at all levels of government and the lack of integrated governance directly affect local service delivery. Coordination failures and disjointed planning and funding have affected the quantity and quality of services and their equitable provision in MCMA, where considerable deficiencies in the coverage and quality of public services are the norm. The failure of the metropolitan commissions, for instance, resulted in a lack of vision with negative effects on the administration of all of MCMA's urban services, whose provision is constantly plagued by problems of coordination, inefficiency and inequality.

All three of the public services examined in this chapter have common patterns of governance constraints, including financial difficulties and coordination failures. They all also suffer from significant limitations in terms of service quality and frequency. Provision can be precarious, particularly in low-income or informal contexts. But the different characteristics of these services translate into variations with respect to their spatial coverage and access. Transport services have more limited coverage than other services within the metropolitan area. Water services have a more or less well-defined spatial pattern. The coverage of these two services may contribute to explaining broader spatial inequality patterns within MCMA. Moreover, in the context of increasing scarcity some inhabitants with very limited access to formal water or transport services end up paying a significant percentage of their income to secure them. Frequently such cost transference is to the detriment of low-income households.

The pattern of the existing, often informal, development of public service delivery makes improvement both economically and politically difficult and expensive. Part of the solution to many of the problems deriving from inadequate metropolitan governance is to rethink the structures of the existing formal government, the instruments of finance and the mechanisms for participation in the definition of priorities and courses of action, with collective action called for when seeking to improve organisations and outcomes.

Even if there are limits to what can be achieved without adjusting the underlying political, administrative and legal conditions, governments and other actors should make changes to support local governance and service delivery. Besides improving local actors' practices, it is clear that intergovernmental metropolitan coordination, between local authorities as well as between government sectors, needs to be made compulsory. It is also necessary to explore new forms of cooperation and community involvement. Adequate funding for metropolitan projects and policies is also needed to meet the financial requirements for water, transport, solid waste and other urban services on a metropolitan basis.

References

Aguilar, A. & López, F. (2018). 'The City-Region of Mexico City: Social Inequality and a Vacuum in Development Planning'. *International Development Planning Review*, 40(1), 51–74.

Bayón, M. C. & Saraví, G. A. (2013). 'The Cultural Dimension of Urban Fragmentation: Segregation, Sociability, and Inequality in Mexico City'. *Latin American Perspectives*, 40(2), 35–52.

Cenizal, C. (2015). 'Governing the Metropolis: The Evolution of Cooperative Metropolitan Governance in Mexico City's Public Transportation'. Master's Thesis, Massachusetts Institute of Technology, Boston.

CONAGUA. (2013). 'Estadísticas del Agua de la Región Hidrológico-Administrativa XIII'. *Organismo de Cuenca Aguas del Valle de México*. Comisión Nacional del Agua, Mexico.

CONAGUA. (2014). 'Situación del subsector agua potable, drenaje y saneamiento'. *Secretaría de Medio ambiente y Recursos Naturales*, Comisión Nacional del Agua, Mexico.

Díaz Aldret, A. (2018). 'Gobernanza metropolitana en México: Instituciones e instrumentos'. *Revista del CLAD, Reforma y Democracia*, 71, 121–154.

Fernández, J. (2002). *Servicios Públicos Municipales*. Instituto Nacional de Administración Pública, México.

Gilbert, L., Khosla, P. & De Jong, F. (2016). 'Precarización y crecimiento urbano en la zona metropolitana de México'. *Espacialidades*, 6(2), 5–32. At: http://espacialidades.cua.uam.mx/ojs/index.php/espacialidades/article/view/133

Government of the State of Mexico. (2009). 'Programa para la prevención y gestión integral de residuos sólidos urbanos y de manejo especial del Estado de México'. *Gaceta del gobierno 69*, Gobierno del Estado de México, Mexico.

Harris, D. & Wild, L. (2013). 'Finding Solutions: Making Sense of the Politics of Service Delivery'. Research reports and studies, ODI Politics and Governance, London. At: https://www.odi.org/sites/odi.org.uk/files/odi-assets/publications-opinion-files/8331.pdf

IMCO. (2012). *Propuestas transversales. Acciones urgentes para las ciudades del futuro*. Instituto Mexicano para la Competitividad, México.

INEGI. (2010). *Censo de Población y Vivienda 2010*. Instituto Nacional de Estadística y Geografía, México. At: http://www.inegi.org.mx/est/contenidos/proyectos/ccpv/cpv2010/

INEGI. (2016). *Inventario Nacional de Viviendas*. Instituto Nacional de Estadística y Geografía, México. At: https://www.inegi.org.mx/app/mapa/inv/

Lámbarri, F., Rivas, L., Trujillo, M. & Martínez, J. (2014). 'La gestión de residuos sólidos en México'. In *Residuos en Hispanoamérica: De lo ambiental a lo social*. Ediciones EAN, Colombia, pp. 117–202.

Legorreta, J. (1991). 'Expansión urbana, mercado del suelo y estructura de poder en la ciudad de México'. *Revista mexicana de ciencias políticas y sociales*, 36(145), 45–76.

LSE Cities. (2015). *Urban Age*. London School of Economics Cities, United Kingdom. At: https://urbanage.lsecities.net/data

Meza, O. (2018). 'Urban Development Governance: A Proposed Framework to Investigate Municipal Infrastructure Inequalities in Chaotic Mexican cities'. DTAP No. 306. CIDE, Mexico City.

National Research Council. (1995). *Mexico City's Water Supply: Improving the Outlook for Sustainability.* Washington, DC: The National Academies Press. At: https://doi.org/10.17226/4937

Navarro, A. (2012). "*La gestión metropolitana de los residuos sólidos municipales*". Reporte CESOP, Cámara de Diputados, (51), 30–35.

OECD. (2015). 'Getting Mobility in the Valle de México on the Right Track'. In *OECD Territorial Reviews: Valle de México, Mexico.* Paris: OECD Publishing. At: http://dx.doi.org/10.1787/9789264245174-7-en

Paquette, C. & Negrete, M. E. (2011). 'La interacción entre transporte público y urbanización en la Zona Metropolitana de la Ciudad de México: Un modelo expansivo que llega a sus límites'. *Territorios* (25), 15–33.

Parnreiter, C. (2012). 'More than an Ordinary City: The Role of Mexico City in Global Commodity Chains'. In Derudder, B. Hoyler, M. Taylor, P.J. and Witlox, F., (eds.) *International Handbook of Globalization and World Cities.* Cheltenham: Edward Elgar, pp. 437–446.

Parnreiter, C. (2005). 'Tendencias de desarrollo en las metrópolis latinoamericanas en la era de la globalización: Los casos de Ciudad de México y Santiago de Chile'. *EURE*, 31(92), 5–28.

Perlman, B., & De Dios Pineda Guadarrama, J. (2011). 'Rethinking a Megalopolis: A Metropolitan Government Proposal for the Mexico City Metro Area'. *State & Local Government Review*, 43(2), 144–150. At: www.jstor.org/stable/41303185

Raich, U. (2006). Unequal development: Decentralization and Fiscal Disparities in the Metropolitan Zone of the Valley of Mexico. PhD Thesis, Dept. of Urban Studies and Planning, Massachusetts Institute of Technology.

Rosales, A. (2015). Economía política del servicio de agua y saneamiento en la Ciudad de México. PhD Thesis in Urban and Enrironmental Studies. CEDUA, El Colegio de México, México.

Rubalcava, R. & Schteingart, M. (2000). Segregación socio-espacial. In G. Garza (ed.) *La Ciudad de México en el fin del segundo milenio.* México: Gobierno del Distrito Federal/ COLMEX.

Salinas-Arreortua, L. A. (2017). 'Gestión metropolitana en la Zona Metropolitana del Valle de México: entre la legalidad y la voluntad política'. *Papeles de población*, 23(91), 143–169. At: https://doi.org/10.22185/24487147.2017.91.007

Sánchez Almanza, A. (2012). 'La evolución de la Ciudad de México. Factores para el desarrollo social'. Consejo de Evaluación del Desarrollo Social del Distrito Federal, Mexico City.

Saraví, G. A. (2008). 'Mundos aislados: segregación urbana y desigualdad en la ciudad de México'. *EURE*, 34(103), 93–110. At: https://dx.doi.org/10.4067/S0250-71612008000300005

SCT. (2012). 'Libro Blanco. Sistema 1 del tren suburbano Ruta Buenavista-Cuautitlán'. Secretaría de Comunicaciones y Transportes, México.

SEDATU, CONAPO & INEGI. (2018). *Delimitación de las zonas metropolitanas de México 2015. Secretaría de Desarrollo Agrario*, Territorial y Urbano, Consejo Nacional de Población, Instituto Nacional de Estadística y Geografía. Mexico City. At: http://www.gob.mx/conapo/documentos/delimitacion-de-las-zonas-metropolitanas-de-mexico-2015

SEDESOL (NA). 'Manual técnico sobre generación, recolección y transferencia de residuos sólidos municipales.' México, D. F.: Secretaria de Desarrollo Social, Subsecretaria de Desarrollo Urbano y Vivienda.

SEMOVI. (NA). 'Transporte de pasajeros'. At: http://www.semovi.cdmx.gob.mx/tramites-y-servicios/transporte-de-pasajeros

Trejo Nieto, A. (2020). *Metropolitan Economic Development: The Political Economy of Urbanisation in Mexico.* London: Routledge. At: https://doi.org/10.4324/9780429456053

Trejo Nieto, A. B., Niño Amézquita, J. L. & Vasquez, M. L. (2018). 'Governance of Metropolitan Areas for Delivery of Public Services in Latin America'. *REGION*, 5(3), 49–73. DOI: 10.18335/region.v5i3.224

Unikel, L. (2016). '*El desarrollo urbano de México: Diagnóstico e Implicaciones Futuras*'. México, DF: El Colegio de México.

World Bank. (2013). 'Agua urbana en el Valle de México'. Washington, DC: World Bank. At: http://www-wds.worldbank.org/external/default/WDSContentServer/WDSP/IB/2013/03/12/000425962_20130312111818/Rendered/PDF/759170WP0P11990n0el0Valle0de0Mexico.pdf

Ziccardi, A. (2016). 'Poverty and Urban Inequality: The Case of Mexico City Metropolitan Region'. *International Social Science Journal*, 56(217–218), 205–219.

5 The challenging evolution of integrated governance in metropolitan Buenos Aires

Gabriel Lanfranchi

Introduction

Located at the bank of the Río de la Plata, also known as La Plata River or River Plate, is the federal capital of the Republic of Argentina and was founded in 1536 by Pedro de Mendoza. It was later re-established in 1580 by Juan de Garay and its development began at the current Plaza de Mayo, or May Square. During the eighteenth century, it was declared as the Capital of the Viceroyalty of the Río de la Plata, giving it an important position in the commercial markets due to its port and the vast connections to the rest of the country which depended on it. By the end of the nineteenth century, Buenos Aires became the federal capital of Argentina, exploiting its strategic commercial location in a country known as "the world's barn" and as the entry point to large migratory waves which came to populate the nation. At the time, an ambitious plan defined how land was to be parcelled in a city which was already recognised as one of the most significant metropolises of the world, and that had already been designed to triple in urban footprint. The metropolitan system of Buenos Aires has since been continuously expanding, becoming the present Metropolitan Region with a population of 16,706,015 inhabitants and a surface of 13,947 square kilometres (Indec, 2003). This region is formed by the Autonomous City of Buenos Aires (CABA) and 40 municipalities located at its perimeter, representing 0.4 per cent of the country's surface, 36 per cent of the Argentine population and generating approximately 50 per cent of the national Gross Domestic Product.

The city earns its autonomy a century later, following the reform of the National Constitution in 1994. Since this modification, the executive power now belongs to the Governor elected by the citizens. Previously, the mayor was designated by the President, the legislative system was composed by the City Legislature and presided by the Vice-Governor and the autonomous judicial system. More than 3 million people live within the 200 square kilometres of CABA, but the metropolitan region which it is located in surpasses that number significantly.

To make matters more complicated, there is no single definition regarding the extent of the metropolis. It is worthy to mention the difference between

DOI: 10.4324/9781003105541-8

the Buenos Aires Metropolitan Region (BAMR), the Metropolitan Area (AMBA) and the Agglomeration of Great Buenos Aires (AGBA). Although there are other defining terms for the general area, these three are the focal categories in this chapter.

The AMBA encompasses CABA and 24 other municipalities within the province of Buenos Aires, which create a unified area of the city, also known as Great Buenos Aires. This area was also identified as "conurbano bonaerense", however the Indec ceased the use of this term in 2003 (Indec, 2003).

Simultaneously, the AGBA is defined as the area within the urban footprint, made up of CABA and 32 municipalities, some engulfed completely and others partially (Figure 5.1). The Great Buenos Aires differs from the AGBA by referring to a conjunction of complete municipalities, while the latter alludes to an area that changes with time and can include parts of municipalities (Indec, 2003; Lanfranchi et al., 2017).

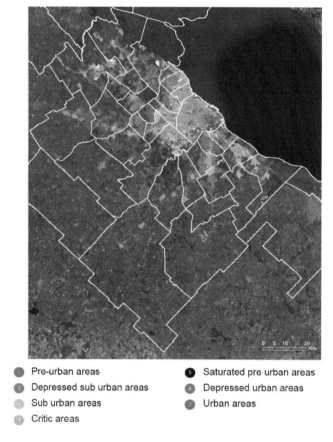

- ● Pre-urban areas
- ● Depressed sub urban areas
- ○ Sub urban areas
- ● Critic areas
- ⑤ Saturated pre urban areas
- ⑥ Depressed urban areas
- ⑦ Urban areas

Figure 5.1 Agglomeration of Great Buenos Aires

Source: Lanfranchi (2017).

All three regions are in constant and uninterrupted development and defining them is neither simple nor definitive as they are dynamic and ever-growing systems. The intercensal population growth is notorious, and the urban expansion is constant and lacking in metropolitan-scaled planning.

Finally, the BAMR includes CABA and 40 municipalities of the conurbation, extending to the neighbouring Great La Plata and delineated by the provincial route 7 and the La Plata River (Figure 5.2).

This chapter reviews BAMR's advances and difficulties in metropolitan management and service provision, and offers a series of recommendations

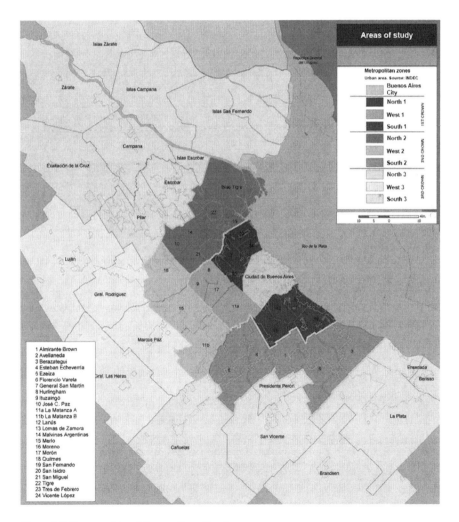

Figure 5.2 Buenos Aires Metropolitan Region

Source: Lanfranchi (2017).

for a better urban and regional planning, to ensure governance for a sustainable and inclusive metropolitan development in the twenty-first century.

Primary challenges of cities

Cities today act as stages for the main challenges facing contemporary societies. To reach sustainable development, radical transformations are required to improve equality, promote climate change resilience, encourage digitalisation in governmental management and incentivise metropolitan governance (Lanfranchi & Yañez, 2018). The expansion of the BAMR reflects the complex institutional structure to coordinate, composed by 43 governments at four governmental levels (national government, provincial government and city government, and 40 municipalities). Most of the social, economic and environmental challenges which face cities today don't adhere to jurisdictional boundaries, which is why diagnoses need to be carried out using a metropolitan framework, considering it as the fourth challenge and a great opportunity. This approach would ensure and promote coordination between the different sectors involved as well as the jurisdictions and governmental levels, keeping in mind that the region in question harbours one-third of the country's population.

This topic is also of interest to international organisations, such as the New Urban Agenda, adopted at the United Nations Conference on Housing and Sustainable Urban Development (Habitat III). This generated a significant precedent that serves as a guide, similar to Chapters 11 and 17 of the Sustainable Development Goal (SDG), which establish the objective to achieve inclusive, safe, resilient and sustainable cities and to revitalise the global alliance for sustainable development. It is important to also understand how essential cities are in the Paris Agreement and in city networks such as C40 (a network which unites megacities worldwide with the common ambition to tackle climate change, proposing carbon neutrality by 2050). Even in the G20 framework, cities have asked for a platform where their voices can be heard, and as of 2018 they began forming teams to tackle a variety of specific urban issues and challenges. This is how the U20 was created, where the governors of capital cities of the G20 bring forth ideas and recommendations for public policies so that participating countries can achieve the objectives of the various international agendas. The topic of metropolitan areas is also discussed in these frameworks, where a new governance is required to take on these difficult challenges. Another example is the United Cities and Local Governments (UCLG), a global network with the objective to represent, defend and amplify local and regional governments in support of the SDGs.

The BAMR is no exception to the challenges that other Latin American metropolises are faced with. Complications in areas such as service provision inequality, resilience and productivity, among others, are typically present in large conurbations. Inequity standards, for instance, can be seen directly applied in the Region: according to the DNA urban indicator (Lanfranchi,

2017) 60 per cent of demographic growth, between the 2001 and 2010 census, took place in vulnerable, critical or rural areas.

First, the concentration of capital generated in central cities is coupled with social and territorial inequities, representing a great challenge in developing urban centres environmentally sustainable, economically efficient and socially equitable. A large percentage of the low-income population lacks adequate infrastructure, urban services, and safety due to the lack of planning for accessible housing and lack of effective urban management.

In time, it has become increasingly evident that anthropogenic activities are responsible for a great portion of the rise in average global temperatures, which brings Climate Change to one of the top challenges that cities need to address. Urban agglomerations will have seen an average temperature rise of over 1.5° in relation to pre-industrial temperatures by mid-century. This creates an increase in the frequency and intensity of extreme climate events, which will in turn directly affect the vulnerability of urban areas and generate a greater social and economic risk. One example of recent resilience in Argentina is the major flooding events which happened in the city of La Plata in 2013, when 400 mm of rain precipitated within four hours, causing the death of over 100 people and generating an economic cost of ARG$3,000,000 in damages (Campanario, 2013).

The third challenge is regarding digitalisation, with the use and access of technology being essential when managing modern and inclusive cities. When technology is applied directly to the city, it is considered as a Smart City, where creativity is combined with new technologies to improve communication and citizen participation. A comprehensive approach to city development is necessary, intertwining its actors and organisations transversely (such as governmental, educational, social, civil and private entities) to effectively tackle the risks of climate change and accomplish wealth redistribution to evade social and economic inequalities. The availability and analysis of real-time data, the campaign for an open and transparent government and the search for efficient solutions to present and future problems are characteristics of this focus.

None of these three challenges are solved within the jurisdictional limits and boundaries of a single city. Hence why metropolitan governance is the fourth challenge and transverses the other three. An effective governance depends on local governments as much as the inhabitants of the region, emphasising citizen participation as a fundamental pillar for this governance model to succeed. Having feedback from the city dwellers about the local community needs is essential to achieve realistic city planning, simultaneously creating a sense of trust in future planned expansions and developments, having felt a part of the planning process, which further gives it legitimacy and efficiency. On the other hand, metropolitan government entities tend to focus on integral development, including mostly transport and the territorial and economic organisation. With this in mind, each metropolitan region needs to calculate how much coordination they can achieve, taking into account their assigned budget and finances, human resources and citizen understanding of the metropolis. The creation of this type of institution does not have to entail removing function and authority from the other existing governmental roles and levels but does complement and generate policies which are more efficient in handling each sector as an entity that reaches beyond jurisdictional boundaries (Lanfranchi & Yañez, 2018).

Governance in the Buenos Aires Metropolitan Region

Latin American and Caribbean cities harbour 80 per cent of the national population, while the global average is 55 per cent (Lanfranchi & Bidart, 2016). This accelerated growth does not go unnoticed in the unplanned growth of metropolitan regions, and the lack of standards, transport systems, infrastructure and public services may bring dire consequences to society.

According to the document "Gobernanza Metropolitana en América Latina y el Caribe" (Metropolitan Governance in Latin America and the Caribbean) (ibid), of the 64 metropolitan areas analysed, 65 per cent feature a metropolitan plan (varying between a strategic, sectoral or territorial plan of the metropolitan scale), but only 50 per cent have a metropolitan entity as a governing body which encompasses the territory. Still, there are numerous coordinating sectoral agencies that focus on tackling a sole issue at the metropolitan scale. In Latin America, the sectoral coordination is mostly found in urban planning and in the management of water and sanitation, followed by transport, solid waste management and basin management. The economic development and energy sectors, however, tend to be less coordinated.

In the BAMR some efforts have been made to create coordinative agencies since mid-twentieth century for water and sanitation, waste management, public transport and other sectors: Central Market Corporation (1967); Metropolitan Area Ecological Corporation (Coordinación Ecológica Área Metropolitana Sociedad del Estado – CEAMSE) (1976); River Reconquista Basin Committee (ComiRec) (2001); Argentine Water and Sanitation SA (AySA) (2006); Matanza Riachuelo Basin Authority (ACuMaR) (2006); Metropolitan Transport Agency (ATM) (2012); and, River Lujan Basin Committee (ComiLu) (2015).

Central Market Corporation

The Buenos Aires Central Market is the central vendor for fruits and vegetables that supplies the metropolitan region. The corporation was created in 1967 with the objective of administrating, constructing and protecting a distribution centre dedicated to the concentration of food supplied by national and international producers, as well as the conservation, packaging and storage of the products for sale, internal distribution and exportation.

The market building was built in the 1970s and has since been one of the most important market centres for fruits and vegetables in Latin America, presently supplying goods for over 13 million people. It not only contributes to the organisation, packaging, and distribution of these goods, but also to certifying the quality of the products by utilising their own bromatology, microbiology and phytopathology laboratories as well as fishing products, being the only commercial entity that systemically monitors the quality of the goods.

Since its creation, the Directory is the one that oversees and manages the Market. It is integrated by national government representatives, the province of Buenos Aires, and the Autonomous City of Buenos Aires in equal parts, functioning as a public entity with public and private legal capacities. Similarly, the initial funding was provided in equal parts by the three government levels and the rights, rates, taxes, leases and concession rights are split evenly among them (Mercado Central, 2021).

The market's metropolitan character is not solely reflected through its administration but is also evident in the market's physical dimensions – occupying approximately 540 hectares in La Matanza municipality – and in the 5,000 jobs generated and the 500 companies involved in the commerce of over 1,400,000 tons of goods sold presently. In addition, the market offers two fairs for small retailers, as their offers, variety and quality attract customers of all social classes. These fairs also provide cereals, milk products, meats, farm and warehouse products, and baked goods, generating interest from a variety of gastronomic personnel.

On the other hand, the Market is part of the program "The State in your Neighbourhood", organised by the national government and present in the provinces of Buenos Aires, Entre Ríos, Neuquén, Santa Fé and Mendoza. This program consists of transporting the products from the market to various neighbourhoods in the provinces through nomadic fairs, changing locations every week to ensure that all citizens have access to quality and affordable goods, coming directly from the suppliers. The Market was the first institution created with a metropolitan perspective and had a significant impact in the policies for management and distribution of food products in all regions.

Metropolitan Area Ecological Corporation (Coordinación Ecológica Área Metropolitana Sociedad del Estado – CEAMSE)

The Metropolitan Area Ecological Corporation (CEAMSE) was created in 1977 as a public firm dedicated to the incorporated management of the AMBA's urban solid waste. It was established by the City of Buenos Aires and the Province of Buenos Aires government (CEAMSE, 2021). Currently, the interference area includes the City and 33 municipalities within the metropolitan region, treating around 17,000 tons of waste daily, approximately 40 per cent of the waste generated in the entire country (Figure 5.3).

Figure 5.3 CEAMSE's landfills at the North III Environmental Complex

Source: Buenos Aires City Government (2021).

The creation of CEAMSE took place after the prohibition of incinerating solid waste and the closure of power plants that were previously active. Along with CEAMSE, sanitary filters began being utilised and are still being used today.

Per the law 25.916 which regulates the Integrated Management of Urban Solid Waste (USW), the stages of the treatment process would be the following: generation, initial disposal, collection, transfer, transport, treatment, final disposal. CEAMSE is not responsible for all stages of this process; transport is the responsibility of each municipality, even though CEAMSE generally supervises and controls the urban hygiene services offered by third parties. This way, CEAMSE's primary role is the management of the waste treatment plants where the USW is treated and disposed of. Another task they are responsible for is the closure and post-closure of the disposal sites once they've reached their end-of-life stage. There are currently three active waste treatment plants and one in this post-closure stage.

On the other hand, parallel to these USW tasks, CEAMSE is the owner of the Camino Parque del Buen Ayre freeway – which crosses six municipalities in the metropolitan area – and is responsible for the cleaning and maintenance of some rivers in the Province of Buenos Aires. This includes quality checks and monitoring the waters on the surface and in aquifers, controlling the air quality and gas emissions, the state of the soil, fauna and flora, as well as training national and international entities and academics in environmental matters. It also has a Centre for Research and Development in which technological advances are studied with the objective to improve environmental services and care.

In the last few years, CEAMSE has been attempting to position itself as a firm that promotes the circular economy, experimenting with different mechanisms to improve processes and convert waste into resources.

Argentine waters and sanitation (AySA/ Aguas y Saneamientos Argentinos S.A.)

One of the last agencies created was the Argentine Waters and Sanitation Corporation (Aguas y Saneamientos Argentinos S.A. – AySA) in 2006, although in reality it is part of the last stage in the transformation process of the nation's Sanitation Works, founded at the end of the nineteenth century as a response to the yellow fever epidemic. Its composition is interesting, since 90 per cent of the social funds correspond to the National State while the remaining 10 per cent belongs to the personnel, thanks to the Employee Shareholder Program. At first, the company would offer services for potable water and sewage treatment in the City of Buenos Aires and in 17 other municipalities of the metropolitan area. In the last few years, new areas were incorporated, reaching a total of 26 municipalities outside of the City and supplying 14 million people.

Since the seventeenth century, with the creation of the Río de la Plata Viceroyalty, plans and processes were created to manage the city's sanitation, with the main objective to avoid infections and the propagation of epidemics, such as measles and smallpox, among others, but this was done to no avail. Only during the mid-nineteenth century came the distribution of purified water, after the first epidemic outbreaks of cholera and yellow fever which, like the current pandemic, had a significant impact on society and people's way of life.

Economic activity was halted and the neighbourhoods in the southern region of the city were abandoned, like San Telmo and Barracas, in search for healthier and cleaner air to the north, leading to a densification of Recoleta and Retiro and expanding the urban footprint towards Palermo and Belgrano. During 1869, the first running water system in Latin America was introduced to Buenos Aires, reaching 8 per cent of the city's population. The network was slowly but steadily expanded, and reservoirs were constructed, as well as purification plants and pumping stations. The Palacio de las Aguas Corrientes (Palace of the Running Waters) is an example of these emblematic constructions: it was built in 1894 as a lift station and is still used as such. The building quality and imposing design shows the importance that was bestowed upon sanitation at the time, and how significant the technological advancement and quality of life was for the growing city.

Only in 1909 was the first National Sanitation Plan approved, creating more plants and expanding those existing ones. At the time, 40 per cent of homes in the City of Buenos Aires were connected to the sewage system. A few years later, the National Sanitation Works (OSN) was created, being the first national firm in charge of water and sewer services, setting an important precedent in sanitation works throughout the continent.

During the first decade of the twentieth century, the city's growth was such that the OSN Directory projected an expansion of the current water and sanitation network for a population four times the size of the population at the time. The Palermo Potable Water Treatment Plant was inaugurated in that context, and it continues to function after 93 years of use, providing service not only to the City of Buenos Aires, but also to eight other municipalities in the metropolitan area, leading the OSN to be one of the first agencies to offer metropolitan services and ignoring the jurisdictional boundaries of the city. At the end of the 1980s and with an ongoing decentralisation, the services provided by Argentine Waters to the City and 16 jurisdictions in the metropolitan area were privatised.

In 2006, potable water and sanitation was again nationalised with the creation of AySa, who continues the expansion of those services and the construction of treatment plants in the various municipalities of the metropolis, reaching the 26 jurisdictions supplied presently, aside from the Capital.

Achieving universal potable water in the concession area was proposed, as was increasing the population's access to sanitation systems to more than 80 per cent. To achieve this, the last ten years saw monumental developments such as the Paraná de las Palmas Potable Water Treatment Plant, or the left margin collector construction of Riachuelo, which is one of the primary infrastructure projects in the entire region.

Matanza riachuelo basin authority – ACuMaR

There are three agencies that handle basin management, the River Lujan Basin Committee (ComiLu), the River Reconquista Basin Committee (ComiRec) and the Matanza Riachuelo Basin Authority (ACuMaR), the last of which influences the largest population and which is described below (Acumar, 2021).

Acumar is an autonomous and intermunicipal entity that coordinates at the three government levels in the area: the nation, the province, and the city. It was created in 2006 through law 26.1668 due to the basin's grave environmental situation and after a lawsuit presented by a group of neighbours who held the national, provincial, and city States, along with 14 municipalities and 44 companies, accountable for damages caused by the contamination of the Matanza-Riachuelo River. This lawsuit, known as the Mendoza Cause, was the catalyst that illustrated the lack of historic coordination between all governmental levels that have authority over the basin. In its creation, the Authority was given power to regulate, control, and foster industrial activities, public services, and other activities which could jeopardise the basin's environmental state. Although it was created under the hand of the national state, Acumar is a tri-party entity that relies on powers delegated by the three jurisdictions it encompasses.

According to Article 5 of the creation law, the Authority's powers are the following:

i Unify the applicable regime in the matter of effluent discharges to receptive bodies of water and gaseous emissions.
ii Plan the environmental management of the territory affected.
iii Establish and collect fees for rendered services.
iv Carry out any type of legal act or administrative procedure necessary or convenient to execute the Comprehensive Pollution Control and Environmental Reconstruction Plan.
v Manage and administer, as the Central Executing Unit, the funds necessary to carry out the Comprehensive Pollution Control and Environmental Reconstruction Act.

At the same time, the faculties and powers of Acumar in environmental matters take precedent over any other concurrent authority in the basin area, needing to establish its articulation to local competences.

In 2008, the National Supreme Court of Law mandated that Acumar created an environmental sanitation plan to improve the basin's inhabitants' quality of life, not only recovering the water but also the air and soil involved and avoiding future damages. Hence why the Comprehensive Environmental Sanitation Plan (PISA) was created in 2009, detailing the management and control framework for the Authority. The PISA was updated in 2015, per the Justice's request, and revisions were done to the actions carried out, incorporating new ones to fulfil the primary objectives of the Plan.

The basin's water's main course runs 64 kilometres and through 14 municipalities of the metropolitan area as well as the southern portion of the City of Buenos Aires. The basin is home to approximately 5.8 million people, or 15 per cent of the country's population. These numbers take into account the high population density of the area, which creates a significant impact on the environment. This is what fuelled the creation of 12 environmental protection areas where they aim to conserve high biological biodiversity and contribute to growth control, flood mitigation, aquifer recharge, climate change mitigation, erosion control, and purification of contaminated water. Likewise, biodiversity contributes to the biological control of agricultural plagues, plant pollination, soil fertility recovery, and carbon dioxide sequestration, among other benefits. Despite the great impact caused by anthropic activities seen in the basin, it still maintains certain biological components of its original ecosystem. Some of these include wetlands, which have fundamental environmental functions such as rainwater and overflow retention which could cause flooding, and the ability to retain contaminants in the water, since the vegetation acts as a filter that absorbs heavy metals and decomposes organic compounds. To improve its protection, a CONICET

(National Council of Scientific and Technical Investigations) agreement was signed in 2019 to carry out a combined Matanza Riachuelo Basin Wetlands Inventory.

Having the objective of carrying out the previously mentioned actions, Acumar was organised in six action axes, each having individual functions (Lanfranchi et al., 2018):

i   Control and monitoring. Controls specifically the industries or establishments that may generate an environmental impact on air or water quality in the Basin.
ii Institutional strengthening.
iii Solid waste management. This axis carries out the Master Plan for Comprehensive Urban Solid Waste Management, within which environmental damage must be restored by cleaning open-air dumps, removal of waste present on the water surface and the river margins on one hand and prevents damage on the other, through actions related to waste recovery in the Basin.
iv Construction and infrastructure. Supports the strategic planning for the expansion of drinking water and sewage networks in the Basin, along with AySA and ABSA, companies that provide services in the area. Acumar also executes and plans water infrastructure works that regulate the use of water in the basin.
v   Territorial planning. Focuses on the recovery of public spaces, improving the population's housing conditions, and implementing actions related to land use planning.
vi Health. This area works with the Emergency Health Plan, focusing on six main aspects: identifying environmental rusk and vulnerable populations in order to assist them; incorporating Primary Healthcare strategies to improve access to healthcare systems; recognise health as common right; promote health in the territory and strengthen health networks; strengthen local health services and monitor the problems detected; and, train interdisciplinary teams.

Over ten years since its creation, Acumar has not been able to achieve the objectives for which it was created. However, the institutionalisation is advancing and can be a suitable platform for metropolitan governance, if aligning political interests with operational capacities of the institution is at all possible.

Metropolitan transport agency

The agency, made up of representatives from the province and the Autonomous City of Buenos Aires along with the national government, aims to solve the transport and mobility challenges faced by the BAMR. Some of them include the comprehensive multimodal planning of public transport, resource optimisation and data analysis using data provided by the SUBE system (Sole System for Electronic Tickets), the coordinated work between technical teams and the gender policies in transport. The agency was created in 2012 but had no major activity until recently. It is a consultancy body, lacking in executive power over metropolitan transport nor authority.

In the AMBA alone, 390 bus lines circulate the city with more than 1000 routes, and there are 79 kilometres of Metrobus (the local Bus Rapid Transit system – BRT), 62 kilometres of subway and 800 kilometres of train rails. Of the different transport methods, the national government controls the railways, freeways, and bus lines. Contrarily, the city government has authority over the subway and transit while the province controls the provincial routes and buses. Lastly, each municipality manages transit and bus lines within their own jurisdictional boundaries. The need to initiate the ATM and bestow authority to coordinate, control, and plan is evident in order to have a more efficient, orderly, and economic metropolitan circulation for all parties involved (Ministerio de Transporte de la Nación, 2020).

Recent advances in the region's coordination

There have been more recent advances in coordination within the BAMR due the Coronavirus pandemic, which demanded a joint management of decision-making by uniting the different levels of government. The heads of the national, provincial, and city governments spent ten months negotiating and discussing, at the time this chapter was written, where interjurisdictional governance was fundamental. As explained throughout this book, there are numerous variables that are oblivious to municipal boundaries, and a global pandemic has not been the exception. The growth of infection rates within the AMBA was highly analysed during all these months and the efforts to flatten the curve and control the health system in the region could not have been accomplished had it not been for the joint work that was done in terms of isolation measures, business closures, and circulation restrictions, being that, according to estimates, approximately 3 million people enter the city each day from the various municipalities in the metropolitan area.

Problems in key metropolitan services

Even if it isn't easy to get accurate and complete information (Public Services Program, 2009), AySA has shown interest and efforts to increase water coverage in the BAMR by implementing public works, learning projects, and joint programmes of sewerage and water supply networks. These programmes are carried out together with cooperatives, society and municipal authorities, thus triggering public-private linkages to increase coverage (Tobías & Fernández, 2018).

The problems that most directly affect the population are the centralised evolution of service coverage and significant backlogs in water sanitation.

Table 5.1 AySA, operational results

	2019	2018
Gross profits	6039	7012
Operative results	(190)	(19566)
Financial and holding results	750	(8704)
Other incomes and expenditures	(26)	166
Net result (profit/loss)	(18291)	(28104)

Note: The figures are presented in millions of pesos.

Source: General Syndicate of the Nation.

Because network expansion develops in an enveloping manner, most peripheral areas are left behind. Thus, inequality does not decrease but persists regardless of the implemented changes (ibid).

AySA has a significant financial dependence on the central government, which, at the same time, finances AySA with resources obtained from multilateral organisations. Therefore, the central government has a direct impact on the execution and fulfilment of investment and performance plans. Table 5.1 shows the financial losses for 2018 and 2019 (Presidency of the Nation, 2020), which were covered by the central government. There are also significant problems in controlling water quality because it is difficult to access information from private firms regarding the form and standards of treatment of watercourses (Cáceres, 2017).

Waste collection's regulation is centralised since the provincial authority is the one which, almost exclusively, evaluates and makes the most fundamental decisions. Although citizen participation laws have been implemented, they only apply to education and awareness-raising initiatives, while the central government has the power to decide the implementation of policies (Vallejos & Pohl Schnake, 2007). As far as institutions are concerned, fundamental problems need to be solved. Among these, fragmentation and weak coordination between the involved authorities. The management of the system is divided into 17 jurisdictions spread over three levels of the federal government and 39 participatory bodies at the territorial level. This means responsibilities are not specified or clear, which generate different institutional dysfunctionalities (Minaverry & Ferro, 2016).

The quality of service provision is acceptable for the province if only collection and transport solid are taken into account. These tasks are done directly by municipalities or through agreements with (a) private and specialised entities or (b) cooperatives. Disposal becomes deficient when waste is transported to clandestine open-air deposits that are potentially dangerous and very difficult to inspect (Center for Federal Studies, 2013). Usually providers cannot recover the costs of their activity but this depends on each municipal authority capacity (Regulatory Authority Water and Sanitation, 2020).

In the BAMR, there are different modes of transport such as the train, the underground network and buses, which together are part of the relevant modal interchange system. In addition, they offer, based on high subsidies to supply, the service at affordable fares for broad population sectors (Borthagaray & Natale, 2017). Pérez (2020) reviews the 90-year history of the buses that provide the service and observe a significant lack of comprehensive planning that directly affects the population. In the 1990s, concessions were granted to private operators. The regulations applied to them produced an intense process of power concentration that configured new networks of relations between the state and companies. As a result, it is difficult to identify adequate guidelines to plan the system correctly. In some regions, there are rates of up to 35.5 per cent of the population without access to any of the different modes of public transport (Center for Federal Studies, 2013).

There is a backlog of the railway network, which has not shown significant improvements in terms of capacity. In the beginning, it offered the service for approximately two million inhabitants compared to the current 15 million population. Problems arise in management, policy disruption, different pricing criteria, delays in investment and non-compliance with the frequency for passengers and freight (Borthagaray & Natale, 2017). Political decisions have focused on macroeconomic issues generally harming the system and deepening its failures. The criteria on which different price adjustments and subsidies are made are not linked to the real dynamics of the transport sector (Pérez, 2020). Therefore, significant subsidies are necessary.

To solve problems in policy implementation and service delivery different metropolitan approaches have been suggested as discussed next.

Proposed metropolitan approaches

Lefèvre (2005) suggests that metropolitan governance can be divided into two categories, which in turn can be organised in various subtypes. On one hand, Lefèvre mentions the institutional construction category, in which he differentiates between the institutions that were created through supra-municipal arrangements and those that emerged as a product of intermunicipal cooperation. The metropolitan supra-municipal government model is the least frequent and is characterised by the existence of a metropolitan authority with political legitimacy, by a jurisdictional territory equal to that of the metropolis and by managing its own financial resources.

Within this model, there is the "Intermunicipal Arrangements" subtype, where the joint authorities base their actions on cooperation between the municipalities that are part of the metropolitan area. Simultaneously, three subtypes of arrangements are distinguished as follows: "supra-municipal" in which intermunicipal authorities of the metropolitan area participate; "infra-metropolis" where only some of the municipalities of the metropolis coordinate; and the mono-sector authorities dealing with a specific sector. All three cases lack political legitimacy, since the agencies that administer these institutional arrangements are not directly elected.

The second subtype found is the "non-institutional governance modes", in which there is a tendency to coordinate polities in the different sectors through local agreements with contracts being formalised through specific tools. There are also collaboration subtypes within this typology: on the one hand, metropolitan areas where public policies result from infra-metropolitan sector organisations, and on the other, agreements made for the policy coordination between single-sector public actors. These are subject to local governments' will and to change in political parties.

Tomàs (2015) describes in "Metropolitan Governance in Europe: Models and Challenges" a typology that is based on the interrelation of the elements that occur in metropolitan areas: territorial fragmentation, competencies of a metropolitan nature, type of financing and representation form. Based on the following variables, four types of institutional governance arrangements are identified.

i   Monocentric or polycentric municipalities. Creating metropolitan institutions depends on the degree of fragmentation existing in the territory, which is why the author considers all the administrations that operate in the metropolitan area.
ii Competencies of the entities that act in the area and the binding nature of their decisions. Difference between hard policies (those related to the entire physical environment) and soft policies (including education and health, among others).
iii Financing, since it helps to determine the margin of autonomy of an institution according to the origin of the financial resources.
iv Entity representation. This can be done through direct election or indirect election where the authorities of the metropolitan body are made up of representatives of the different municipalities.

The four metropolitan governance models are defined according to the institutionalisation degree:

1   Metropolitan governments. They are created specifically for this task. Both its powers and its financing are set by law.
2   Sectoral metropolitan agencies. They are dedicated to managing a single service or planning a single sector.
3   Models of vertical coordination. They manage policies based on de facto coordination between exiting governments, without creating a metropolitan institution.
4   Model of voluntary cooperation of municipalities (horizontal cooperation). Characterized in that local representatives organise themselves on their own initiative.

In the BAMR, there is no comprehensive coordination body, however, in Latin America, 32 of the 64 metropolitan areas had some level of coordination in 2015. There is no universal model that can be implemented in every city, given that each country has its own legal institutional characteristics, political tradition and culture. However, the study of several cases allows us to find patterns when organising, which are worthy of review before making any proposals (Lanfranchi, et al., 2018).

Some conclusions were reached in Lanfranchi et al.'s research regarding metropolitan governance models in Buenos Aires. Based on that research some alternatives for the BAMR are outlined. In order to identify the functions and sectors frequently treated in governance models applied worldwide, the study carried out a survey to be able to compare and relate it to the reality of the BAMR. The following categories were identified to classify the functions according to the sectors: monitor, coordinate, plan, promote, execute works, manage and control (Figure 5.4).

Two aspects can be deduced: the models studied have greater influence in the economic development, public space, waste, land use, transport and housing sectors. In turn, the most common actions in these sectors are to monitor, coordinate, plan and promote. To a lesser extent, water and sanitation monitoring, coordination and risk management planning are repeated. Models have less influence in the health and safety sectors, as well as in the execution of works, management and control of all sectors.

As a second stage, the grid of functions of the analysed organisations is superimposed with that of the sectors covered by the BAMR. The coordinated sectors are shown from left to right, whose logos indicate: water and sanitation, watersheds, economic development, public space, waste, risk management, health, safety and use, transport, housing and others. On the

What do the studied entities do?

	💧	Basin	$	🌲	🗑	☁	✚	badge	Land Use	🚌	🏠	...
Control	2	3	4	4	6	4	1	3	5	5	5	4
Manage	3	2	6	4	5	6	1	3	5	4	6	6
Construct	4	5	3	6	5	5	2	2	4	7	7	6
Promote	6	4	8	9	9	6	3	3	10	7	8	7
Plan	7	6	8	10	11	9	2	4	13	11	9	11
Coordinate	8	6	8	10	10	5	3	3	11	10	10	9
Monitor	8	7	7	9	11	7	3	3	11	10	8	10

Figure 5.4 What do the studied entities do? Resume of the international entities' functions

Source: Author's elaboration.

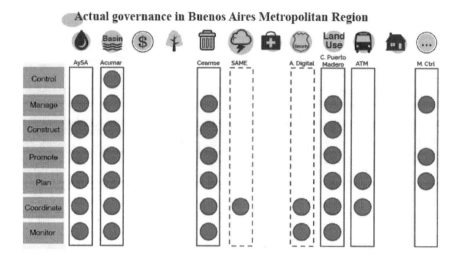

Figure 5.5 Roles and responsibilities of the BAMR's institutions

Source: Author's elaboration.

vertical axis are the organisation functions which were previously identified (Figure 5.5).

Unlike most of the governance models studied, the BAMR lacks coordination in sectors that include economic development, public spaces, land use and housing. On the other hand, there are agencies such as Aysa, Acumar and CEAMSE which manage a considerable number of functions such as managing and controlling of urban functions.

It is worth highlighting the importance of creating a metropolitan body with a clear objective for economic and social development, which intertwines the existing sectors and coordinate their functions. Current proposals are metropolitan institute; metropolitan Corporation; the Metropolitan Agency; Metropolitan Parliament and, the AMBA as a national region.

Metropolitan institute

The Buenos Aires Metropolitan Region institute could be the collaboration between two entities, the City of Buenos Aires and the province of Buenos Aires, and a possible third entity being the national government, with the aim of generating evidence for the decision-making process. The institute could initially function as an observatory dedicated to the monitoring of critical information, such as the number of COVID cases, transport, among others, and then could evolve according to relevant needs, such as in the coordination of decision making across different sectors or the planning of future urban expansion.

Metropolitan corporation

A metropolitan corporation would require the unification of existing metropolitan public utilities companies under one umbrella corporation with the management capable of promoting integrated decisions instead of sectoral ones. This corporation could also result in the creation of new public companies that address new issues, such as the promotion of tourism, economic development, the conversion of urban land, or the development and maintenance of parks. Both strategies for the development of a metropolitan corporation are valid as long as the corporation is able to generate its own revenue. The corporation can also have evolved from the institute but requires the capacity and authority to act.

Metropolitan Agency

Devised by two national Congressmen, the bill that creates the Agency was presented in July 2020 at a virtual event organised by the Metropolitan Citizenship Institute. It includes members of the national government, the city, and the province, and would work on various sectors such as the environment, waste, drinking water, sanitation, transport, mobility, basins, regional planning, infrastructure, land use and risk management, among others. It is required to create an Annual and Multi Annual Action Plan, have opinionated studies and databases and generate agreements with international organisations to finance projects. The monetary contributions of each level of government would be defined by the Congress.

Metropolitan Parliament

Architect Artemio Abba, general coordinator of the Buenos Aires Metropolitan Local Urban Observatory, proposes the creation of an Inter-Parliamentary Commission for metropolitan issues, composed of elected members from the legislatures of the city of Buenos Aires and the province of Buenos Aires. Specific parliamentary functions for the metropolitan region would need to be defined, and the special legislative commission would establish metropolitan public policies that would then be implemented by the executive branch of the appropriate national, provincial, or municipal governments. Thus, it would not create a new parliament but would be an Inter-Parliamentary Commission with powers to formulate inter-judicial policies that would later be validated by the respective parliaments. On the other hand, by partially updating the seats during election time, there would be a greater continuity in the formulation and monitoring of public policies (Observatorio AMBA, 2020).

Metropolitan Region

Finally, Pedro de Piero, former President of the Metropolitan Foundation, proposes the creation of the metropolitan region, as established in Article 124 of the National Constitution: "The provinces may create regions for economic and social development and establish bodies with authority to fulfil their purposes, and may also celebrate international agreements as long as they are not incompatible with the foreign policy of the Nation and do not affect the powers delegated to the federal Government or the public credit of the Nation; under National Congress awareness. The City of Buenos Aires will have an established regime for this purpose". The Region would include the city and province of Buenos Aires and calls on the relevant national and municipal governments to join.

"PlanificAcción": a new method for promoting a culture of metropolitan planning during the revision of the Urban Environmental Plan of Buenos Aires City

Previously, urban development plans were highly technocratic with the understanding that the plans would be implemented by the corresponding agencies. The time and development of the metropolisation of cities have demonstrated that today that is no longer possible. It is necessary to explore new methods that allow the beginnings of a wider political and social consensus capable of setting a course for medium- and long-term development. Otherwise, the plans end up in the libraries of universities without ever having influencing real-world politics or the territory.

"PlanificAcción" (translated into English as "Plan + Action") thus arises out of an innovative proposal for the co-creation of urban development plans, starting with the premise of creating a "culture of planning" through public consultations and the co-creation of specific action plans throughout the planning process. The focus on creating concrete actions helps to build social capital among the stakeholders, which is not common in our societies. The building of trust and the promotion of "a culture of planning" are necessary for the plan to become a true social pact that transcends government administrations and that lasts as an urban planning instrument.

Since 2008, the City of Buenos Aires has required the Urban Environmental Plan (enacted by Ordinance 2930), which is the framework law for urban planning and public works and under which function the City's business license law and zoning, building, and environmental codes. The process of revision for the Urban Environmental Plan began in July 2020 based on an innovative proposal from the Urban Environmental Plan Council: the co-creation of three development strategies with key institutions – the Comunas, the public and the City Legislature. Each line of work has its own objective.

The urban strategy is developed in collaboration with the Strategic Plan Council, which has been around for more than 20 years and consists of around 200 civil society organisations. Around 10 workshops were held, focusing on strengths and weaknesses and putting forth proposals and designs for addressing the principal challenges of the city: growth inequality, climate change resilience, digitalization and metropolitan governance.

Considering the concept of the 15-minute city, workshops with the city's Comunas (the level of government closest to the citizenry) were held. The City of Buenos Aires is composed of 15 Comunas, each with a "junta comunal" (neighborhood council) that is directly elected by the inhabitants of each Comuna. The workshops in each Comuna collaborated with the "junta comunal" as well as the Consejos Consultivos (Consultative Council) that consisted of neighbourhood organisations with direct links to each Comuna. The Comunas are highly politicised spaces but up until now they lacked any medium- to long-term plans. The co-creation of these plans utilised tools from urban anthropology and permitted the locals to identify and prioritize strategic actions for each Comuna. The plan would last past the current administration and would evaluate the plan's achievements on a yearly basis. The participatory process has managed to collect more than 1000 proposals for the 15 Comunas, which are in the process of being refined through a new mechanism of citizen consultation in the streets.

Normally, the City Legislature gets to the planning process at the end of its legislative cycle when the ordinance must be revised (once it has been presented by the executive branch and been voted on). This mechanism has resulted in endless debate in some cases, such as the current Urban Environmental Plan that was debated for more than eight years. In the current process of revision, it was proposed to include the legislators from the beginning of the process to get their buy-in from the start. The City Legislature, having created the Office of Metropolitan Affairs, was invited to lead an inter-institutional dialogue with all of the municipal legislatures of the BAMR. Experts contribute to the metropolitan-themed debates on transport, watershed management, urban solid waste management, economic development, territorial planning and public spaces. These efforts not only help create a metropolitan consciousness in those responsible for legislating but also help to catalyse the need for dialogue and to promote "a culture of planning" that is so necessary for our cities today.

The process of revision for the Urban Environmental Plan is currently in its final phase as of writing, for which it is too early to share conclusions. Nevertheless, the process is very encouraging and is worth considering in future studies of Buenos Aires.

Final comments

The metropolitan governance of one of the main Latin American megacities such as Buenos Aires is challenging and difficult to solve, but urgently needed, given the current context of growing threats like pandemics or climate change. Over the last few decades, the BAMR has been able to develop a series of sectoral institutions with reasonable levels of response to the urban demands in the mestropolis. Some sectors already have organisations capable of managing very complex processes and presenting adequate solutions. There are still several issues still to be resolved in terms of access to drinking water or sanitation or the modernization of the solid waste management system. It should also be noted that a large part of these organisations (such as the CEAMSE or the Central Market) were created, not as a result of an impulse of maturing political institutions, but during the military government, or by the ruling of the Supreme Court (in the case of ACUMAR) before a judicial ruling.

The lack of an intersectoral metropolitan entity is not attributable to the current lack of political synergy. From 2015 to 2019, the national government, the Province of Buenos Aires, and the City of Buenos Aires were led by authorities from the same political party (who had been part of the same City government administration until 2015). Despite this, progress in advancing metropolitan governance was timid. This could lead us to believe that any possibility of better organisation faces significant obstacles or interests by present politicians.

This challenge needs to be resolved urgently. The management of the COVID emergency is a clear example. While the mayors of Santa Cruz de la Sierra Metropolitan Area, Bolivia, managed to accelerate its institutionalisation process to respond to the health emergency, the political leaders in AMBA went from being publicly seen together on prime-time television in 2020 to waging an ongoing media war about resuming in-person attendance of children in schools amid the second COVID wave of 2021.

All citizens, through their social organisations, academy or the media, must strengthen their voice and demand greater integration and more effective mechanisms for solving these challenges that do not recognize jurisdictional limits but affect the quality of daily life. This will only be possible if society manages to understand the importance of having a medium- and long-term perspective and develops the tools (metropolitan plans) and the structure to implement them. The Buenos Aires Urban Environmental Plan in an attempt to tackle this cultural battle.

We are living in times of the greatest access to information in the history of humanity but also in times of unprecedented uncertainty. Only those societies with the greatest capacity to plan and organise will emerge stronger from the global context of the pandemic. Developing better metropolitan governance mechanisms may be one of the key practices to achieve this.

References

ACUMAR (2021). *Institucional*. At: https://www.acumar.gob.ar/institucional/

AySA (2021). *Nuestra historia*. At: https://www.aysa.com.ar/Quienes-Somos/nuestra_historia

Borthagaray, A. & Natale, D. (2017). Estructura urbana, transporte y movilidad en la Región Metropolitana de Buenos Aires. In Soldano, D. (ed.), *Viajeros del conurbano bonaerense. Una investigación sobre las experiencias de movilidad en la periferia*. Buenos Aires: Universidad Nacional de General Sarmiento, pp. 61–80. At: https://ediciones.ungs.edu.ar/wp-content/uploads/2017/06/9789876302692-completo.pdf#page=61

Buenos Aires City Government (2021). Historia de Buenos Aires. *Gobierno de la Ciudad de Buenos Aires.* At: https://turismo.buenosaires.gob.ar/es/article/historia-de-buenos-aires

Cáceres, V. L. (2017). 'La Regulación ambiental de los Servicios de agua y saneamiento en Argentina'. *Revista Electrónica del Instituto de Investigación Ambrosio*, 18, 71–100. At: http://www.derecho.uba.ar/revistas-digitales/index.php/revista-electronica-gioja/article/viewFile/314/246

Campanario, S. (2013). Álter eco. Catástrofe en el Excel: el costo real de la inundación de La Plata. La Nación, Economía. At: https://www.lanacion.com.ar/economia/catastrofe-en-el-excel-el-costo-real-de-la-inundacion-de-la-plata-nid1587463/

CEAMSE (2021). At: https://www.ceamse.gov.ar/

Center for Federal Studies (2013). *Infraestructura productiva y social en la provincia de Buenos Aires.* Buenos Aires: Consejo Federal de Inversiones. At: http://biblioteca.cfi.org.ar/wp-content/uploads/sites/2/2013/01/49771.pdf

Indec (2003). *Qué es el Gran Buenos Aires?* Buenos Aires: *INDEC* At: https://www.indec.gob.ar/dbindec/folleto_gba.pdf

Lanfranchi, G. (2017). *ADN Urbano - Aglomerado Gran Buenos.* Documento de Políticas Públicas, Recomendación No. 183, CIPPEC. Buenos Aires: CIPPEC. At: https://www.cippec.org/wp-content/uploads/2017/03/970.pdf

Lanfranchi, G. & Bidart, M. (2016). *Gobernanza metropolitana en América Latina y el Caribe.* Documento de trabajo No. 151, CIPPEC. Buenos Aires: CIPPEC. At: https://www.cippec.org/wp-content/uploads/2017/03/1069.pdf

Lanfranchi, G. & Yañez, F. (2018). *Urban challenges in the 21st century.* Urban 20 White Paper, CIPPEC. Buenos Aires: CIPPEC. At: https://www.cippec.org/en/publicacion/urban-challenges-in-the-21st-century-urban-20-white-paper/

Lanfranchi, G., Bercovich, F., Rezaval, M. V., Gonzalez Canada, D. & Simone, V. (2018). *Gobernanza Metropolitana. Análisis de modelos y posibles aplicaciones en la Región Metropolitana de Buenos Aires.* Documento de trabajo No. 170, CIPPEC. Buenos Aires: CIPPEC. At: https://www.cippec.org/publicacion/gobernanza-metropolitana-analisis-de-modelos-y-posibles-aplicaciones-en-la-region-metropolitana-de-buenos-aires/

Lanfranchi, G., Garay, A., Baer, L. & Bidart, M. (2017). *Revisión de los Lineamientos Estratégicos para la Región Metropolitana de Buenos Aires 2007–2017.* Documento de trabajo No. 168, CIPPEC. Buenos Aires: CIPPEC. At: https://www.cippec.org/publicacion/revision-de-los-lineamientos-estrategicos-para-la-region-metropolitana-de-buenos-aires-2007-2017/

Lefèvre, C. (2005). Gobernabilidad democrática de las áreas metropolitanas. Experiencias y lecciones internacionales para las ciudades latinoamericanas. In Rojas, E., Cuadrado-Roura, J. R. & Fernández Güell, J. M. (eds.), *Gobernar las metrópolis.* Washington: Banco Interamericano de Desarrollo, pp. 195–262. At: https://publications.iadb.org/publications/spanish/document/Gobernar-las-metrópolis.pdf

Mercado Central (2021). *Qué es el Mercado Central?* At: http://www.mercadocentral.gob.ar/paginas/quper centC3per centA9-es-el-mercado-central

Minaverry, C. M. & Ferro, M. (2016). La fragmentación jurídico-institucional como obstáculo para aplicar el paradigma ambiental. *Revista Reflexiones*, 95 (1), 115–129. At: https://www.scielo.sa.cr/pdf/reflexiones/v95n1/1659-2859-reflexiones-95-01-00115.pdf

Ministerio de Transporte de la Nación (2020). *Transporte impulsa la Agencia Metropolitana.* At: https://www.argentina.gob.ar/noticias/transporte-impulsa-la-agencia-metropolitana-1

Observatorio AMBA (2020). *Interview to Artemio Abba.* At: https://observatorioamba.
    org/noticias-y-agenda/noticia/artemio-abba-el-crecimiento-metropolitano-y-la-
    complejizacion-de-su-interjurisdiccionalidad-no-fue-acompanada-por-una-adecuada-
    institucionalidad

Pérez, V. (2020). 'A 90 años de la aparición del colectivo. Reflexiones sobre la partic-
    ipación del Estado en un servicio público esencial en la Región Metropolitana de
    Buenos Aires (1928–2018)'. *Sociohistórica*, (47), 1–20. At: https://www.sociohistorica.
    fahce.unlp.edu.ar/article/view/SHe119/13500

Presidency of the Nation (2020). Informe situación empresa, Agua y Saneamientos
    Argentinos S.A.

Public Services Program (2009). El acceso a agua segura en el Área Metropolitana de
    Buenos Aires. Una obligación impostergable. [Online] At: https://www.cels.org.ar/
    common/documentos/agua_INFORME_COMPLETO.pdf

Regulatory Authority Water and Sanitation (2020). Resumen Ejecutivo Memoria y
    Estados Contables de AySA. [Online] At: https://www.argentina.gob.ar/sites/default/
    files/INFORMACIÓN ECONÓMICO-FINANCIERA DE AYSA/informes_ge/
    Informe-Memoria-y-estados-contables-Aysa-al-31-12-18.pdf

Tobías, M. & Fernández, L. (2018). 'La circulación del agua en Buenos Aires: Resonancias
    geográficas y desigualdades socioespaciales en el acceso al servicio'. *Cuadernos de
    Geografía*, 28 (2), 423–441. At: http://www.scielo.org.co/pdf/rcdg/v28n2/2256-
    5442-rcdg-28-02-423.pdf

Tomàs, M. (2015). *La gobernanza metropolitana en Europa: modelos y retos.* Barcelona: European
    Metropolitan Authorities. At: http://webcache.googleusercontent.com/search?q=
    cache:XRhebWvl564J:www.ub.edu/grel/ca/descarregar%3Fseccio%3Drepositori%26
    id%3D33+&cd=1&hl=es-419&ct=clnk&gl=mx

Vallejos, V. H. & Pohl Schnake, V. (2007). La gestión integral de residuos sólidos urbanos
    en la provincia de Buenos Aires ¿El modelo CEAMSE continúa y amplía su escala
    territorial? [Online] At: http://www.memoria.fahce.unlp.edu.ar/trab_eventos/ev.733/
    ev.733.pdf

6 Metropolitan Santiago

The challenge of moving from dispersion and inequality to effective intergovernmental governance

Esteban Valenzuela Van Treek, Claudia Toledo A. and Osvaldo Henríquez O.

Introduction

Santiago is relatively well rated in various rankings of international cities, in clear contrast to the obvious inequalities that increased with the social outbreak of 2019 and more recently in the pandemic. For instance Mercer (2019) considers it an attractive city for new investment projects. Data indicate that of the 34 communes that make up the Santiago Metropolitan Area (SMA), the five wealthiest, in the north-east of the city, have seen deaths from COVID at only a quarter of the number of those in low-income communes on the periphery and have on average three times as much green space, the highest educational indicators in the country, and the lowest degree of pollution. Added to this, despite improved public opinion on the transport system, increased intermodality and annual investment of 407 billion Chilean pesos from 2003 to 2016 – an important proportion of the country's budget – there is strong criticism of the service, which is cost-inefficient with tariff evasion at 30 per cent (Comptroller General of the Republic, 2016).

Behind Santiago's economic success is high economic inequality creating spatial segregation that was exacerbated by the 1981 Urban Policy, which stated that "land is not a scarce resource" and established a neoliberal style of urban land management that became dependent on the free market and produced "natural" growth of urban areas without restrictions, laying the foundations for the current urban development of Greater Santiago. Urban expansion exacerbated by population growth made the management of the metropolitan area increasingly complex due to the lack of institutional strength to address urban problems in an integrated manner. Today this complexity is exacerbated by institutional fragmentation and intraregional centralism, which is even more pronounced in this metropolitan area under the weak authority of the current mayor, who is often absent from decision-making on the metropolitan territory. This could change in 2022 with the implementation of Law 21.074, fostered by the Presidential Advisory Commission on Decentralisation and Regional Development (2014), which aims to strengthen the regionalisation of the country (Law 21.074, 2018) and could substantially transform the administration of the metropolitan area. This law

DOI: 10.4324/9781003105541-9

will support the articulation of the powers of future regional governors in a context of greater horizontal intergovernmental relations (Henríquez, 2020) that seek to cooperatively involve central agencies (ministries), municipalities and a new metropolitan institutionalism. Under this approach regional governments are expected to take the lead on managing transport, environmental issues and urban planning.

The integrated governance of the SMA thus remains prominent in Chile's public agenda due to the longstanding challenges to social equity and urban sustainability that threaten both the quality of life in the capital and the country's competitiveness. This chapter examines how the SMA's highly complex institutional governance structure has evolved in the last four decades. This type of governance has produced segregated and unequal outcomes across its urban services. It also reviews the most recent roadmaps proposed to build institutional spaces and operational strategies through which multilevel political coordination has been expected to advance towards a shared, long-term vision of inclusive and sustainable metropolitan development.

Dispersion and inequality in Santiago Metropolitan Area

Chile is a highly urbanised country, more than 87 per cent of whose population lives in urban areas and an expansion rate of 17.8 per cent according to the last census (INE, 2017). Approximately 8 million of its 19 million inhabitants are concentrated in an area of 107,000 hectares in its three main metropolitan areas: Greater Santiago, Greater Concepción and Greater Valparaíso. In all three, urban growth has accelerated urbanisation, which in turn has generated various problems affecting citizens' quality of life.

With a population of 6.1 million and a surface area of 78,000 hectares of which 10,000 hectares were added in 2002–2017, Greater Santiago is the largest city in the country (INE, 2017). The figures indicate the complexity and accelerated growth of this urban agglomeration, which occupies the 2 per cent of the Santiago's regional surface. It holds 86 per cent of the region's and 35 per cent of the country's population, which is why the demographic evolution of Santiago has a decisive impact on that of the country (Rodríguez, et al., 2017). Santiago is the strategic economic, cultural, educational (especially higher education), trade and services centre of Chile (BID, 2018). The main headquarters of many private and public companies are located in a small part of its territory. A significant proportion of the country's productive and creative capacities are also found in Santiago (Galetovic and Jordan, 2006; De Mattos and Hidalgo, 2007; Dureau et al., 2014; Fuentes and Sierralta, 2014). Multiple national and international rankings position Santiago among successful emerging cities with a high level of security, services, economic activity, value chains and mega service areas (Castells 1995; Castells & Borja, 1997, Castells, 2001; Veltz, 1999; Sassen, 2003). However, this view is not consistent with the level of the country's social development (Orellana, 2009). The Mercer quality-of-life ranking of

230 cities of the world is led by European (Vienna ranking first), Canadian and Australian cities. In Latin America the best-positioned is Montevideo (78th), followed by Buenos Aires (91st), with Santiago in 93rd place (Mercer, 2019); however Sassen's (1991, 2001) concept of a global city – a metropolis with a world brand, airports as international connection centres, a transport network, advanced telecommunications infrastructure, scientific and cultural weight, a business platform hosting the headquarters of mega-companies – ranked Santiago 60th in 2019 (AT Kearney, 2019).

While there is consensus that from the administrative political point of view Greater Santiago comprises 34 communes, there are several different definitions of the metropolitan area:

- Santiago's central macrozone has 10 million people. This includes the 7.4 million in the Santiago Metropolitan Region, 600,000 in the Rancagua-Rengo-San Fernando area (120 kilometres to the south), and the two million inhabitants of Gran Puerto de Valparaíso and its inland area (approximately 120 km northeast of Santiago). This includes the communes (municipalities) of Valparaíso, Viña del Mar, Concón, Casablanca, Quilpué, Villa Alemana, Quillota, La Calera, Los Andes and San Felipe. All of this area is an hour to an hour and a half from the centre of Santiago and have intermediate levels of commuting (Orellana and Fuentes, 2008). Valparaíso has no fast train, while Rancagua has had a high-frequency metro-train to Santiago and direct trains taking only 45 minutes since 2016.
- An integrated Metropolitan Region and one of the fifteen regions of Chile (an intermediate level of government in Chile) with 7 million inhabitants (INE, 2017). The smallest of all of Chile's regions with an area of 15,403.2 square kilometres, this is the most densely inhabited. This delimitation does not include the province of Melipilla or the Andean area of the city. The Port Region of Valparaíso is in the northwest of this definition of the metropolitan region, Argentina is in the east and the Region of Libertador General Bernardo O'Higgins, Rancagua's capital, is in the south.
- The urban nucleus of the Functional Urban Area of Greater Santiago (INE, MINVU and SECTRA, 2020) stands out as the largest in the country, consisting of the consolidated urban area that includes the urban centres of the Province of Santiago, in addition to Puente Alto, San Bernardo, Colina, Lampa, Padre Hurtado, Peñaflor, Calera de Tango and Talagante, with a hinterland of the populated centres of Lampa, Pudahuel, Maipú, Padre Hurtado, Peñaflor, Talagante, Calera de Tango, San Bernardo, Puente Alto, La Florida and Lo Barnechea. This definition as a functional urban area has 6.2 million inhabitants.
- The consolidated area of 34 suburban communes which is widely recognised as the SMA, which has a population of 6.1 million. It includes 32 communes in the province of Santiago (Quilicura, Huechuraba,

Vitacura, Lo Barnechea, Pudahuel, Renca, Conchalí, Independencia, Recoleta, Providencia, Las Condes, Cerro Navia, Lo Prado, Quinta Normal, Estación Central, Santiago, Ñuñoa, La Reina, Maipú, Cerrillos, Pedro Aguirre Cerda, Lo Espejo, San Miguel, La Cisterna, San Joaquín, San Ramón, La Granja, Macul, Peñalolén, La Florida, El Bosque and La Pintana) plus the municipalities of Puente Alto in the province of Cordillera, and San Bernardo in the province of Maipo. This definition excludes a set of municipalities less than 20 kilometres away that are dormitory towns or strongly linked to the city centre. This is the definition we look at in this chapter.

Santiago's complexity and dynamics create a series of structural problems, which despite several public policies and investment in tackling them have not been solved. The main problems and challenges of this metropolis are high segregation and inequality, the provision of key services such as transport, water and waste management, high pollution and lack of public safety.

Santiago's urban development is characterised by its expansion and segregation, with a significant shortage of land for social housing and high levels of sociospatial inequality evident in its urban quality index, evidencing the wide differences between northern communes such as Vitacura (75.6 points) and La Pintana in the south-east (38.08 points). Such differences show clear social fragmentation (Orellana and Marshall, 2019). Urban inequality in Santiago is geographically expressed in the division between the east of the city, the Barrio Alto, at the foot of the Andes mountain range with a population of one million, and the poor peripheries in the south and north-west areas of the city, with fewer services and precarious housing (Sabatini, 2006; Agostini, 2010). Santiago's urban growth is occurring not only on its peripheries but also in its conurbations and dense city centre (Contreras, 2012).

Its high segregation and inequality have been aggravated by the absence of a metropolitan government that internally redistributes income, triggering asymmetric provision of public services and urban infrastructure. Despite the existence of a Municipal Common Fund, which gives part of the taxes collected from rich municipalities to the poor ones, the combination of centralism (funds administered by central agencies), the high exemption of payment of property taxes and the lack of a dedicated metropolitan government perpetuate the inequality. High-income citizens are concentrated in only six communes that occupy 18 per cent of the urban area, as identified by the Index of Territorial Welfare which measures the gaps and imbalances in welfare in the metropolitan area (TECHO, 2016; IBT, 2021).

The key element of the historical displacement of the poor population towards the periphery following the urban policy introduced in the 1980s has been the lack of urban land regulation. Land for social housing is not acquired in consolidated areas and additional taxes are not charged to those who obtain high earnings constructing in high-density areas. This has exacerbated social and territorial exclusion, making it difficult for those on the peripheries to access good-quality public goods and services. This pattern of land management has created deep ruptures in the communities, complex processes of urban restructuring, and the marginalisation and spatial concentration of poverty, increasing the problems in less-favoured areas of the metropolis (Ortega, 2014).

The COVID-19 pandemic has made these inequalities more evident. A recent study confirming that socioeconomic status determines the incidence of COVID-19 and mortality in Chile (Mena et al., 2021) found that the commune with the highest socioeconomic level was Vitacura, with 93.7 points, which saw 22.6 weekly cases per 10,000 people in May 2020, while at the other extreme La Pintana, scoring only 17.0 points, saw 76.4 cases in June 2020. In terms of deaths from COVID-19 per 10,000 inhabitants, once again Vitacura had the lowest rate with a maximum of 1.6 deaths per week, in contrast to San Ramón, with 4.4 deaths. The study concludes that these figures reflect the inequality and disparities in medical care across a segregated city.

Another acute issue in the metropolitan area is service provision, and most critically, that of public transport. The dramatic implementation of Transantiago, the integrated transport system, was imposed in 2007 by the Ministry of Transport without involving the municipalities in its decision-making. Several drawbacks affecting the general public transport system have become apparent in both its design and its operation since its implementation. One of the main problems was the excessive increase in demand for the Metro network, practically doubling it, which created considerable congestion and consequently service provision problems (OECD, 2009). In 2006, the Metro transported around 331 million passengers; in 2007, the year the integrated transport system was implemented, this jumped to 600 million, using the same infrastructure.

Various measures have been introduced, including modernising the infrastructure, more, and more frequent trains, the addition of new Metro lines, and information campaigns, particularly on preventing fare evasion. These have involved heavy public investment and use of resources, leading to protests from other regions who demanded similar benefits. In response the government of Chile issued a compensatory law Mirror Law subsidising national public transport elsewhere except for the province of Santiago and the municipalities of Puente Alto and San Bernardo, by the same amount as that allocated to Transantiago.

Despite these problems with the integration of the transport system, an international study of such systems in 84 cities ranks Santiago top in America, surpassing New York and Curitiba (La Tercera, 2014). Another study reports that Transantiago's travel times were similar to those of Bogotá, surpassing those of Mexico, Lima and Porto Alegre (UC, 2016). Regular service-user evaluations conducted by the Metropolitan Public Directory (DTP, 2021) rated the service at 4.3 in 2016 and 4.6 in 2019, with an important improvement in 2020 reaching a maximum rating of 5.0 attributable to the implementation of a new system called Red, focusing mainly on new bus standards. Red has involved considerable investment by central government and has led to increased positive evaluation.

High pollution is a by-product of the structural conditions of the Mapocho River valley, which in winter suffers from poor fresh air and high thermal inversion that inhibit the dispersal of smog. Added to this natural disadvantage there is no control of fixed sources of pollution, streets are not cleaned, the number of vehicles on the roads has increased and consolidated green areas in eroded hills are not developed. To mitigate this situation an air pollution control process has reduced fine PM2.5 particles, the emissions most harmful to health, by 68 per cent as part of various decontamination plans emanating from the Ministry of the Environment since 1998. The current plan, in force since 2018, applies the Euro VI Standard to Transantiago's buses with emission standards and incentives for cleaner and more efficient light and midsize vehicles, absolute prohibition of heating using wood throughout Greater Santiago, and restriction of the use of catalytic vehicles registered before 2012 (Ladera Sur, 2018).

In Santiago, there was an increase in assaults and robberies with intimidation previous to 2016 (Emol, 2016). A study by the Association of Municipalities of Chile (AMUCH) between 2014 and 2015 concludes that there was a substantial increase in three categories of crime: violent crime, especially in Santiago, La Reina, Maipú, La Florida and Lo Barnechea; property crime, particularly in Las Condes, San Miguel, Cerrillos and Pudahuel; and other crimes in Peñalolén, Puente Alto, La Pintana and others (AMUCH, 2015). Santiago cannot be considered a world-class city when a high percentage of its population faces insecurity and violence every day (Dammert and Oviedo, 2005). Rather it is what is called a dual city, where the cosmopolitan and globalised city coexists with a poor, marginal and criminalised counterpart, each segregated from the other (Sassen, 2001).

Centrally coordinated governance

To a large extent the above-mentioned urban problems have their origin in the current lack of integration and coordination of public and municipal institutions to address the complexity of the territory that makes up Greater Santiago. In Chile, the issue of metropolitan governance of the SMA has been a legal issue. Attempts at coordinated governance have been the result of regulatory improvisations since coordination was first discussed in 1974 in the wake of regionalisation. The fundamentals of the proposed new regulation included excessive economic concentration in the city of Santiago and the necessity for advancing decentralisation across regions, provinces, communes and metropolitan areas (DL 573, 1974). Proposed future legislation would define metropolitan areas and establish special regimes for their government and administration with integral metropolitan development planning and the coordination of investment and of state and municipal services.

The initial proposal for restructuring the Chile's territorial administration under regionalisation envisioned the organisation and regulation of the SMA through the establishment of a higher metropolitan authority with specific functions, with adequate participation by the municipal authorities (Hernández, 1977). However, subsequent regulation through DL 1317 (1976) subsumed the metropolitan area category into the same model of general application as that for the rest of the regions, which was based on the establishment of a deconcentrated regional administration model mirroring that of the central organisation (Henríquez, 2020).

The metropolitan region played a decisive and relevant role in national performance but included rural areas and various urban centres with their own functionality (Aylwin, 1991). Of the original proposal only the planning function of the metropolitan area was maintained by approval of the Intercommunal Regulatory Plans (PRI), which regulated the physical development of urban and rural areas of communes that, due to their functional relationships, were integrated into an urban agglomeration. The formulation of such plans was one of the functions of the Regional Ministerial Secretariats of Housing and Urban Development, with the Ministry of Housing and Urban Development responsible for their implementation (DL 1305, 1976). Between 1974 and 1993 the implementation of public functions in the metropolitan area – defined as the set of communes that due to their relationships were integrated into an urban agglomeration with over 500,000 inhabitants – was structured on the basis of relationships between national ministries and municipalities, as Figure 6.1 illustrates (DTO 458, 1976).

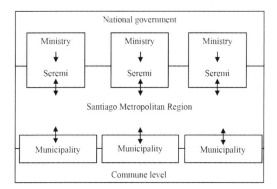

Figure 6.1 Centrally coordinated governance of the Santiago Metropolitan Area (1974–1992)

Source: Based on DL 573 (1974), DL 575 (1974), DL 1317 (1976) and DTO 458 (1976).

The governance model for metropolitan areas was dissolved by the Political Constitution of 1980, which returned to the strongly centralised coordinated governance model, although the existing regulation promoted metropolitan management by intermunicipal coordination and municipalities were allowed to solve common problems (DS 1.150, 1980: Art. 112). Intermunicipal coordination was regulated by municipal rules authorising the collaboration of two or more municipalities for the implementation of services or the accomplishment of common public works (DL 1289, 1975: Art. 67). One example of this model is the collaboration of 14 Greater Santiago municipalities that established the non-profit Metropolitan Waste Company (Empresa Metropolitana de Residuos Ltda., or EMERES) in 1986 under municipal law. Its objective was to provide the collection, transportation and disposal of household solid waste (Pizarro, 2018). The discussion of city issues and city organisation was strongly influenced by the Urban Development Policy of 1979 and implementation of the neoliberal paradigm based on deregulation and the elimination of restrictions to allow the natural growth of urban areas following market trends (Daher, 1991; Trivelli, 1991).

The debate on the management and organisation of SMA resumed in the 1990s within the framework of the democratisation of the country (Orellana, 2013). In 1991, the regional administration was reorganised through an agreement between the different political parties with parliamentary representation. Regional governments were created and municipalities democratised in a new constitutional reform under Law 19.097. The reorganisation of the regional administration in 1991 maintained the 1980 Constitution's original conceptual definition of metropolitan areas of based on intermunicipal coordination and public services.

Discussion of the problem of metropolitan management and organisation continued in 1993 with a proposal for a new definition of the metropolitan area as the territory formed by two or more population cores linked by built areas and sharing the use of urban infrastructure and services (Law 19.175, 1993: Art. 90). The creation of a Regional Coordinating Council for Municipal Action to plan and coordinate joint municipal action aimed to prevent and resolve problems affecting the communes within a metropolitan area, and required joint treatment (Figure 6.2). This coordination model implied, in the first instance, less influence on the part of the regional mayor, but the approach has rarely been applied. One example is the application of the SCAT program in 1999 to improve the efficiency of the existing road infrastructure supply and road users' safety by managing the road traffic system using synchronised traffic lights. The metropolitan area's 34 municipalities signed an agreement transferring the coordination of the system to the regional administration and collaborated with the Ministry of Transport and Telecommunications to finance this program (DIPRES, 2000). SCAT did not work well due to political differences and municipalities' fear of losing their autonomy (Schiappacasse and Müller, 2012).

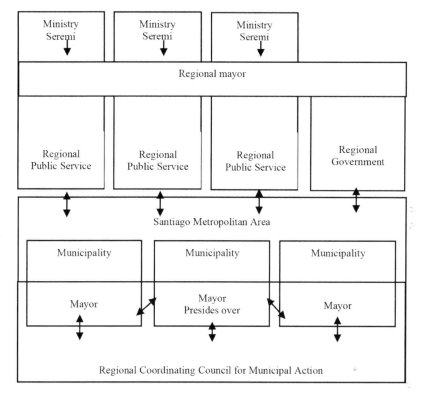

Figure 6.2 Coordinated governance of Santiago Metropolitan Area (1993–2017)
Source: Based on Law 19.175 (1993).

The coordinated SMA governance model has seen no major modifications since its inception in 1974. The main adjustment was the transfer of competences to the regional governments in 1993 on the approval of the Metropolitan Regulatory Plan of Santiago (PRMS). This instrument had clear implications for social equity and environmental sustainability, problems that continue to threaten both citizens' quality of life and urban competitiveness. The constitutional reform of 2009 (Law 20.390, 2009) resumed the discussion of metropolitan issues, arguing that they seriously hindered the management of the State as a result of obsolete and deficient institutional capacity to deal with urban issues (Presidential Advisory Commission for Urban Mobility, 2014). In the same tone, the Presidential Advisory Commission on Decentralisation and Regional Development (2014) raised the issue as a bottleneck in public management. The Commission urged that adjustment of the approach to metropolitan management was necessary to create an efficient and responsive administration system providing appropriate responses to citizens' demands. Administrative fragmentation has generated fissures in the administration of functional urban areas, particularly

Table 6.1 Proposed governance approaches for Metropolitan Areas

Entity	Approach to metropolitan governance
Presidential Advisory Commission on Decentralization and Regional Development (2014)	The administration of metropolitan areas will be of shared responsibility, which will fall on the Regional Government with the collaboration of municipalities (communes) that comprise them
Presidential Advisory Commission for Urban Mobility (2014)	A unique city authority capable of managing and governing the metropolis, intervening effectively and consistently on the problems of the city including land use and urban mobility
Ministry of Housing and Urban Development (2014)	Metropolitan governments involving the reordering of powers, competences and functions of both, the regional and commune levels. In a first phase, this metropolitan government is exercised by the regional government
OCDE (2013)	Metropolitan authority led by a metropolitan council, provided with sufficient autonomy. Capable of mitigating the impact of institutional fragmentation, establishing development strategies for metropolitan areas, prioritising planning and promoting coherence in the implementation of urban initiatives, including service delivery and sectoral policies

Source: Based on OCDE (2013), Presidential Advisory Commission for Urban Mobility (2014), Presidential Advisory Commission on Decentralisation and Regional Development (2014) and Ministry of Housing and Urban Development (2014).

metropolitan territories. Each municipality in a metropolitan area is administered independently with no mechanism for overseeing the wider economic and productive context (OECD, 2013). The Urban Development Policy of 2014 defines metropolitan governance as a fragmented, reactive, centralised and not very participatory decision-making process.

Various alternative solutions have been proposed in the new constitutional framework, given that urban functions implicate jurisdictional limits, administrative responsibilities, and policies on the provision of services and infrastructure (Table 6.1). With some of these proposals in mind, the discussion has progressed.

From a centrally coordinated governance model to a regional metropolitan government

Table 6.1 shows the diversity of proposals for the organisation and management of metropolitan areas, all of which propose reformation of the current system of centrally coordinated governance to create a metropolitan authority, the limits of whose administrative competences and services to be clearly established while maintaining the jurisdictional boundaries of the communes. The growing need for coordination in metropolitan management should now encompass public action centred on a single body of public law. The institutional economic approach promoted in Chile and applied in the new regulatory framework concentrates the new metropolitan management in the existing institutional context, granting new powers to regional governments (Law 21.074, 2018).

From 2021, the regional government will consist of a regional governor, directly elected by citizens, with an executive function, plus a regional council as a decision-making body. The regional governor is the new political entity created under the stipulations of the constitutional reform (Law 20.990, 2017) and the regulation specified by Law 21.073 (2018). The regional government will implement its metropolitan functions in regions with a territorial extension formed by two or more communes of the same region linked by a continuum of urban built areas that share the use of infrastructure and urban services and have over 250,000 inhabitants (Law 21.074, 2018: Art. 104 bis). The metropolitan governance structure will be made up of the regional government as an administrative body and an advisory committee of the mayors within the metropolitan area, and will be chaired by the regional governor. This is intended to be the space where different government actors interact on the formulation of policies and provision of collective goods and services on a metropolitan scale (Figure 6.3). The articulation of central policies with metropolitan strategies will be the responsibility of the regional government through new metropolitan area departments based in the planning divisions of the respective regional governments, aiming to strengthen the management and administration of metropolitan areas. Additionally, a metropolitan investment fund may be created, which will require the reorganisation of the regional budget to keep the resources of the investments that correspond to this area.

The new metropolitan governance structure can only be implemented if the existence of a metropolitan area is verified. Proposed metropolitan areas must comply with the minimum standards established in the regulation (Table 6.2). The declaration of a metropolitan area will be formalised in a

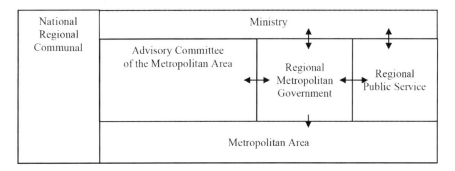

Figure 6.3 Metropolitan Regional Government in Santiago, 2018

Source: Based on Law 21.074 (2018).

Table 6.2 Minimum conditions to define the metropolitan area and its basic competencies

Territorial criteria	Area formed by two or more communes in the same region and according to the communes' limits
Demographic threshold	The number of inhabitants exceeds 250,000 based on the current official population Census
Continuum of the urban built area	Area which is made up of contiguous buildings and/or infrastructure which has urban functions, in accordance with the morphological criteria and functional standards
Use of urban infrastructure and services	Urban infrastructure, equipment and services that have influence on an intercommunal scale, and allow the generation and sharing of complementary functions among the communes in the metropolitan area
Morphological criteria	Housing density, distance to clusters and identification of buildings; exclusion of non-habitable buildings, urban parks, hills and uncultivated sites
Functional criteria	Existing spatial interaction between the communes capable of forming a metropolitan area, identifying the functional area based on the functional dependence between two or more urban centres, or the urban centres with their hinterland, depending on the type of urban sub-system. Dependence will be determined by a percentage greater than 15 per cent of trips for work purposes
Basic and initial competences	a Approve the Master Plan for Metropolitan Urban Transport b The direction of vehicular traffic on urban roads defined as intercommunal c The collection, transportation and/or final disposal of household solid waste from one or more municipalities of the metropolitan area d Approve the metropolitan or intercommunal regulatory plan e Approve the intercommunal investment plan in mobility infrastructure and public space f Give their opinion on the prevention or de-contamination plans

Source: Based on Law 21.074 (2018) and Reglamento DS 98 (2020).

supreme decree at the initiative of the President of the Republic of Chile or at the request of the regional government, for instance the Metropolitan Region of Santiago, for which prior consultation with its mayors will be required. This new institutional framework, the metropolitan regional government, is endowed with a set of basic and initial administrative competencies with the option of acquiring new competencies from central ministries through the transfer system stipulated by law. Administrative decentralisation in Chile involves the transfer of powers from ministries and public services offices to regional governments, regulated by Law 21.074.

Competencies can include sectors such as transport and investment in housing, the environment, and public works for the effective management of household solid waste, by prior agreement with the metropolitan municipalities. As powers are transferred to the metropolitan regional government and the metropolitan investment fund is created, the regional governor's influence and action in the metropolitan territory will gradually increase.

Governance and the provision of metropolitan services

The management of public services in Chilean cities experienced a period of openness and liberalisation in the 1980s and 1990s. At the same time, urban expansion accelerated in some cities. Strong growth in the production and consumption of urban services and infrastructure in Santiago and its metropolitan area also occurred during this period. The interlinked functionality between services and urban expansion acquired at least two forms: in some cases services pushed the development and expansion of the city, while in others they developed in response to increasing demand (Figueroa, 2003).

The centrally managed water company and the Metro had been progressively separated from national ministries since the mid-1970s to become publicly owned anonymous companies financing their own operations. In contrast, the urban bus services, already privately owned and operated, were subjected to strong deregulation. Household waste collection was also largely transferred to private companies. Table 6.3 shows the varied forms of management of these liberalised services (ibid).

Potable water was one of the services to be partially privatised through the sale of state assets. In 1988, Chile initiated a new regulatory regime for water and sanitation whose rates reflected the full cost of providing the services. The government first reorganised the sector into 13 state-owned regional companies and then started to partially privatise some of these in 1998 (WB, 2003). The tariff-setting mechanisms defined for privatised services, and in particular for water companies, were such that consumer payments covered the total investment made in the long term (Figueroa, 2003).

Table 6.3 Models of liberalised services in Santiago in the 1980s and 1990s

Service	Type of property	Model	Regulation	Tariffs
Water	Mixed	Sector monopoly	Superintendence	Superintendence
Metro	Public	Monopoly	The firm	The firm
Bus services	Private	Deregulated	National ministry	Firms
Waste management	Private (public in some cases)	Local monopolies	Municipalities	By law

Source: Based on Figueroa (2003).

Private delivery appeared to provide a powerful boost to meeting the investment needs of such a highly capital-intensive sector as water and sanitation in Santiago. A social consensus emerged that made the higher water tariffs acceptable given the important improvements to service quality and the addition of further services such as sewerage (WB, 2003). Water is now provided to the metropolitan area by a single company covering 99.9 per cent of SMA, with centralised metropolitan management.

Transantiago, SMA's current public transport system, comprises a Bus Rapid Transit (BRT) service, feeder bus lines and a metro system. Before this the public transport system was run by private operators with a total fleet of 8,000 buses. Transport services were characterised by fragmentation, inefficiency, the absence of fare integration, competition for passengers, low quality and insecurity. Poor maintenance contributed a high level of noise and environmental pollution. A survey in 2003 rated the bus system the worst public service. Transantiago, considered one of the most ambitious transport reforms in a developing country, started operating in 2007 across the entire metropolitan area. However, the system's performance has been rather poor, plagued by several flaws (Global Mass Transit, 2011). It quickly became evident that a bigger bus fleet and more infrastructure were needed, among other problems, and state funding had to be incorporated into its operation (CEPAL, 2017). As mentioned, Transantiago is one of the greatest challenges in the metropolitan area.

Solid waste services became the responsibility of each local municipality subject to the norms and standards of the National System of Health Services. In 1980, a decree forced the municipalities to transfer the management of these services to the private sector via public tenders. This service has historically suffered from inadequate financing. Users used to be those in households registered by the Internal Revenue Service (subject to the payment of land tax) and all companies that had to pay for a commercial license. Because the majority (67.7 per cent) of urban properties were exempt from land tax they did not have to pay for waste services either. In the mid-1990s, the law empowered municipalities to directly charge a considerable proportion of exempt households for this service. However, due to the type of service provided a large number of defaulters persisted (Figueroa, 2003).

Transferring the collection of waste to municipalities with very different realities revealed that their management capacity, especially that of those with fewer resources, differed significantly. As a result the quality of this service varies according to the socioeconomic capacity of each municipality's population because financing comes from contributions to real estate while local governments have no resources from which to increase their budgets for better management (ibid).

Solid waste management still poses important challenges in the SMA. The creation of the Ministry of Environment, the resolution and implementation of a Plan for Solid Waste Management in the Metropolitan Region and the revival of the Metropolitan Waste Company (EMERES) offered new opportunities to address these long-term challenges (Vásquez, 2011). Earlier we described the EMERES metropolitan governance model, which is based on intermunicipal coordination among some of the metropolitan municipalities.

Finally, despite the universality of services such as water, Cortés (2021) finds that the accessibility of other local public services such as transport is unequally distributed among metropolitan residents, mainly low-income groups, which suffer from significant deficits in the provision of local public services. Geographically the periphery of the SMA, where the poorer municipalities and large housing social projects are located, are worst affected. Thus low-income populations face a double disadvantage: socio-economic exclusion and limited access to essential services such as transport, reinforcing residential segregation.

Final remarks

Discussion about the governance of the SMA has been going on for more than 40 years. Initially, in the absence of regulation, centrally managed coordination implemented mainly by the central ministries was established as a predominant metropolitan area governance model. The Ministry of Housing and Urban Development has exercised hegemonic administration through several instruments: the control and regulation of the PRMS; communal regulatory instruments; the Higher Council of Transport, and the National Council for Urban Development created in 2014. The attempt in the 1990s to modify the centrally coordinated metropolitan administration system into a model based on intermunicipal coordination through the creation of a Regional Coordination Council for Municipal Action failed. This approach left the local authorities without effective competencies and with few links with the central and regional authorities. In practice the new system led to the strengthening of the centrally coordinated system.

Demand for effective territorial decentralisation in the last decade and reforms to the constitution have acted as critical junctures promoting institutional change from a centrally coordinated governance model to one based on the regional government as a metropolitan authority, strengthening a local coordination approach through the formation of an Advisory Committee of municipal mayors in the metropolitan area. In turn, multilevel coordination, especially with the central level, will be implemented through interaction between the ministries, public services and the Metropolitan Regional Government, with the latter responsible for approving territorial planning instruments, the regulation of land use, economic activities, urban equipment and the organisation of urban transport.

Solving the SMA's problems requires urgent, efficient and coordinated action. The new governance system offers possibilities for generating the structural changes that the city and its citizens require for an improved quality of life. Changes to the current juxtaposition of functions in a context of fragmented and centralised institutions depends on the implementation of the proposed governance model, the Metropolitan Regional Government, which promotes coordination and multilevel relationships among the agents in the same territory. The challenge lies with the Regional Governor who will preside over the Advisory Council, the relationships to be established with the 34 mayors, and the interaction with the other government institutions to reach political, technical and administrative agreements and influence the management of this complex and highly segregated territorial system.

While there are successful cases of the provision of urban services such as water, that of others including transport services, waste collection and roads have not achieved the same performance. The problems of such services demonstrate the need for improved conditions to ensure the success of metropolitan management, one of which is the institutional governance arrangements to be implemented in 2021.

References

Agostini, C. (2010). 'Pobreza, desigualdad y segregación en la Región Metropolitana". *Estudios Públicos*, 117 (Verano), 220–270.

AMUCH (2015). *Mapa del delito. El caso de la Región Metropolitana y la comuna de Santiago.* Santiago: Asociación de Municipalidades de Chile. At: https://www.amuch.cl/pdf/mapa_del_delito.pdf

AT Kearney (2019). 2019 Global Cities Report. *AT Kearney.* [Online] At: https://www.kearney.com/documents/20152/4977718/A+Question+of+Talent2019+Global+Cities+Report.pdf/106f30b1-83db-25b3-2802-fa04343a36e4?t=1578677670798

Aylwin, A. (1991). 'Interrogante y Planteamientos sobre un gobierno metropolitano para Santiago de Chile'. *EURE*, XVII (52/53), 143–156.

BID. (2018). *Construyendo Gobernanza Metropolitana: El caso de Chile.* Washington, DC: Banco Interamericano de Desarrollo. At: https://publications.iadb.org/publications/spanish/document/Construyendo_gobernanza_metropolitana_el_caso_de_Chile._es.pdf

Castells, M. (2001). *La Era de la Información.* Ciudad de México: Siglo XXI.

Castells, M. & Borja, J. (1997). *Local y global. La gestión de las ciudades en la era de la información.* Madrid: Taurus.

Castells, M. (1995). *La ciudad informacional. Tecnologías de la Información, reestructuración económica y el proceso urbano-regional.* Madrid: Alianza Editorial.

CEPAL (2017). 'Implementation of the Transantiago system in Chile and its impact on the transport sector labour market'. *CEPAL, Transporte*, 360 (8). At: https://www.cepal.org/sites/default/files/publication/files/43409/S1701288_en.pdf

Comptroller General of the Republic (2016). *Marco legal y estimación del gasto público asociado al sistema de Transporte Público de Santiago: periodo 2003–2016.* Santiago: División de Infraestructura y Regulación División de Análisis Contable.

Contreras, Y. (2012). '*Cambios socio-espaciales en el centro de Santiago de Chile: Formas de anclarse y prácticas urbanas de los nuevos habitantes'.* PhD Thesis, Pontificia Universidad Católica de Chile and Universidad de Poitiers. At: https://tel.archives-ouvertes.fr/tel-00684955/document

Cortés, Y. (2021). 'Spatial accessibility to local public services in an unequal place: An analysis from patterns of residential segregation in the Metropolitan Area of Santiago, Chile'. *Sustainability* 13 (2), 442. At: https://doi.org/10.3390/su13020442

Daher, A. (1991). 'Neoliberalismo Urbano en Chile'. *Estudios Públicos*, (43), 281–299.

Dammert, L. & Oviedo, E. (2005). 'Santiago: Delitos y violencia urbana en una ciudad segregada'. In C. De Mattos et al., (eds.) *Santiago en la globalización: ¿Una nueva ciudad?* Santiago: Ediciones SUR y EURE, pp. 273–294.

De Mattos, C. & Hidalgo, R. (eds.) (2007). *Santiago de Chile: Movilidad espacial y reconfiguración metropolitana*. Santiago, Chile: Pontificia Universidad Católica de Chile, Instituto de Estudios Urbanos. Serie GEOlibros No. 8.

DIPRES (2000). Sistema de Control de Áreas de Tráfico para Santiago (SCAT). Evaluación de Programas Gubernamentales, *Proceso de Evaluación* 2000.

DL 1289 (1975). *Ley Orgánica de las Municipalidades*. Biblioteca Congreso Nacional.

DL 1305 (1976). *Reestructuración y Regionaliza el Ministerio de Vivienda y Urbanismo*. Biblioteca Congreso Nacional.

DL 1317 (1976). *Divide las regiones y Provincias*. Biblioteca Congreso Nacional.

DL 573 (1974). *Estatuto del Gobierno y Administración Interior del Estado*. Biblioteca Congreso Nacional.

DL 575 (1974). *Regionalización del País*. Biblioteca Congreso Nacional.

DS 1.150 (1980). *Constitución Política de la República de Chile*. Biblioteca Congreso Nacional.

DS 98 (2020). *Fija los estándares mínimos para el establecimiento de las áreas metropolitanas y establece normas para su constitución*. Biblioteca Congreso Nacional.

DTO 458 (1976). *Ley General de Urbanismo y Construcciones*. Biblioteca Congreso Nacional.

DTP (2021). Transporte Público Metropolitano alcanza histórica alza en evaluación y usuarios valoran incorporación de buses Red. At: https://www.dtpm.cl/index.php/homepage/noticias/647-transporte-publico-metropolitano-alcanza-historica-alza-en-evaluacion-y-usuarios-valoran-incorporacion-de-buses-red

Dureau, F., Lulle, T., Souchaud, S. & Contreras, Y. (eds.) (2014). *Mobilités et changement urbain. Bogotá, Santiago et São Paulo*. Rennes: Presses Universitaires de Rennes.

Emol (2016). Paz Ciudadana: Robo con violencia aumenta de forma significativa en 56 comunas del país. Emol, January 11th. At: https://www.emol.com/noticias/Nacional/2016/01/11/767956/Paz-Ciudadana-Robo-con-violencia-aumenta-en-56-comunas-del-pais.html

Figueroa, O. (2005). 'Infraestructura, servicios públicos y expansión urbana en Santiago'. In C. De Mattos et al. (eds.) *Santiago en la globalización: ¿Una nueva ciudad?* Santiago: Ediciones SUR y EURE, pp. 243–272.

Fuentes, L. & Sierralta, C. (2014). 'Santiago de Chile, ¿ejemplo de una reestructuración capitalista global?' *EURE*, (30)91, 7–28. At: http://dx.doi.org/10.4067/S0250-71612004009100002

Galetovic, A. & Jordan, P. (2006). 'Santiago: ¿dónde estamos?, ¿hacia dónde vamos?' *Revista Estudios Públicos*, (101), 87–146. At: http://www.cepchile.cl/santiago-donde-estamos-hacia-donde-vamos/cep/2016-03-04/093914.html

Global Mass Transit (2011). Transantiago, Chile: Attempts to fix a beleaguered system. Global Mass Transit, May 1st. At: https://www.globalmasstransit.net/archive.php?id=6461

Henríquez, O. (2020). 'Descentralización y regionalización en Chile 1974-2020: de la desconcentración autoritaria al Estado unitario descentralizado con mayor empoderamiento regional'. *Revista Territorios y Regionalismos*, (3), 61–81. At: https://doi.org/10.29393/RTR3-5OHDR10005

Hernández, D. (1977). *Estatuto Jurídico de la Regionalización*. Ediciones Jurídicas de América. Santiago.

IBT (2021). Indicador de Bienestar Territorial. Bienestar territorial. At: https://bienestarterritorial.cl

INE, MINVU & SECTRA (2020). Metodología para determinar áreas funcionales de las ciudades chilenas. Instituto Nacional de Estadísticas, Ministerio de Vivienda y Urbanismo & Secretaría de Planificación de Transporte. At: http://observatoriodoc.colabora.minvu.cl/Documentos%20compartidos/Metodolog%C3%ADa%20Áreas%20Funcionales_2020.pdf

INE (2017). Censo de población y vivienda 2017. Instituto Nacional de Estadística. At: https://www.censo2017.cl/

La Tercera (2014). Estudio evalúa al transporte público de Santiago como el mejor de Latinoamérica. 11 October. At: https://www.latercera.com/noticia/estudio-evalua-al-transporte-publico-de-santiago-como-el-mejor-de-latinoamerica/

Ladera Sur (2018). Todos los detalles del Plan de Descontaminación de Santiago. Ladera Sur, 24 April. At: https://laderasur.com/estapasando/todos-los-detalles-del-plan-de-descontaminacion-de-santiago/

Law 19.175 (1993). *Gobierno y administración Regional.* Biblioteca Congreso Nacional.

Law 20.390 (2009). *Reforma Constitucional en materia de gobierno y administración regional.* Biblioteca Congreso Nacional.

Law 20.990 (2017). *Dispone elección popular del órgano ejecutivo del gobierno regional.* Biblioteca del Congreso Nacional.

Law 21.073 (2018). *Regula la elección de gobernadores regionales.* Biblioteca Congreso Nacional.

Law 21.074 (2018). *Fortalecimiento de la regionalización.* Biblioteca Congreso Nacional.

Mena, G., et al. (2021). 'Socioeconomic status determines COVID-19 incidence and related mortality in Santiago, Chile'. *medRxiv*, preprint version. DOI: https://doi.org/10.1101/2021.01.12.21249682

Mercer (2019). 'Ranking de calidad de vida 2019'. Mercer, Latam. [Online] At: https://www.latam.mercer.com/newsroom/estudio-calidad-de-vida.html. Revisado abril 2021.

Ministry of Housing and Urban Development (2014). *Política Nacional de Desarrollo Urbano. Hacia una nueva política urbana para Chile.* Santiago: Ministerio de Vivienda y Urbanismo.

OECD. (2013). *Estudio de la Política Urbana de OCDE el caso de Chile.* Paris: OECD.

OECD. (2009). *OECD Territorial Reviews.* Chile 2009. Paris: OECD.

Orellana, A. (2013). 'Gobiernos metropolitanos para Chile: La necesidad versus la factibilidad'. *Centro de Políticas Públicas*, 8 (63), 1–17.

Orellana, A. (2009). 'La gobernabilidad metropolitana de Santiago: La dispar relación de poder de los municipios'. *EURE*, XXXV (104), 101–120.

Orellana, A. & Fuentes, L. (2008). 'El arco, los conos y los clusters: geometrías espaciales para la gobernabilidad metropolitana y local de Santiago'. In Yáñez, G. et al., (eds.) *Ciudad, Poder, Gobernanza.* Colección RIDEAL, Serie GEO Libros EURE, No. 9. Santiago: LOM, pp. 111–132.

Orellana, A. & Marshall, C. (2019). 'Análisis de la complejidad intercomunal para el desarrollo de las áreas metropolitanas en Chile." In Orellana, A., Miralles–Guasch, C. & Fuentes, L. (eds.) *Las Escalas de la Metrópolis: Lejanía versus proximidad.* Santiago: Colección Estudios Urbanos UC, RIL Editores, pp. 251–280.

Ortega, T. (2014). 'Criminalización y concentración de la pobreza urbana en barrios segregados: Síntomas de guetización en La Pintana, Santiago de Chile'. *EURE*, 40(120), 241–263. At: https://dx.doi.org/10.4067/S0250-71612014000200012

Pizarro, F. (2018). *Historia de la Empresa Metropolitana de Residuos.* EMERES Ltda.

Presidential Advisory Commission for Urban Mobility. (2014). *Problemas de la Movilidad Urbana. Estrategia y Medidas para su Mitigación. Comisión Asesora Presidencial Pro Movilidad Urbana*, Ministerio de Transporte y Telecomunicaciones. At: https://www.mtt.gob.cl/wp-content/uploads/2015/01/InformePromovilidad.pdf

Presidential Advisory Commission on Decentralization and Regional Development. (2014). *Propuesta de Política de Estado y Agenda para la Descentralización y el Desarrollo Territorial de Chile Hacia un país desarrollado y justo.* Santiago: Subsecretaria de Desarrollo Regional y Administrativo del Gobierno de Chile.

Rodríguez, J., Páez; K., Abarca, C. & Becker, I. (2017). '¿Perdió el Área Metropolitana del Gran Santiago su atractivo? Sí, pero no. Un examen basado en datos y procedimientos novedosos para la estimación de la migración interna y sus efectos durante el periodo 1977–2013'. *EURE*, 43(128), 5–30. At: https://dx.doi.org/10.4067/S0250-71612017000100001

Sabatini, F. (2006). *The Social Special Segregation in Latin American Cities.* Washington: Banco Interamericano de Desarrollo.

Sassen, S. (2001). *The Global City.* New York: Princeton University Press.

Sassen, S. (2003). 'Globalization or denationalization?' *Review of International Political Economy*, 10 (1), 1–22.

Schiappacasse, P. & Müller, B. (2012). 'Metropolización y Políticas de Planificación: un desafío para Santiago de Chile'. *Revista Urbano*, (25), 31–42.

TECHO. (2016). *Catastro Nacional de Campamentos.* TECHO Chile, Centro de Investigación Social. At: http://datos.techo.org/dataset/catastro-campamentos-2016

Trivelli, P. (1991). 'Reflexiones en torno a la Política Nacional de Desarrollo Urbano'. *EURE*, VIII (22), 16–28.

UC. (2016). *Estudio UC comparó el Transantiago con otros sistemas de transporte de Latinoamérica.* Pontificia Universidad Católica de Chile. At: https://www.ing.uc.cl/noticias/estudio-uc-evaluo-positivamente-a-transantiago/

Vásquez, O. C. (2011). 'Gestión de los residuos sólidos municipales en la ciudad del Gran Santiago de Chile: desafíos y oportunidades'. *Revista internacional de contaminación ambiental*, 27(4), 347–355. At: http://www.scielo.org.mx/scielo.php?script=sci_arttext&pid=S0188-49992011000400007&lng=es&tlng=es

Veltz, P. (1999). *Mundialización, ciudad y territorios.* Madrid: Editorial Ariel.

WB. (2003). '*Water Services in Chile: Public policy for the private sector*'. Note No. 255. New York: The World Bank.

7 An assessment of metropolitan governance and service provision in Latin America

Alejandra Trejo Nieto

Introduction

The authors of this book have underscored the pressing issue of metropolitan governance and its links to service provision and spatial inequality in Latin America, the most urbanised region in the Global South. Chapter 1 began by discussing how metropolitan areas are becoming the predominant mode of human settlement. In an incremental process, they have become a de facto phenomenon in many regions of the world. This development goes hand in hand with three trends: an increasing proportion of residents in metropolitan areas living outside the central city; increasing administrative fragmentation; and disparities within metropolitan areas, mostly between the core city and the peripheries, or suburbs (Sellers et al., 2008).

The book underlines how urban expansion has made defining an adequate geographic scale for planning and public policy increasingly difficult. In metropolitan areas, administrative boundaries generally do not match the urban functional area, and there are many and various obstacles to the management of such large and complex urban territories, from providing basic services to fostering economic development, social wellbeing and urban sustainability. All of these increasingly demand effective policies and frameworks addressing metropolitan-wide phenomena. But the amount of progress made towards authentic political and administrative metropolitan integration remains unclear.

Increasingly, authors such as Bahl (2013) are arguing that while the theory and practice of providing public services in metropolitan areas from an integrated approach have attracted a great deal of attention in advanced countries, they been largely overlooked in less-developed nations. With urbanisation reaching its peak and the rise of megacities, we agree with the idea that time is running out for regions such as Latin America to develop feasible approaches to the management and financing of their metropolitan areas. There is an urgent need to research, evaluate and discuss the governance conditions in metropolitan areas of this region, and how different factors and actors shape the trajectories of development and transformation. This book contributes to this discussion by looking at the metropolitan governance of the provision of urban services and exploring its links with spatial inequalities.

DOI: 10.4324/9781003105541-10

Chapter 1 sets the scene for the analysis of governance issues and the provision of services in Latin America in the face of the growing expansion of several of its metropolitan cities. The empirical Chapters 2–6 began with depictions of metropolitan governance in Bogotá, Lima, Mexico City, Buenos Aires and Santiago, pinpointing the most significant contextual features of their territorial organisation, government structures and administrative arrangements. Using different type of data authors also assessed several issues involved in the implementation of policies and in the provision of urban services, looking mainly at water, public transport and waste collection, but also environmental and other issues. Additionally, our evaluations have identified various areas of inequality linked to the metropolitan provision of services.

In this last chapter, I assess the type of governance observed in Latin American metropolitan areas: how it works, who is involved, the part played by formal/informal or private/public actors, how fragmentation is addressed, the extent to which coordination is advocated, how resources are obtained and spent, and the policy outcomes. I revisit the discussion of metropolitan governance and how it shapes service provision based on the five case studies included in the book, all of which entail different experiences of metropolitan development, and reflect on the broad links between governance, public services and inequality. Because governance in the five metropolises is supported by varied frameworks, this cross-metropolitan evaluation looks for parallels and variations due to the different superstructures in each country and metropolitan area. Sectoral comparisons reveal the importance of the characteristics of each service in shaping governance outcomes.

Several overarching questions apply to service provision: how does the implementation of services compares across metropolitan areas and sectors? How efficient is service provision? What political, territorial, and/or institutional frameworks enable adequate provision of different services? Are there examples of coordinated collective action resolving the issue of service delivery? We provide some answers to these questions.

Below I summarise the main findings of this book. Then I compare service-delivery practices across the metropolitan areas analysed. I offer reflections about governance and service delivery and their links with metropolitan inequality. The final remarks include future avenues for research and the implications of the Latin American cases for broader policy and governance practice.

Governance structures across metropolitan areas

Much scholarly interest has focused on how metropolitan areas are politically and administratively structured because these arrangements determine the operational areas of control, planning and policymaking. As discussed in the introductory chapter, much of the wide variety of public policies in metropolitan areas depends on the general governmental and administrative organisation of their countries and cities. Given the boundary problems of local governments in metropolitan areas (Briffault, 1996) and fragmentation as an inevitable condition of metropolitan growth (Storper, 2014), metropolitan governance supporting the management and planning process in the face of the challenges of a large urban agglomeration is a concept that seeks to distinguish itself from the classical notion of government with its wider vision of policymaking involving sectors of civil and political society and interest groups. Accordingly governance arrangements in metropolitan areas around the world exhibit varying patterns of shared authority (Spink, Ward & Wilson, 2012; Harrison & Hoyler, 2014; Zimmermann, Galland & John, 2020).

The multi-jurisdictional nature of metropolitan areas poses substantial challenges for governance and the politics of scale in Latin America (Aguilar & Ward, 2003). As we noted in Chapter 1, Latin American cities have seen significant changes in their anatomy and the functions of their local governments with the substantial expansion of their urban cores and the decentralisation of fiscal, political, and administrative powers and tasks from central to local government. With urban expansion, the metropolitan area has increasingly become the scale used for decision-making in many areas of development, including urban utilities and public services. On the other hand, decentralisation has brought changes including shifts in municipalities and other local governments' responsibilities and policy areas.

The past four decades have seen a move to decentralised service provision in the region. Neoliberal thinking and the quest for democracy in this period encouraged the allocation of more functions to local government, and many national governments delegated the control of previously centralised services. Financial transfers sometimes followed local governments' new responsibilities, but they were generally required to collect their own resources, which have proved insufficient. The decentralisation of functions and resources was expected to result in greater efficiency, accountability, transparency and participation (Gilbert, 2006); however, as most of the empirical chapters in this book have shown, decentralisation has entailed a contradictory set of implications in metropolitan areas. While the metropolitan area is acknowledged as a functional urban territory, the local government is allotted for public service deliver; this means the former seldom holds the legal status necessary for autonomous decision-making and investment. Jones, Cummings and Nixon (2014) find that while patterns of decentralisation and the structure of local government are critical to a municipal authority's ability to manage service provision, incoherent decentralisation present in metropolitan areas often contributes to poor services.

Central government plays a key role in granting metropolitan authorities legitimacy by establishing a legal and regulatory framework. As in most other Latin American countries, Argentina, Colombia, Chile, Mexico and Peru do not recognise a formal tier of metropolitan government, and municipalities are officially responsible for providing services to populations that are integrated into a single urban functional agglomeration. The institutional mark imposed by decentralisation has been instrumental in decisions about structuring governance in metropolitan areas and has conditioned the activation of the apparatus for managing and planning them adequately. Decentralisation has largely exposed the typical failure of metropolitan government-building by favouring other territorial scales, especially the municipal level (Lefèvre, 2010).

Describing a general pattern of how governance works, who is involved, and what forces and actors interact in metropolitan areas is extremely complex. The heterogeneous settings across countries in terms of the extent and type of metropolisation and decentralisation make establishing any typology problematic. We cannot define, for instance, a Mexican model or an Argentinian system of metropolitan governance. Our analysis confirms that there is no universal formula for advancing towards metropolitan governance, as each case has its own specific characteristics and requirements. The national and local legal frameworks and the institutional and political environments define the features of governance. Local governments have assimilated their political and financial powers to varying extents; local administrations have developed different capabilities for arranging organisational solutions; on occasions intermediate governments have been able to impel metropolitan solutions, and in some cases the centralisation of some urban tasks has been enforced.

Metropolitan governance has been evolving within broader legal frameworks that largely define the scope of political and administrative action at the local level. As stated, the institutional settings for metropolitan governance in Bogotá, Buenos Aires, Lima, Mexico City and Santiago are varied. All are capital cities, but Bogotá, Mexico City and Lima have special legal status. Bogotá, Lima and Santiago are governed under a unitary system, while Mexico City and Buenos Aires are part of federal systems. In most cases, a country's legal framework does not officially recognise or allow for the creation of a metropolitan level of government, although Bogotá has a tradition of efforts to institutionalise and consolidate its metropolitan areas. In all of our cases, while urban expansion has led to the incorporation of multiple local jurisdictions the degree of fragmentation varies due to their individual historical evolution. Although approaches to metropolitan management have been attempted, none of our metropolises have a metropolitan government.

All over the world, efforts have been made to transform metropolitan areas into political spaces with institutional frames and instruments designed to enable and serve metropolitan dynamics even in the absence of an integrated government. The progressive fragmentation of competences following decentralisation has increased the need to implement not only vertical collaboration but also horizontal coordination in decision–making processes and financing. In our case studies, most attempts at metropolitan institutionalisation have been hampered by political competition, lack of enforcement and insufficient resources. Table 7.1 summarises the main characteristics of metropolitan organisation in our case studies.

Table 7.1 Metropolitan organisation in five case studies

Metropolitan Area	Territorial structure (Fragmentation)	Institutional framework	Metropolitan institutionalisation	Coordination
Bogotá	It contains the Bogotá Capital District (CD) which has a special regime and is divided into 20 local jurisdictions or districts. In addition, the metropolitan area includes 19 surrounding municipalities.	The national Constitution and the Special Regime for the CD determine that its administrative structure comprises a central authority (*alcalde mayor*) with wide administrative and taxing powers, and municipal authorities. Municipalities outside the CD have their own government and must provide services.	Constitutional reforms directed to formalise metropolitan areas as legal entities have taken place for over five decades. The powers of metropolitan areas according to Law 1625 include planning and coordination for sustainable development; provision of public services; road infrastructure development and the formulation of guidelines for territorial planning and harmonisation. In practice the metropolitan area does not have an integrated government.	The CD concentrates most population and economic activities. In the 1950s, the CD arbitrarily annexed, by a central government's decision, six surrounding municipalities. The possibility of further annexations has created considerable tension with neighbouring municipalities, specially Soacha. As a consequence, BMA has faced a daunting task for achieving horizontal coordination.
Lima	The metropolitan functional area of Lima is composed of 50 municipalities in two provinces, 43 in Lima, and 7 in Callao. As a capital city, Lima has a special regime.	The province of Callao has a Regional Government and a Provincial Municipality, while the province of Lima has the Metropolitan Municipality of Lima (MML), which also performs the responsibilities of a regional government. Each district municipality has its own mayor and city council which are administratively autonomous in many areas, including the organisation of public services. Thus, local, provincial and regional powers overlap.	There are no metropolitan areas legally created by any rule or regulatory instrument.	Coordination is very problematic. Mancomunidades are an instrument aimed at establishing local coordination but they are not strong.

Santiago	Greater Santiago can be considered a fragmented metropolis that consists of 34 communes. Santiago does not have a special regime.	Each commune has an autonomous municipal government that is directly elected. But there has been intervention from the central government, and responsibilities of the different authorities are blurred. Governance is highly centralised. Administratively, the responsibility is split between the Chief of Government of The Autonomous City of Buenos Aires and the mayors of the surrounding municipalities.	In the country, there is a political resistance to territorially reconfigure the local institutional framework. The aim is to maintain a centralist and sectoral model of government to manage metropolitan affairs. Metropolitan bodies have not been created to address metropolitan issues due to the separation of functions and powers between levels of	Due to local fragmentation and persistent centralisation, collaborative governance and participation to form integrated responses to metropolitan issues are hindered.
Buenos Aires	Buenos Aires Metropolitan Region (BAMR) includes the Federal District and 40 adjacent municipalities all of which are located in the Province of Buenos Aires and the surrounding area.	The Governor of the Province of Buenos Aires has a significant role in metropolitan governance because different public services are under its control. The role of municipalities is generally subordinated, since a bulk of policies are designed and/or financed at the national or provincial level.	government, fragmentation and the political rivalries across the various jurisdictions.	The metropolitan region undergoes the difficulties inherent to a coordinated provision. Fragmentation has been partially offset by de facto centralisation mechanisms by provincial and national governments. It has offered interesting formal attempts in metropolitan coordination, e.g. developmental corridors and consortiums.

(Continued)

Table 7.1 Metropolitan organisation in five case studies (*continued*)

Metropolitan Area	Territorial structure (Fragmentation)	Institutional framework	Metropolitan institutionalisation	Coordination
Mexico City	The metropolitan area includes Mexico City which historically has had a special regime as a capital city and functions as an intermediate government. Mexico City is divided into 16 boroughs with limited autonomy. Additionally, the metropolis includes 59 municipalities in the State of Mexico and 1 municipality in the state of Hidalgo.	A complex territory that includes 76 politically and fiscally heterogeneous local jurisdictions belonging to three different states. Moreover, there is the coexistence of local authorities, three intermediate governments and the central power.	Metropolitan areas are not legally recognised but conurbations are included in the national Law of human settlements. A number of attempts for metropolitan institutionalisation include a Law for metropolitan development, a metropolitan plan and sector specific metropolitan commissions.	The national Constitution allows municipal associativity but the high political-administrative fragmentation translates into scarce horizontal coordination and cooperation.

Source: Author's elaboration.

A decisive question for metropolitan areas that is central to this book is how the different practices of governance influence public policy output. The provision of public services is a policy area of great concern in metropolitan areas. The institutional frameworks for the provision of specific public services where national, sectoral, regional, metropolitan, and local institutions coexist are diverse. Below we summarise the main findings on governance modes for service provision.

Routes to service provision in five Latin American metropolitan areas

Across the world, different approaches have been taken to providing services in metropolitan areas and the variation in the capacity of metropolises to organise their expansion and inclusion has been documented. Diverse outcomes arise, for instance, from different intergovernmental relations that configure the autonomy and capacity to provide public goods and services, or from the degree to which the subnational state is able to deal with the organisation, financing and operation of their functions (Heller, 2017).

Both the quantity and quality of local public services and the efficiency with which they are delivered in a metropolitan area depend to a considerable extent on how its governance works (Jones, Cummings & Nixon, 2014; Slack & Côté, 2014). Effective service provision generally relies on strong institutions and good governance whereas political-economic factors and institutional and governance failures are common elements in ineffective service delivery, typically hitting the poorest the hardest (Jones, Cummings & Nixon, 2014). While most metropolitan comparisons focus on overall institutional structures and general policies, sources of variation within nation-states also influence the outcomes of metropolitan governance.

Sectoral policy differences, regional/local policies, institutions and cultures across metropolitan areas also contribute to the differences. Subnational disparities in these arrangements may outweigh national differences, even in countries with similar national policies and institutions (Sellers, 2010). The provision of public services depends on both the sectoral organisation, the allocation of competences and financial means, and the capacity of subnational authorities to deliver the services for which they are responsible. If services are provided locally by different governments, governmental capacity differences manifest as uneven quality and efficiency. In these ways urban services display both common and individual characteristics. As a result of sector characteristics metropolitan areas display different patterns of governance constraints and challenges to collective action. The characteristics of specific services also influence the political dynamics of their delivery. These features shape the political salience of the service, i.e. the strength of incentives to politicians to devote resources and political capital to effective delivery. The wider political economy shapes the constraints to and opportunities for access and service quality. Governance constraints derive from the contextual factors in each sector (Wild & Foresti, 2013).

The influence of the political economy of governance on the provision of services is attracting increased attention to defining and documenting the specific ways in which these factors influence service delivery. Policy coherence and coordination are central themes in this regard and are appropriate markers of the construction of collective action among governmental actors. Jones, Cummings and Nixon (2014) consider that coordinated governance plays an important role in the effective delivery of services in urban areas alongside financial challenges, technical concerns and the local context. Political-economic factors affecting coordination and integrated governance are just as important for urban service delivery as funding and technical capacity.

There is a gap in the literature that does not allow consistent assessment of the specific nature of key governance challenges and the most important lessons for delivering services in urban areas in the Global South, particularly because only a small number of studies address the links between governance and the effectiveness of service delivery. In turn, studies focusing more on technical aspects of service delivery do not provide explanations about governance and institutions. In this book, we have provided accounts of sectoral governance practices and their impact on service delivery outcomes. Given the relatively few successful instances of formally integrated metropolitan public policies in the region, and the fact that internationally there has not been a direct path to achieving metropolitan integration, pragmatic practices seem to provide a basis for advancing the construction of metropolitan governance for the efficient delivery of services.

We have dedicated the most discussion to the three sectors cited in the introduction: water, waste collection and public transport. As discussed in the introductory chapter, solid waste management is a pressing priority in urban areas with a high concentration of population and waste production. In the vast majority of cities it is primarily a local government responsibility. In its provision there is considerable potential for co-production, e.g. through public-private partnerships. Urban waste management is susceptible to clientelism and politicisation, which can lead to a high incidence of political-economic factors (Jones, Cummings & Nixon, 2014). Water supply is also vulnerable to local patronage politics, which can affect the capacity of water service providers. Local politicians may take advantage of the importance of water in the daily life of urban inhabitants and promise improved access (Mason, Harris & Batley, 2013). Policy incoherence is a major challenge in providing public urban transport, with fragmentation and lack of coordination within and across the agencies and jurisdictions involved perhaps the most evident dangers. Poor vertical coordination, with powers often distributed between central and local levels, is a factor of incoherent decentralisation. High levels of patronage, political interest and poor coordination throughout the urban functional area deeply affect the effective delivery of transport services (Jones, Cummings & Nixon, 2014).

The delivery of these public services is fundamentally local in nature, which is at odds with metropolitan arrangements. As we discuss next, metropolitan areas are prone to access and quality problems in the delivery of these services, and peripheral areas are likely to have especially fragmented services because municipal authorities fail to serve rapidly expanding outer-city areas. Local authorities may lack sufficient power, financial resources and incentive to coordinate the different agencies and local providers involved in supplying services effectively.

Coordination in service delivery

As expounded in Chapter 1, with decentralisation the metropolitan area became a network of decentralised local governments, often municipalities (or *comunas* in Chile), that have to deal with service delivery. In addition, services are frequently provided by parastatal organisations, private producers and public-private associations or community organisations. Informal provision is another salient feature of service delivery in the region, mostly but not exclusively in the periphery.

As Jones, Cummings and Nixon (2014) note, metropolitan areas put pressure on service delivery systems, resulting in numerous often uncoordinated and/or unregulated providers. Therefore coordination is critical in service provision. In the absence of a unified government, mobility, housing and service-delivery issues can be addressed more efficiently via metropolitan-wide coordination than at the municipal level. Effective coordination can contribute to urban productivity and social wellbeing through more efficient and lower-cost service delivery. Indeed, metropolitan coordination serves as an appropriate test of governance (Mashini, 2020), and local interjurisdictional governmental cooperation has increasingly become part of the alternative metropolitan governance arrangements that affect service provision.

Following Sellers (2010), governance arrangements, which are subject to patterns of metropolitan cooperation, can be ordered from low to high by their degree of institutional integration. Figure 7.1 show some categories to characterise particular coordination modes for metropolitan governance.

According to Pioletti, Royer and Urquieta (2019) there is empirical evidence, for instance in countries such as Brazil and Bolivia, showing that horizontal cooperation among municipalities and vertical cooperation among municipal and other levels of government have promoted shared and effective governance through coordination. But while varying mechanisms have been available for coordinated metropolitan governance in other countries, their implementation has failed. Most service delivery has had limited capacity for collective action that boost integrated governance.

In Mexico City Metropolitan Area (MCMA) the presence of many different providers of the three services analysed in Chapter 4 imposes significant limits on policy coherence and collective action to achieve metropolitan coordination. In the provision of waste collection and public transport the

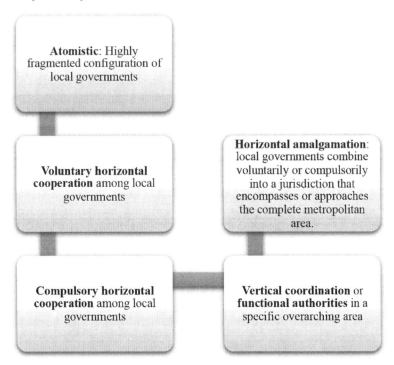

Figure 7.1 Coordination modes for metropolitan governance

Source: Based on Sellers (2010).

atomistic governance approach dominates. There is a single water-service provider in Mexico City, contributing to reducing overall atomisation, which however persists across other metropolitan municipalities. Failures of coordination in the provision of services reflect the fragmented territorial, administrative and political structures, the diverse natures and conflicts of interests – mostly of local actors – and the overlap of powers and interests across levels of government. Rather than vertical coordination, there are a few instances of nationally centralised metropolitan projects that include two metro lines and a suburban train enforced by the national government. But the opportunities to develop municipal associations for public policies have been unexploited.

The expansion of the Buenos Aires Metropolitan Region (BAMR) reflects the complex institutional structure required to coordinate 43 governments at four governmental levels. In the mid-twentieth century, BAMR made efforts to create coordinating agencies for several sectors, including water and sanitation, transport and waste management. Some metropolitan integration in these three sectors has been achieved through coordinative agencies, but these initiatives are more vertically led whereas the metropolitan region lacks horizontal coordination.

The chapter on Santiago Metropolitan Area (SMA) shows that the metropolis exhibits a multifaceted scenario in the realm of centrally integrated governance. The centrally driven metropolitan governance that has been in practice for 40 years has impacted the way in which public authorities address and try to solve urban affairs. Regarding urban services, while there are cases such as water where centralised management solves metropolitan provision, other services like transport, waste collection and roads have not exhibited the same performance. The problems of such services illustrate the need for improved conditions to ensure the integrated metropolitan management based on municipal collaboration.

In Lima Metropolitan Area (LMA) coordination on waste collection and public transport is virtually non-existent. So far these services have been provided by each municipality with no collaboration among them. But whereas waste collection continues to follow an atomistic approach to coordination, the transport sector has made efforts to establish a functional authority. The creation of the central authority for urban transport (ATU) represents an open opportunity for metropolitan integration. Water services are provided in the metropolitan area by the national firm SEDAPAL, which has been able to expand its services without jurisdictional borders acting as barriers. But the lack of coordination on infrastructure projects between SEDAPAL and municipalities contribute to an unplanned, reactive and inefficient mode of expanding the public network.

In Bogotá Metropolitan Area (BMA) efforts at horizontal coordination are few; despite the growing demographic weight of municipalities in the metropolitan area but outside the Capital District (CD) they remain politically and economically subordinated, and on occasion the CD authorities have openly refused to establish links. Metropolitan attempts at coordination have been reduced to collaboration between Bogotá's water company and some metropolitan municipalities, and to the few stations that the Bus Rapid Transit Transmilenio has established in the municipality of Soacha.

Financial challenges

Financial sustainability is a critical area in metropolitan service delivery worldwide. Many local governments are responsible for providing services but lack the finance to meet their obligations. The effectiveness of service delivery relies heavily on the amount of money spent, but their provision is frequently underfunded (Jones, Cummings & Nixon, 2014). Public agencies can succumb to pressure to provide low-cost services, causing chronic underfinancing. The extent to which metropolitan fragmentation and structures impinge on the financial sustainability of service provision is one of this book's central questions.

In MCMA, the financial arrangements for service delivery demonstrate the intricate operational reality of metropolitan governance in a highly fragmented context. Financial balancing is one of the acutest problems because operating costs exceed own revenues. In water management, tariffs and charges are not based on real cost and consumption patterns, and the tariff collection rate is low. This situation varies across jurisdictions. Water rates are set differently across subnational governments, resulting in substantial tariff heterogeneity. Providers' capacity is also heterogeneous. The public company that provides the service in Mexico City has more stable finances than most of the providers in the rest of the metropolitan area. Even in Mexico City subsidies are used to finance investment and cover operating-cost deficits. Decentralised providers in the municipalities depend heavily on central, intermediate and local governments' financial resources. The financial situation is worst in municipalities that provide the service directly.

In Mexico local governments do not charge an official fee for waste collection. In practice the population pays by discretionary tipping. As a consequence the weak user–provider link drives strong deficiencies and a fragile financial capacity for service delivery. The financial situation varies from jurisdiction to jurisdiction depending on the delivery scheme. In public transport, fragmentation across systems and jurisdictions limits the efficient allocation of resources and compromises the financial sustainability of the entire transport sector. Funding schemes and financial sustainability also vary significantly across systems and jurisdictions, and rigorous financial assessment is obstructed by the lack of information on cost structures. In Mexico City most systems are heavily subsidised.

As in many other cases, the transport systems in the BAMR is highly subsidised, in both its investment and operating costs, because own revenues collected via user fees are not sufficient. This need has become more necessary in contexts of tariff freezing. Even though financial sustainability is mostly achieved in operating water services, there are clear challenges for funding the levels of investment needed to achieve the universal coverage objectives. One such challenge is effectively channelling and coordinating financial contributions to ensure the best use of fiscal resources and external financing. For the municipalities that are legally directly responsible for managing waste, the financing system is unsustainable. The financing comes from own resources from their respective budgets with specific rates, and from resources provided by the province directly or indirectly (in the case of Buenos Aires through CEAMSE). Most of the municipalities can only pay with their own resources for the sweeping of streets and public spaces and the collection of waste, with quality standards depending on the possibilities that their budget gives them.

Private delivery appeared to provide a powerful solution to meet the investment needs of a highly capital-intensive sector such as water and sanitation in SMA. High water tariffs seem acceptable given the important improvements in service quality and the addition of services such as sewage. Transantiago, the integrated public transport system, has required state funding for its operation. The collection of waste operates in a fragmented scheme and financial conditions differ significantly across the metropolitan area. The financial resources for provision come from contributions to real estate and there are no resources in local governments to carry out a better management than what their budgets allow.

SEDAPAL has implemented cross-subsidies across LMA; the subsidy system and the centralisation of water provision have contributed to the effective implementation of cost-recovery policies. Although average per-capita revenues from waste collection have increased in the last ten years, the differences across municipalities are large. The lower income levels in some districts are a major constraint to increasing revenues. Additionally, technical restrictions and political costs enforce an efficient payment system. The nonexistence of centralised fare collection in the transport system hampers the establishment of a progressive fare. Some segments of the transport system, such as the metro and the BRT Metropolitano, do achieve relatively affordable fares and are financially efficient, but unless the whole system is integrated the benefits are limited to those who use these segments. Operators of outsourced buses and minibuses face more substantial financial limitations.

In BMA, the CD is in a relatively better financial position to provide services than the periphery. But financial capacity is not without problems, especially to the financing of projects to expand services coverage. On the other hand, restricted budgets and variety of public service delivery mechanisms (public, mixed, and private) limit other municipalities' capacity for service provision. Technical and financial difficulties generate a level of dependence on central transfers, reducing the potential for self-sustainability. With time, the central government has developed infrastructure projects, but these focus on a much broader regional vision and do not necessarily resolve local and metropolitan problems.

Coverage and quality

Significant differences in access to services such as transport, water and sanitation, and waste management persist across and within metropolitan areas, affecting many inhabitants' opportunities. More knowledge of territorial coverage of services helps in designing governance approaches and policies promoting inclusive well-being. According to Sellers (2010), multilevel institutional, policy and governance structures comprise a regime of place equality that shapes local policy outcomes. To disentangle such a regime it is necessary to uncover disparities across the metropolis.

In MCMA, coordination failures and disjointed planning and funding affect the quantity and quality of services and their equitable provision. Deficiencies in the coverage and quality of public services are the norm. Water and public transport services exhibits more unequal coverage across MCMA. While basic service coverage is almost universal in the city centre, it is very limited not only in parts of the periphery but also right across the metropolis and even in some central neighbourhoods. The spatial segmentation of coverage reveals a patchy pattern in water services and a centre-periphery pattern in transport services. Waste collection services in particular have frequency and quality problems.

Overall, basic services are widely covered in BMA's CD. The weaknesses appear in localised parts of the metropolitan periphery, especially in Soacha, due to its high demand for services, and the farthest municipalities. Another problem is the quality of services offered, especially in transport services in areas that Transmilenio does not reach. Bogotá's wide public service coverage implies a change in concern from quantity to quality, unlike in the other metropolitan areas we analysed.

The delivery of services in SMA is a perfect example of the challenges that metropolitan areas in Latin America face today to provide some services in the outer areas of the metropolis. Whereas the access to water is universal, the accessibility to other local public services such as transport is unequally distributed. Geographically, lower accessibility levels are at the periphery of the SMA, where poor municipalities and large housing social projects are located.

In BAMR metropolitan coordination agencies have contributed to improving service coverage. The operating area of the ecology coordination agency that deals with waste management covers the City of Buenos Aires and 33 municipalities, and approximately 40 per cent of the waste generated in the entire country. Argentine Water and Sanitation, now a nationalised company, supplies 14 million people with water and sewerage services across the City of Buenos Aires and 26 municipalities. Evaluating the public transport services is more difficult as the national government controls the railways, freeways, and bus lines, the City government manages the underground, the province controls provincial routes and buses, and each municipality manages transit and bus lines within its own boundaries.

In LMA, SEDAPAL provides water services to the whole metropolitan area and serve areas beyond Lima and Callao where there is territorial continuity and provision is technically feasible. Here the central government has played an important role in the expansion of coverage. However, informal and hilly lands are not fully covered. Other challenges for access to water and sanitation in Lima are found in the periphery beyond the limits of the public network. Although there are difficulties in increasing the quality of the service, it is better than that in other parts of Peru. Almost universal coverage of waste collection services is reported, with strikingly uneven quality across municipalities. The fragmentation of transport services hinders full coverage because it makes it difficult to develop an integrated public network and provide high-quality access to the whole metropolitan area. The creation of a public transport authority, the ATU, in Lima offers the potential to integrate the network and widen its coverage.

In most cases, we found a combination of poor-quality provision and unequal coverage of water, waste and transport. While basic service provision may be increasing generally, limited, paid access to low-quality services persists in the poorest and most peripheral areas. There are several reasons for such failures: weaknesses in financing, capacity and basic infrastructure, and lack of institutional and political capacity to deliver services right across the metropolis. Deeply rooted political structures, power relations and systemic legacies combine to shape the motivation and behaviour of the actors providing services in metropolitan areas (Wild & Foresti, 2013).

Metropolitan governance and service delivery from a comparative perspective

The advancement of a cross metropolitan understanding of governance continues as a growing necessity. There are various reasons for exploring metropolitan governance from a comparative approach: it accounts for policy outcome variations across cities and countries; it helps to advance our understanding of the effects of the interface between national and local political processes; and it reflects the practical need for a comparative understanding of varied forms of governance in different services. Knowledge gaps remain in scholarly debate as there are few systematic cross-country and city comparisons of the institutional and organisational form of metropolitan governance, the performance of metropolitan governance, and the role of metropolitan coordination in delivering strategic urban services.

To discuss governance comparatively we reflect on current practice on the basis of common elements such as coordination, financial sustainability and coverage. These allow the application of an analytical structure combining two central dimensions of governance – political (coordination) and technical (financial sustainability) – with governance outcomes (coverage and quality). The assessment of governance across metropolitan areas in this chapter is based on the ideal of metropolitan-wide capacity to provide public services. Consolidated governance is mostly understood as a condition in which service supply area is metropolitan-wide and can be achieved by means of certain production arrangements or by processes of annexation. Three modes of governance are proposed (Figure 7.2): fragmented, where provision and production organisation preserve the disjointed administrative structure of the metropolitan area, coordination arrangements are ineffective and no other formal or informal efforts to deliver metropolitan wide services are made; consolidated, where a service is provided and produced entirely or mostly by one entity; and in consolidation, where there are arrangements in place to build a metropolitan approach to service supply (Trejo, Niño Amézquita & Vasquez, 2018).

Consolidated
In consolidation
Fragmented

Figure 7.2 Metropolitan modes of service provision

While the metropolitan area has by no means developed perfect govern-ance, and national powers continue to create difficulties for both the poor and the local administration, BMA has been cited in certain respects as an example of 'best practice' (Gilbert, 2006). However, services in the BMA are in a relative state of consolidation because the metropolitan area is pre-dominantly governed by the major of the CD, the political jurisdiction concentrating almost 80 per cent of the population and covers most of the urban area, and provides services to that population. The historical process of the annexation of surrounding municipalities has contributed to advanc-ing this consolidation. This begs the question of whether Bogotá is a model to follow. Certainly, this case illustrates the extent to which metropolitan consolidation can be achieved by historical annexation and the reorgani-sation of public authorities around a more institutionalised conception of metropolitan cities and urban expansion. Moreover, the city's stratification system (*estrato*) can be viewed as an institutionalised mechanism for redis-tributive inclusion. But as Chapter 2 has shown, in recent decades there have been constraints to advancing the implementation of metropolitan institutionalisation.

In contrast, MCMA's service provision remains fragmented because its ser-vices are generally provided by multiple local governments and organisations with an almost total lack of metropolitan cooperation or coordination. Water provision is the least fragmented service as just one water company covers the whole of the Mexico City jurisdiction. In LMA the water service is con-solidated thanks to its provision by a single public company, SEDAPAL, but this is not a metropolitan institution. Intermunicipal agreements on waste collection services have been attempted without success. The transport ser-vice is fragmented, but ATU is an attempt to centralise the system. BAMR similarly has a nationalised water company covering a good proportion of the metropolitan area, is making efforts to integrate its waste management, and has a more fragmented public transport model. In SMA water provi-sion is centralised and partially privatised. Waste collection services remain fragmented whereas transport is centrally managed, but several problems of coverage, quality and sustainability persist.

In the five cases, metropolitan consolidation of service delivery has not been linked with local arrangements to integrate or expand the service area. Whereas metropolitan consolidation ideally emerges from metro-politan authorities or from cooperation and coordination, area-wide pro-vision has been achieved with the intervention of national or regional governments.

Fragmentation has entailed greater financial difficulties, but to the extent that governance structures consolidate the metropolis's services its financial capacity appears to improve. Metropolitan consolidation con-tributes to better coverage and quality, and possibly to more equal access to services.

Governance, service delivery and inequality

The global trend toward metropolisation has profoundly influenced both the form and consequences of inequality and governments and policymakers' efforts to deal with it. In this way, the metropolitan governance of service delivery becomes a governance of inequality (Sellers, 2010). There are stark inequalities in many urban areas and correspondingly clear inequities in service access, with large proportions of the population unable to access good-quality basic services. This is especially true for people living in informal settlements (Jones, Cummings & Nixon, 2014). Uneven access incentivises high-income households to collect in the few neighbourhoods with favourable access, making such neighbourhoods more exclusive and exacerbating spatial inequality (Sun et al., 2016).

The presence of significant disparities in service access is clearly observable in different regions of the Global South. Adama (2012), for instance, reports that the (re)production of spatial inequality in service delivery is a consistent feature of urban planning and policy in African cities. Patchy administrative coverage and uneven service provision are two key outcomes of uneven regulation. Governance practices related to the state's regulatory role have reinforced spatial inequality. Much of this has been happening in the context of neoliberal policies. Governance policies such as privatisation are key strategies in urban policy that have contributed to reproducing spatial inequalities in service delivery. Privatisation has also increased the divergences in the quality of services delivered in different parts of cities. The provision of local public services also varies considerably across Chinese cities, where much of the responsibility for public spending has been devolved to sub-provincial local governments as a result of large disparities in fiscal capacity. The inequality in resource provision for local public services across cities creates both access and inequality differences (Sun et al., 2016).

Governance structures and policies clearly comprise crucial elements for addressing the spatial dynamics of inequality. When individual local governments are responsible for deciding policy on service delivery, fragmentation usually frames segmented agendas that cause intra-metropolitan disparities. In consequence, metropolitan governance must devote much of its attention to addressing spatial disparities in coverage and access to services.

In addressing the link between the governance of service delivery and spatial inequality Sellers et al. (2008) highlight three questions: whether spatial disadvantages arising from concentrations of poverty and related forms of social exclusion have been compounded by disparities in government services; whether the spatial and governance dynamics of metropolitan areas have enabled more affluent citizens to enjoy better service delivery and whether horizontal and vertical arrangements for interlocal coordination within metropolitan areas have tempered or reinforced disparities in service provision. These are questions to be tested empirically.

This book has shown that the metropolitan areas we have examined are at different stages of service inclusion. There is generally tension over access to services between outer- and inner-areas, and the metropolitan peripheries contain more poor populations. The prevalence of informal settlements intensifies many of the constraints to equitable and effective services. The most unequal coverage in service provision pertains to most metropolitan areas' transport services, which are fragmented both territorially and institutionally. This and the increased cost of most other services in the peripheries have been used to explain events such as the protests in Santiago and other cities in the region in recent years, as we pointed out in the introductory chapter. Spatial coverage of water services can be also unequal but in cases such as those of LMA, BMA and SMA, centralised provision contributes to reducing the inequality. Our five case studies lead us to conclude that spatial disparities in service delivery endure, and that horizontal disparities contribute to or compound such inequalities within these metropolitan areas. Further analysis is necessary to confirm how interlocal disparities in governmental services reflect wider patterns of socioeconomic inequality and to what extent they can aggravate or add to them.

According to Pírez (2000), it was in the neoliberal period that service provision in Latin American cities ceased to function as a mechanism for redistribution and instead began to reinforce social inequality due to increased private participation in producing services. Neither powerful public intervention in essential services nor such increased private participation succeeded in reducing the prevailing pattern of inequality. Following Antúnez and Galilea (2003), decentralised and mixed provision resulted in a complex city structure which is socially inefficient by providing more expensive services.

The question of how patterns of interlocal and multilevel institutional dynamics produce inequalities in the delivery of goods and services involves multifarious factors: the participation of national institutions and policies in service delivery influences metropolitan-wide access to services; depending on the level of national centralisation of services, the disparities will be larger or smaller; fragmentation, local politics, efforts at coordination and geography all impact differently on the extent of spatial inequality. Under the conditions of territorial inequality that have become characteristic of fragmented metropolitan settlements in the Global South generally and metropolises in Latin America in particular, privileged communities seem to have the advantage. More equitable distribution of services essentially depends on the implementation of management schemes that allow inclusive provision. This in turn depends on the specific roles of different state agencies, their political definition, and their control over service management (Pírez, 2000). Egalitarian or compensatory regimes are urgently needed in the metropolitan areas we studied to impose less unequal conditions or compensate for local disadvantage.

Concluding remarks and future research

Research on metropolitan governance and urban service provision in Latin America is valuable, as there is a dearth of literature on the impact of the organisation of government and society in metropolitan areas on strategic urban functions such as how their infrastructure and public services are developed and financed. Analysing the extent to which the governance setup fosters the provision of public services in an inclusive and efficient manner is essential to understanding the developmental problems of most metropolitan areas in the region.

The experience of urban governance in Latin American depicted in this book has shown that metropolitan areas are distinctive arenas of conflicting interests and power struggles among different agencies and across municipalities and other levels of government. Accordingly, metropolitan areas must reorganise their governments and reconfigure their governance if they are to overcome the existing questions of political legitimacy and urban functionality, because in most cases there is poor progress towards metropolitan institutionalisation.

Decentralisation has been an important hurdle in this legitimisation. According to our findings, the responsibility for providing the bulk of urban public services is mostly given to municipal governments or other local government bodies that have very little technical, political and financial capacity to provide them directly. But intermediate and central governments still play a role as providers of services in several cases, such as in the provision of water in LMA. Higher levels of government have served as corrective mechanisms to support the delivery of metropolitan services in a more inclusive manner via centralised provision. Given the poor advancement in building governance through horizontal coordination, we have found that metropolitan-wide governance is seldom a product of local-level initiatives. A number of metropolitan projects such as the case of the suburban train and couple of metro lines in MCMA have depended on institutional arrangements at a higher level. In all five of the metropolises we have analysed, even where local authorities are the statutory service providers service delivery is frequently outsourced to the private sector to some degree. Community providers (e.g. of water services in MCMA) and informal actors in practically all of the metropolises have been needed to fill gaps in the formal provision of some services. There are instances where different arrangements such as waste scavenging have been built organically on existing practices. Although local sources of service delivery can be informal as well as formal, clientelistic links between local authorities and the population are not uncommon in the provision of services to low-income or disadvantaged groups.

Implementing a more efficient and inclusive structure of metropolitan governance appears to be easier where there is more comprehensive geographic consolidation of a metropolitan area, where its geographical limits coincide most with the limits of the functional urban area and where coordination in providing services is achieved with neighbouring jurisdictions. These contribute to a capacity for self-financing that gives metropolitan areas more tools for managing their local services with less dependence on intergovernmental transfers and other competing financial agents. Informal practices have become necessary, but should be minimised as they imply lower quality or higher costs for low-income populations and those living far from the centre whom the formal services network does not reach.

Overall, the evidence suggests that effective, efficient and legitimate metropolitan governance remains a work in progress. This can be explained not only by the sheer magnitude of the prevailing challenges and often suboptimal and incoherent policymaking and implementation but also by the nature of contemporary Latin American big-city governance itself. Metropolitan administrative organisation is complicated, ambiguous and horizontally and vertically non-cooperative. Local governments rarely participate in collective decision-making on metropolitan-wide issues such as service provision. Although there have been attempts to implement mechanisms for the delivery of metropolitan services, most of them guided by centralised initiatives, so far the experience in Latin America is of a substantial lack of metropolitan approaches to delivering efficient and equitable services. Technical, institutional and financial constraints to providing area-wide services have caused marked disparities and segments of the population still lacking access to basic public services. The process of providing services across metropolitan areas has shaped patterns of spatial inequality. The poorest population faces constraints to service access because of their peripheral or/and irregular location. The differential provision of services can in turn reinforce socioeconomic inequalities across space.

Politics, policies and institutional arrangements could provide means of limiting spatial inequality. Some of these policies and institutions may be situated at the national or other higher levels. Others may be found to initiatives within metropolitan areas themselves. The more governance equips metropolitan-wide capacity and dialogue and promotes interlocal cooperation the more it contributes to diminishing metropolitan disparities. But equity in service provision is usually at most a secondary objective of most metropolitan policies, and metropolitan arrangements that have succeeded in reducing socio-spatial inequality have taken the form of either amalgamated general jurisdictions or unified local governments (Sellers et al., 2008). Political capacity and desire, institutional support from higher levels and citizen participation are necessary elements of equitable and effective service provision. Intersectoral and multilevel coordination is also a contributing factor.

We conclude by recognising that the available evidence shows that there is no master logic in the construction of metropolitan governance, which depends on history and context, intergovernmental relations, the capacity of municipal authorities, the pace of urban expansion, financing, and the local political economy. The actors are diverse and include national and subnational state agencies, political parties, private interests and civil society, and the institutions and practices involved can be both formal and informal. The empirical studies presented in this book contribute to reducing the gap in our knowledge about metropolitan governance in Latin America. But there remain broad empirical questions to resolve, such as how to reconcile the struggle to alienate the subsidiarity ideals present in decentralisation processes and metropolitan integration; how can political legitimacy be improved for metropolitan authorities in the presence of decentralised structures of government?; to what extent recentralisation is an option in metropolitan management and financing; how best practices can guide general models of governance; how to adequately construct tailor-made and flexible metropolitan strategies; what are the best schemes to efficiently finance metropolitan policies and what are the best mechanisms for incentivising metropolitan coordination. Civil participation and transparency are two significant governance issues that have not addressed in this book, but they deserve thorough attention.

Further research based on case studies and comparative and comprehensive perspectives is also required in the analysis of service provision, because significant challenges remain. Analysing and addressing the social, economic and political implications of spatial disparities in access to services should be at the top of the both the policy and the academic agenda. Further research on these questions will help to build different routes towards better metropolitan management and governance in metropolitan areas worldwide.

References

Adama, O. (2012). 'Urban Governance and Spatial Inequality in Service Delivery: A Case Study of Solid Waste Management in Abuja, Nigeria'. *Waste Management & Research*, 30(9), 991–998. DOI: 10.1177/0734242X12454694

Aguilar, A. & Ward, P. (2003). 'Globalization, Regional Development, and Mega-City Expansion in Latin America: Analyzing Mexico City's Peri-Urban Hinterland'. *Cities*, 20(1), 3–21. At: http://www.sciencedirect.com/science/article/pii/S0264275102000926

Antúnez, I. & Galilea, S. (2003). *Servicios públicos urbanos y gestión local en América Latina y el Caribe: problemas, metodologías y políticas*. Serie Medio ambiente y desarrollo, No. 69. Santiago: CEPAL/ECLAC. At: https://repositorio.cepal.org/bitstream/handle/11362/5770/1/S039607_es.pdf

Bahl, R. (2013). 'The Decentralization of Governance in Metropolitan Areas'. In Bahl, R., Linn, J., Wetzel, D., (eds.), *Financing Metropolitan Governments in Developing Countries*. Cambridge: Lincoln Institute of Land Policy, pp. 85–106.

Briffault, R. (1996). 'The Local Government Boundary Problem in Metropolitan Areas'. *Stanford Law Review*, 48(5), 1115–1171. DOI: 10.2307/1229382

Gilbert, A. (2006). 'Good Urban Governance: Evidence from a Model City?' *Bulletin of Latin American Research*, 25(3), 392–419. At: http://www.jstor.org/stable/2773387

Harrison, J. & Hoyler, M. (2014). 'Governing the New Metropolis'. *Urban Studies*, 51(11), 2249–2266. DOI: 10.1177/0042098013500699

Heller, P. (2017). 'Development in the City: Growth and Inclusion in India, Brazil, and South Africa'. In M. Centeno, A. Kohli & D. Yashar (eds.), *States in the Developing World*. Cambridge: Cambridge University Press, pp. 309–338.

Jones, H., Cummings, C. & Nixon, H. (2014). 'Services in the City: Governance and political economy in urban service delivery'. Discussion paper. Overseas Development Institute: London. At: https://www.odi.org/sites/odi.org.uk/files/odi-assets/publications-opinion-files/9382.pdf

Lefèvre, C. (2010). 'The Improbable Metropolis: Decentralization, Local Democracy and Metropolitan Areas in the Western World'. *Análise Social*, 45(197), 623–637. At: http://www.jstor.org/stable/41012827

Mashini, D. (2020). 'Metropolitan Dialogues: Steps towards the Institutional Construction of Metropolitan Governance'. Blog Post, *Ciudades Sostenibles*. At: https://blogs.iadb.org/ciudades-sostenibles/en/metropolitan-dialogues-steps-towards-the-institutional-construction-of-metropolitan-governance/

Mason, N., Harris, D. & Batley, R. (2013). *The Technical is Political: Understanding the Political Implications of Sector Characteristics for the Delivery of Drinking Water Services*. London: Overseas Development Institute and University of Birmingham.

Pioletti, M., Royer, L. & Urquieta, P. (2019). 'Institutional Patterns for Metropolitan Governance in LAC Countries: The Differentiated Evidence from Bolivia and Brazil'. Book of Papers, AESOP 2019 Planning for Transition Conference.

Pírez, P. (2000). *Servicios urbanos y equidad en América Latina. Un panorama con base en algunos casos*. Serie Medio ambiente y desarrollo, No. 26. Santiago: CEPAL/ECLAC.

Sellers, J., Hoffmann-Martinot, V., Kitayama, T. & Kübler, D. (2008). 'Metropolitan Governance and Social Inequalities'. Paper to be presented at Metropolitan Governance and Social Inequality workshop, ECPR Joint Sessions Rennes, 11–16 April 2008. At: https://ecpr.eu/Filestore/PaperProposal/d6a24760-050e-4a85-971d-f34137c6fc5d.pdf

Sellers, J. M. (2010). 'Place, Metropolitan Inequality and Governance: A Framework for Comparative Analysis'. Paper presented at Centre for Metropolitan Studies Seminar on Metropolis and Inequalities, University of São Paulo, 24–26 March 2010. At: http://centrodametropole.fflch.usp.br/sites/centrodametropole.fflch.usp.br/files/inline-images/sem_metropolis_J_Sellers.pdf

Slack, E. & Côté, A. (2014). *Comparative Urban Governance*. London: Foresight, Government Office of Science. At: https://assets.publishing.service.gov.uk/government/uploads/system/uploads/attachment_data/file/360420/14-810-urban-governance.pdf

Spink, P. K., Ward, P. & Wilson, R. (2012). *Metropolitan Governance in the Federalist Americas: Strategies for Equitable and Integrated Development*. Indiana: University of Notre Dame Press.

Storper, M. (2014). 'Governing the Large Metropolis'. *Territory, Politics and Governance*, 2(2), 115–134. DOI: 10.1080/21622671.2014.919874

Trejo Nieto, A., Niño Amézquita, J. L. & Vasquez, M. L. (2018). 'Governance of Metropolitan Areas for Delivery of Public Services: The Cases of Bogotá, Lima and Mexico City'. *Region*, 5(3), 49–73. At: https://openjournals.wu.ac.at/region/paper_224/224.html

Sun, W., Zheng, S. & Fu, Y. (2016). 'Local Public Service Provision and Spatial Inequality in Chinese Cities'. 56th Congress of the European Regional Science Association, 23–26 August 2016, Vienna, Austria. At: https://www.econstor.eu/handle/10419/174683

Wild, W. & Foresti, M. (2013). 'Working with the Politics: How to Improve Public Services for the Poor'. Briefing No. 83. London: Overseas Development Institute. At: https://www.odi.org/sites/odi.org.uk/files/odi-assets/publications-opinion-files/8587.pdf

Zimmermann, K., Galland, D. & John, H. (eds.) (2020). *Metropolitan Regions, Planning and Governance*. Berlin: Springer.

Index

Printed in the United States
by Baker & Taylor Publisher Services